A SIMPLE GUIDE TO COMMON MUSHROOMS

Mushrooms
of the
Upper Midwest
2ND EDITION

T0021264

by Teresa Marrone and Kathy Yerich

Adventure Publications
Cambridge, Minnesota

Acknowledgments

Special thanks to Ron Spinosa for his advice and assistance throughout the writing of this book and also for his review of the final manuscript. (See Ron's biography on pg. 304.)

Cover, book design and illustrations by Jonathan Norberg
Page layout by Teresa Marrone
Edited by Brett Ortler
Cover photo: *Tylopilus felleus* by Teresa Marrone
All photos by Teresa Marrone and Kathy Yerich unless noted (see pg. 302 for additional photos).

The authors would like to gratefully acknowledge fellow mycophile Walt Sturgeon (co-author of *Mushrooms of the Northeast*, with Teresa Marrone), who provided valuable information on various mushrooms, assisted with changes in this second edition, and took a number of photos that appear in this book.

PHOTOS BY WALT STURGEON: 16, *Hericium* teeth. **28**, Shaggy Manes. **31**, *Sparassis americana.* **34**, *Pleurotus ostreatus.* **40**, *Cantharellus appalachiensis.* **43**, Skull-Shaped Puffball. **47**, *Porphyrellus indecisus.* **49**, *Hericium americanum.* **58**, Deadly Galerina. **66**, Yellow Patches. **75**, *Conocybe apala.* **79**, Shaggy Parasol. **85**, *Tricholoma subsejunctum.* **87**, Decorated Pholiota, *Pholiota squarrosoides.* **89**, Spring Fieldcap. **95**, Clustered Collybia. **99**, Rooting Collybia. **107**, Common Funnel Cap. **111**, *Armillaria solidipes.* **119**, The Blusher. **127**, Red-Gilled Cort, Dappled Cort, Orange Webcap. **133**, *Hygrocybe miniata, Hygrocybe cuspidata.* **141**, Amethyst Laccaria. **143**, Young Blewits. **147**, *Lactarius chelidonium.* **148**, Fairy Inkcap. **158**, The Gypsy. **160**, "Fairy Ring Fungus." **163**, Platterful Mushroom. **181**, all three. **183**, *Tylopilus plumbeoviolaceus.* **186**, Graceful Bolete. **199**, Netted Stinkhorn. **211**, Young Oak Bracket. **218**, Lacquered Polypore. **235**, Yellow-Red Gill Polypore. **241**, Common Earthball. **245**, Black Bulgar. **263**, Orange Hydnellum. **278**, Scaly Chanterelle.

IMAGES USED UNDER LICENSE FROM SHUTTERSTOCK.COM: 7, BGSmith. **10**, Egg-shaped: mikeledray. **12, Mycelium:** Martin Fowler; **Bulbous base:** Maxim Blinkov. **13, Ring zone:** Alba Casals Mitja; **Patterned/ reticulated:** CCat82. **22, Atypical Caps:** Sergiy Palamarchuk. **26, middle:** Tony Campbell. **27**, *Gyromitra esculenta,* Kletr. **56, bottom right:** Kletr. **62, middle:** Kirsanov Valeriy Vladimirovich; **right:** Lumir Jurka Lumis. **63**, Serg Zastavkin. **145, bottom right:** Vassiliy Fedorenko. **155**, Nevada31. **177, top:** Digoarpi. **199, top left:** Sergiy Palamarchuk. **237, After releasing spores:** Lippert Photography. **247, bottom left:** Medwether. **259, top left:** N. F. Photography.

15 14 13 12 11 10
Mushrooms of the Upper Midwest
First Edition 2014, Second Edition 2020
Copyright © 2014 and 2020 by Teresa Marrone and Kathy Yerich
Published by Adventure Publications, an imprint of AdventureKEEN
310 Garfield Street South, Cambridge, Minnesota 55008
(800) 678-7006
www.adventurepublications.net
All rights reserved
Printed in China
ISBN 978-1-59193-960-3 (pbk.); ISBN 978-1-64755-029-5 (ebook)

Table of Contents

About This Book

This book was written with the beginning mushroom enthusiast in mind. It is a pocket-sized field guide featuring hundreds of the most common species in the Upper Midwest, with clear pictures and additional comparisons for each species. Many "beginner" books feature just the top eminently edible and deadly toxic varieties, while leaving out the hundreds—maybe thousands—of other species that grow in the area. Some books are generalized and may present descriptions and photos of mushrooms that don't grow in our area, the Upper Midwest. Given the sheer number of mushroom species in the Upper Midwest alone, one book cannot completely cover every species you are likely to find … especially not one you'd care to carry into the field!

This book includes North Dakota, South Dakota, Minnesota, Iowa, Wisconsin, Michigan, Illinois and Indiana

Our hope is that this book will both spark your interest about mushrooms and provide you with the means to learn more. A list of useful resources is included at the end of this book, as is a list of some mushroom terms you may encounter in those and other resources. First and foremost, we have arranged the entries in this book by what they look like, or their *morphology*. Many of the genus and species names that originally placed a mushroom in a certain family were assigned by experts because of the mushroom's physical appearance, and many other books arrange species based on their names or the scientific classification. But it is hard to look up a mushroom in a book by its name when you don't have a clue what it is yet.

Many misidentifications start with a hopeful guess that guides you to a book entry that, while incorrect, may have numerous features that seem to match the specimen you have found. The temptation is strong to "force" the description to fit what you have in hand. This can be a dangerous path to travel when attempting to identify wild mushrooms; a mistaken identification may prove harmful or, in the worst case, even fatal if a misidentified mushroom is eaten because the reader attempted to make the specimen "fit" the description given in a book. **For this reason, we strongly advise that novice mushroom enthusiasts consult multiple reliable references or, better still, a local authority who can verify the identity of the mushroom in question before it is eaten.**

Remember, too, that when attempting to compare features of mushrooms in various references or when discussing them with other enthusiasts, the scientific name (which is always in Latin) must be used. The colorful, sometimes descriptive and often humorous common names of mushrooms are fun but can vary by region and are not a truly reliable way to label a species. Using the Latin genus and species name, referred to as **taxonomy**, is the standard and most respected way of referring to a specific variety. However, without a microscope it is often impossible to determine the difference between species with similar appearances. Even some scientists have been overheard in the field referring to a drab specimen simply as an LBM ("little brown mushroom").

To make things more complicated, as more species are discovered and scientists have the ability to study them in more depth with microscopic examination, mating studies and DNA sequencing, authorities are finding that many of the mushrooms that were given their Latin name hundreds of years ago may belong to a different genus than that to which they were originally assigned. In fact, some of the names remain in constant flux, creating so much confusion that at any one time a specific mushroom could be referred to by multiple names, depending on your source. Again, we've attempted to list as many species as possible while keeping this a pocket-sized book. We've also used single quotes around names (such as *Russula 'densifolia'*) used for species which appear in, say, Europe but not in North America; this means that specimens found in North America are very similar but not exactly the same as their European counterparts, but a new name has not yet been published.

There is also a complete index starting on pg. 290 referencing both common and Latin names, and you'll see that we have included both on the ID pages.

We have been greatly aided in our decades-long studies by numerous people who generously shared their expertise with us over the years, and particularly those who helped us as we developed this book. Ron Spinosa has been a wonderful mentor and friend during the work on this project, and his assistance helped make this book possible. We'd also like to thank Lee Moellerman for coordinating the Minnesota Mycological Society field forays, as well as the many MMS members who shared their knowledge in the field and also helped us locate species to photograph on various forays.

In writing this book we have also consulted many excellent books and other sources; a list of the best is included in Helpful Resources and Bibliography, starting on pg. 282.

What Is a Mushroom?

Mycology is the study of mushrooms. In very general terms, mushrooms are the fruiting body of an organism from the Kingdom Fungi. Indeed, many references refer to the aboveground portion of a fungal organism as a *fruitbody*, although the word *mushroom* is far more common in everyday use. Mushrooms are not plants, because unlike plants they do not use sunlight to photosynthesize their food. More like animals, they use enzymes to break down what they consume. In their role as decomposers of organic material, fungi are essential to life on earth, because without them, the world would be buried in its own debris. In the forest, fungi break down dead or dying organic matter and render it into soil, making it usable for new growth.

The *mycelium* or "roots" of the organism may spread for miles underground, or inhabit an entire tree. The part that we see (and harvest, if we so choose) is comparable to the fruit we pick from a tree; the tree—and the mycelium—remains to bear fruit the following season. Like fruits, mushrooms can also assist in reproduction; just as an apple produces seeds that can grow into a new tree, mushrooms produce microscopic *spores* that are dispersed by wind, insects or other vectors, allowing the larger organism to spread into new areas. Of course, that is a very simple description. There are thousands of species of fungi with complicated life cycles and growth patterns. Learning some basic mycological terms and understanding how mushrooms grow and reproduce will help you understand some of what you'll encounter, but because of the staggering amount of diversity you'll run into, it is more important to learn **how** to decipher what you are seeing.

How to Look at Mushrooms

The main goal of an identification book is to teach the reader how to identify, name and understand more about something. With mushrooms, the sheer number of possibilities makes them a challenging but fascinating subject. Besides the large number of different species, there is an amazing variety of characteristics among those species. Additionally, some of the features are tactile or even sensory elements, like smell or taste, which can be described in a book but should really be experienced firsthand. Other features are too small to be seen without a microscope. This book will cover only criteria visible to the naked eye or through a magnifying glass or loupe (called a *hand lens* in this book), or observable by the senses. Removing microscopic features from our view leaves no shortage of traits that can be observed to positively identify a species. These traits provide a wealth of interesting content for a book, but firsthand experience in the field is even more fascinating! So, what we are really sharing in this book is **how to look at a**

mushroom. Reading about different traits and studying the images refines our ability to notice them.

Modern digital photography captures details that may not be readily noticed by the naked eye, making it easier to spot subtle ID features. Multiple photos can be taken and reviewed at home, perhaps even shared on blogs and social media sites, creating an almost instant digital field record. Many universities, mycological societies and individuals have created virtual

The store-bought white button mushroom, the brown cremini and the Portobello (all shown above) are different growth stages of the same species, *Agaricus bisporus*.

field guides with amazing photos and descriptions (see a list of recommended websites on pgs. 282), but as noted, the best learning experience is a trip to the woods with an experienced teacher.

The practice of taking notes and making drawings to highlight features of the specimens you've found is an old exercise but a good way to become aware of important details. Dr. Michael Kuo's wonderful book, *100 Edible Mushrooms* (see Bibliography), recommends trying this with store-bought mushrooms. He suggests studying button mushrooms and Portobellos to observe and compare the features of different stages of growth in the same species (both of these familiar mushrooms are forms of *Agaricus bisporus*, a species that also grows in the wild; see pg. 82 of this book). Some mushrooms have similar features at different stages of growth, beginning their life as a smaller version of the mature mushroom. Other mushrooms, however, change quite drastically as they grow, going through stages that would be described quite differently. Weather also has a huge effect on the growth, development and size of a mushroom. That is why it is important to look at not only the entire mushroom, but also multiple specimens, if possible. Most proper identification depends on evaluating many distinct features, some of which occur only at certain stages of growth, during specific types of weather or with other various factors. Due to all the factors noted, your mushroom may not look exactly like the ones in the photos.

In this book, we have listed the key identification features for each species in **green**. One of those key elements, which you'll see listed even before the description on the page, is habitat. When you see a mushroom, get used to looking around you. What type of terrain is there? What other plants or trees are nearby? What is your mushroom really growing on? Sometimes, it may look like a mushroom is growing from the soil when in reality it is growing from a buried piece of wood or an underground tree root. Many species are *saprobes*, mushrooms that get their nutrients from decaying or dead organic matter, whether from a specific type of tree or other vegetation. Other mushrooms grow from the soil in association with certain trees, in a symbiotic relationship that is called *mycorrhizal*. Getting to know your trees is a good way to look for certain species of mushrooms.

Learning the parts of a mushroom will help you examine them more closely. Many books take a scientific approach to terminology; this book will not. The diagram below gives an overall view of the parts of a mushroom we'll be mentioning in the upcoming descriptions. Rather than list all of the possible variations of those parts, let's start looking at some pictures and save the terminology and definitions for the Glossary at the back of this book. Some of the features you'll need to consider are easier to distinguish in a picture, so we've included closeup photos on the next pages that clearly show these elements.

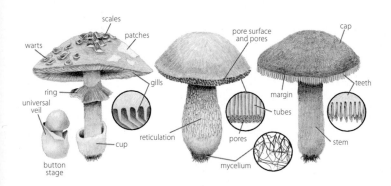

GROWTH STAGES

This discussion focuses on mushrooms—fruiting bodies, actually—that have a distinct cap and stem, resembling familiar store-bought species. Some types of mushrooms take different forms; shelf mushrooms, for example, have no distinct stem, puffballs have neither a traditional stem nor a cap in the common sense of the word, and others, such as coral fungi, are simply structured differently.

Young mushrooms arise from the *mycelium*, microscopic threadlike fungal roots that are underground or growing in another substrate such as rotting wood. Most emerge from the substrate as a *pinhead*, a small rounded bit of tissue that grows rapidly, soon becoming recognizable as what we call a mushroom. The photo sequence below shows a Green-Spored Lepiota (pgs. 60–61) over the course of four days. Some cap-and-stem mushrooms don't develop this quickly, but the stages are similar. (Note that some mushrooms, such as Amanitas and Volvariellas, are encased in a **universal veil**, a thin membrane that encircles the entire developing mushroom; see pg. 62 for photos that show the early growth stages of an Amanita.)

In the photo below at left, the mushroom has emerged from the ground; the cap and stem are distinct and recognizable. At this point, the cap is about 1½ inches wide. The next day, the cap has expanded dramatically to about 4½ inches wide. The photo at right shows the fully expanded cap, which is now about 7½ inches wide. The cap is almost completely flat, with just a slight curve on top, and the darkened gills are visible underneath.

Different species mature at different rates and in different ways. Development is also affected by the weather; mushrooms tend to mature quickly during periods of warm, wet weather and more slowly when it is cool and dry.

CAPS

The cap is generally the first thing that is seen, and its features such as shape, color, size and texture are a good starting point for identification.

As shown on the previous page, the cap's **shape** can change dramatically over the life of a mushroom. The size increases as well; this is particularly dramatic on mushrooms that have the traditional cap-and-stem shape, but caps become larger on other shapes such as shelf mushrooms. Here's a look at some of the common cap shapes.

In the *button stage*—when the specimen has recently emerged from the ground—most caps are *spherical* or *egg-shaped*. As the mushroom grows, the cap expands and begins to open up like an umbrella. Common shapes are shown at right and below.

Spherical

Egg-shaped

Bell-shaped

Conical

Knobbed

Elongated/cylindrical

Rounded/convex

Flat

Bowl-shaped/depressed

Funnel-shaped/vase-shaped

In addition to the shape of the cap, its **texture** must be considered. Some textures are obvious; the egg-shaped cap above is *patchy* (covered with small, slightly raised patches), while the elongated example is *shaggy* (covered with scales that curl or create an irregular, highly textured surface). The rounded example above is *smooth*; however, a smooth cap may feel dry, velvety or slimy, and the best way to know is to touch the cap.

Irregular/ wavy edge

Scalloped edge

Upturned edge

Ribbed/ striated edge

Cap **edges** also play a part in identification. The edge may be smooth, irregular, scalloped or upturned. It may have faint ribbing; in technical literature, this ribbed texture is referred to as *striated*. Edges also may have fine hairs or *veil fragments* (tissue-like pieces) hanging on them. A hand lens is sometimes needed to observe these characteristics.

Hairs on edge

Veil fragments on edge

The **color** of the cap may be uniform over the entire surface, but it may also have variations that may be subtle or very obvious. Some are mottled or streaky; others appear to have faint stripes, bands or rings. The center may be a different color than the outer edges; many mushrooms also fade or darken over time. It's not uncommon to have a mushroom change color substantially after it is picked; a digital photo taken before the specimen is picked can be helpful in later identification.

Sometimes, cap colors change on the same specimens depending on the weather. The photo sequence below shows the same group of mushrooms over a three-day period during which the weather changed from rainy to dry and back to rainy (a few of the individuals fell over or were removed from photo to photo). A mushroom whose cap changes color in response to moisture is referred to as *hygrophanous*. If you can observe specimens over the course of a few days, this can be a diagnostic characteristic. Hygrophanous genera include *Agrocybe*, *Galerina*, *Panaeolus*, *Psathyrella* and *Psilocybe*.

Day 1: Wet

Day 2: Dry

Day 3: Wet

STEMS

After you've inspected the cap, take a look at the stem underneath it. It's a good idea to study the stem a bit before picking the mushroom, as there are several things you should look for.

Study the base of the stem to look for *mycelium*, thin fungal roots that look like fine threads, cotton or a fuzzy coating. The color, texture and quantity of the mycelium (if present) provide a clue to the mushroom's identity. Mycelium may be found on any substrate that provides a growing medium for mushrooms: soil, decaying wood, live trees—even soggy carpet!

Mycelium

Volva

Next, look for any sign of a *volva*, a fragile, cup-like structure that surrounds the stem base on Amanitas and Volvariellas. You may need to dig around carefully in the dirt at the base of the stem to find the volva, but if you do find one, you're well on your way to identifying the mushroom, since very few types of mushrooms have them. The volva is a remnant of a universal veil; see pgs. 62-63 for more information about this.

Look at the shape, length and thickness of the stem. It may be fairly even in thickness from top to bottom, or it might taper at the top, becoming thicker towards the base. Many can be said to have a *club-shaped* base; this resembles the shape of a baseball bat or may be slightly wider, but generally

Club-shaped base

Bulbous base

the taper is smooth. A *bulbous* base is also broader at the bottom, but the swelling is generally more abrupt and the stem appears to bulge at the base.

Now it is time to pick the mushroom and turn it over. Note whether the stem is centered on the cap, or if it is off-center (mycologists call this positioning *eccentric*). What do you see under the cap? There may be *gills*, thin blade-like structures that run radially (like spokes of a wheel) between the cap edge and the stem. Instead of gills, some mushrooms have *pores* that look like a very fine sponge. A few, such as Chanterelles (pgs. 38–40), have neither gills nor pores. Gills and pores are discussed in detail on pgs. 14–15.

| Velvety | Scaly | Ridged/grooved | Patterned/reticulated |

Like the cap, the stem may be smooth and fairly featureless, or it may be highly textured. Some of the common textures are illustrated above. Textures can be crucial to identifying your mushroom, so study them carefully; a hand lens may be helpful in some cases. If the stem appears smooth, touch it and note whether it is velvety, slimy or dry.

You may notice a ring on the upper part of the stem. This is a remnant of the **partial veil**, a thin tissue that covers the developing gills or pores on some mushroom species (this is not the same thing as the universal veil mentioned at left and discussed in more detail on pgs. 62-63). If you look at a common button mushroom from the grocery store, you'll see a partial veil on small specimens. As the mushroom grows, the cap expands and

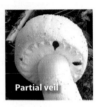
Partial veil

opens up, tearing the veil away from the cap and allowing the spores to disperse from the gills or pores. The veil remains attached to the stem. It may persist as a **ring** or it may deteriorate, leaving behind a **ring zone**, a sticky band that is often colored by falling spores; sometimes it dis-

| Skirt-like ring | Simple ring | Ring zone |

integrates completely, leaving no trace. The photos above illustrate these features. Note that pieces of the veil may also remain attached to the cap edge, as shown in the photo of veil fragments on pg. 11.

Some species have veils that are extremely thin and cob-web-like; this type of veil is called a **cortina**, and it is found on *Cortinarius* species as well as several others. Because the cortina is so insubstantial, it does not leave a classic ring; at most, a faint ring zone remains behind on the stem.

Cortina

UNDER THE CAP

Some of the most important mushroom features are found under the cap. On cap-and-stem or shelf mushrooms, this area produces **spores**, microscopic particles that function like seeds to help the mushroom reproduce.

Gills

Many mushrooms, including common grocery-store mushrooms (*Agaricus bisporus*), have **gills**, thin blade-like structures (referred to as **lamellae** by mycologists) that grow like the spokes of a wheel between the cap edge and the stem. Spores are produced on the flat faces of the gills and are forcibly ejected when they are mature. The spore color often affects the color of the gills; if you look at a young button mushroom from the grocery store, you'll notice that the gills are pinkish, but on mature specimens the gills have turned chocolate-brown from the spores. (Indeed, you may often find a dusting of brownish spores on the tray underneath Portobello caps.) When collecting wild mushrooms, it's always a good idea to make a spore print as described on pg. 17; this is the best way to determine the color of the mature spores, which is often key to properly identifying your find.

When you're holding a gilled mushroom you've picked, look closely at the way that the gills are attached to the stem. Mycologists use numerous terms to describe a wide variety of attachment methods; the differences between some of them are so subtle that it's difficult for the layperson to detect them. In this book, we're going to focus on those attachments that are easy to see with the eye, or perhaps with use of a hand lens. Other attachment methods can be included broadly in the three described here.

Attached gills are just what they sound like: the gills are attached to the stem. **Decurrent gills** are attached gills that run down the stem, slightly or a fair distance, rather than ending abruptly. **Free gills** stop short of the stem; when viewed from above, it looks like there is a miniature racetrack around the stem. It's often helpful to cut the mushroom in half from top to bottom to get a clearer view of the attachment, as shown in the first and last photos below.

Attached gills, cross-section

Decurrent gills

Free gills

Free gills, cross-section

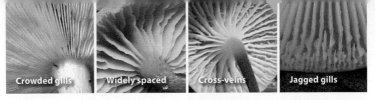

Crowded gills   Widely spaced   Cross-veins   Jagged gills

The spacing of the gills is an important identification point. From tight to loose, spacing is described in this book as crowded, closely spaced, moderately widely spaced, or widely spaced. They may be as straight as a knife blade, or wavy as shown in the photo of decurrent gills on the facing page. Sometimes there are short *cross-veins*, small ridges that connect the gills in a net-like fashion; a hand lens is often needed to see these. Some gills have a jagged texture on the edge; others are forked near the edge of the cap. The color of the gills is an important identifying factor; also note that some species have gills that are a different color along the thin edge. And as previously noted, gills often change color over time as spores collect on them.

Pores

Rather than gills, some mushrooms have *pores*, created by a sponge-like layer of very thin tubes attached to the underside of the cap. The spores develop inside the tubes, then drop down through the open bottom ends of the tubes when they are mature. *Boletes* are the most well-known of the cap-and-stem mushrooms that bear pores.

Bolete tubes, cross-section

The pore layer of a bolete can be peeled away from the cap as a fairly cohesive unit; this differentiates it from the pore layer on *polypores*, short-stalked or shelf-like mushrooms that grow on wood.

Like gills, pore surfaces are various colors. The pores may be extremely tiny or fine, appearing almost like a solid, featureless layer unless studied through a hand lens; they may also be large and coarse enough to see easily with the naked eye. Pores may be rounded, angular or hexagonal. Many species have pores that *bruise*, or change color when handled, cut or damaged.

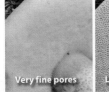

Very fine pores   Larger pores   Angular pores   Bruised pores

Teeth

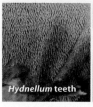

Hydnellum teeth

Hericium teeth

Rather than gills or pores, some mushrooms have **teeth**, spine-like structures on which the spores develop. Members of the *Hydnum* genus (pgs. 52–53) and the *Hydnellum* genus (pgs. 250–251) look like standard mushrooms when viewed from above, but they have short teeth on their undersides. *Hericium* species (pgs. 48–49), on the other hand, seem to be composed of nothing but long, dangling teeth.

Folds

These spore-bearing structures look like gills at a quick glance, but further inspection reveals that they are not separate, individual structures like true gills; they are merely thin, raised veins that are part of the mushroom body. Chanterelles (pgs. 38–40) are the best example of this, and the folds are not the only features that differentiate them from lookalikes. They do not have a distinct cap and separate stem; rather, the entire mushroom is a single item that is somewhat trumpet-shaped. Chanterelles are one of

Chanterelle folds

the top edibles and are highly prized, but care must be taken to ensure that the specimen really has folds rather than gills in order to distinguish it from the Jack O'Lantern (pgs. 72-73, a **toxic** lookalike. Black Trumpet (pgs. 50–51) is another mushroom in this book that has spore-bearing folds rather than gills.

Other spore-bearing structures

The mushroom world is complex, and the examples above are only part of the story of how mushrooms spread their spores. Morels (pgs. 24–27) carry their spores on pits between external ridges. Puffballs (pgs. 41–43, 226, 232) are solid sphere-like mushrooms with spores located in the interior flesh; when the spores ripen, the mushroom becomes shrunken and will burst open when lightly touched, scattering its spores. Other mushrooms are shaped like cups, coral or shapes that are too numerous to list here; each shape of mushroom has its own unique way of dispersing its spores.

SPORE PRINTS

As noted on pg. 14, the color of the spores is often a major clue to the identity of a mushroom, and we're including information about spore color for every species discussed in this book. Sometimes, a mushroom that is still standing in the woods or field has deposited spores on surrounding vegetation, logs or other mushrooms; in cases like this, you can determine the spore color without any further action. At right is a photo of a Purple-Gilled Laccaria (pg. 140) that has deposited its whitish spores on the green leaf of a nearby plant.

Spore deposit

Most of the time, however, you'll have to make your own spore print at home. It's easy to do and fun to see the results. The spore deposit may be white, black, or nearly any color of the rainbow. White prints won't show up on white paper, and black prints won't show up on black paper, so the best way to make a print is to use a piece of paper that is half-white and half-black; it's easy to run sheets of paper on a laser printer that have a large black field covering half of the paper.

You'll need a completely developed but still-fresh mushroom; specimens that are too young or too old probably won't produce spores. It should not have any trace of a partial veil over the gills. Cut off the stem so it is just a stub that fits inside the cap; a scissors often works better than a knife. Place your black-and-white paper on a table where it can sit undisturbed. Carefully place the mushroom with the spore-producing surface down, positioning it so half of it is over the white paper

and half is over the black area. Cover it with a bowl or glass and let it sit for a half-day, or overnight. Carefully remove the bowl, then the mushroom cap; with any luck, you'll have something that looks like the example at left.

The benefit of the two-colored paper is obvious. The spore print shown here is whitish to pale cream-colored; it shows up well on the black part of the paper, and just a slight trace of it can be seen on the white part of the paper.

Eating Mushrooms

Identifying mushrooms from a book is a good way to begin learning about them, but when edibility is your goal you must be extremely careful. It is recommended to obtain a first-hand, positive ID from an expert before eating any mushroom, as many of the toxic varieties look similar to the edible ones and could make you very ill, or even kill you! Join a local mycological society (see information in the Resources section on pg. 282), or hook up with an experienced forager who is familiar with local species.

Even after you have a positively identified a good edible, always try just a small portion the first time to assess your body's tolerance to it. Never eat more than one new species at a time the first time you try it, because if you combine several and have problems, you won't know which mushroom was the culprit. Don't assume that because others can enjoy a particular species, it will be OK for you, too; a friend who is an amazing outdoorsman recently shared his unfortunate discovery that even though he loves the taste of morels, he found that eating them made him nauseous. Also remember that **wild mushrooms should never be eaten raw**.

It is tempting to look for a simple rule or test that tells you whether an unknown mushroom is edible, but unfortunately no such rule exists. Taking the time to learn how to identify each species by its unique characteristics (even though some may be hard to see) is the only appropriate method. Also read Top Edibles and Top Toxics on pg. 21 for additional guidance.

Some mushroom folklore to ignore

- If a mushroom was eaten by animals or insects, it isn't poisonous.
- If you cook a mushroom with a silver utensil or coin in the pot and the metal doesn't turn black, the mushroom isn't poisonous.
- If a mushroom smells and tastes good, it isn't poisonous.
- If a mushroom peels easily, it isn't poisonous.
- Brightly colored mushrooms are the only poisonous ones.
- Pickling or boiling eliminates toxins from poisonous mushrooms.
- Rice will turn red if cooked with poisonous mushrooms.

Digging Deeper into Mycology

Physical features that can be observed with the eye (possibly aided by a hand lens) are enough to identify some mushrooms positively. Many other mushrooms, however, are difficult or impossible to identify unless the spores (the reproductive units) are studied microscopically. Mycologists classify mushrooms into groups (called *phyla*) based on how the spores are dispersed. Two major groups are described briefly below: basidiomycetes and ascomycetes.

Most mushrooms in this book fall into the *basidiomycetes* group, which includes all mushrooms with gills or pores and others such as puffballs. The spores are carried on the surface of club-shaped appendages called *basidia*. The surface of the gills on gilled mushrooms, and the insides of pore tubes on boletes and polypores, are covered with basidia. Each basidium (the singular form of basidia) holds several spores on tiny prongs at the end of the appendage. By the time the tiny spores are on the mycologist's slide, however, they have often been ejected from the basidium, so this appendage is not visible in most microscopic views of the spores.

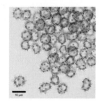

Ascomycetes are also called sac fungi because the spores are contained in a sac-like container called an *ascus*. These sacs are carried on the spore-bearing surface of non-gilled and non-pored mushrooms, including morels, cup fungi and others.

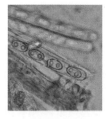

When the spores are ripe, the end of the sac opens to eject the spores. The number and shape of spores in each ascus may vary, although many asci (the plural form of ascus) contain eight spores. As with basidiomycetes, the spores have often been ejected out of the ascus before they are collected for analysis; however, mycologists sometimes shave off a section of the mushroom before the spores are ejected, in order to observe the asci (shown in the detail at left).

This discussion may seem highly technical to the novice; however, it is actually an extremely simplified overview. Mycologists who study mushrooms microscopically use terms that are baffling to the novice when describing the shape and other characteristics of the pores. Should you wish to learn more, check with your local mycological society or a university; some mycological societies offer periodic seminars on studying mushrooms microscopically.

How to Use This Book

As noted in the Introduction, this is an abbreviated field guide designed for ease of use by a layperson—one who is not intimately familiar with mushrooms in the field or on the written page. It focuses on mushroom features that can be seen without the aid of a microscope, so it is organized a bit differently than other field guides you may have seen.

Many books organize the entries based on an alphabetical listing of the *genus*, which might be thought of as the mushroom's "last name." That is followed by an alphabetical sub-listing of the exact *species*, the mushroom's "first name" that makes it different from other members of its genus. This listing is referred to as the mushroom's *scientific name*, and it is always in Latin. This is a much more reliable system than using "common names" which change depending on the language being spoken; indeed, common names can change from one state to another, making them unreliable.

The King Bolete (pgs. 44–47), for example, is referred to as the Porcini in Italy and the Cep in France. Its scientific name, however, is listed as *Boletus edulis* in all references, regardless of language. *Boletus* is the genus name; *edulis* is the species name. This tells us that this mushroom is closely related to, say, *Boletus subvelutipes*. However, while *Boletus edulis* is a choice, highly prized edible with a brown cap and whitish pores, *Boletus subvelutipes* is toxic, with a reddish cap and bright red pores. Thus, within the same genus, you may have a listing for a brown mushroom followed by a red one; a white one may follow that and another brown one after that. If you know what you're looking for, this type of organization is easy to follow, but if you're not sure what genus your mushroom belongs to, it's difficult to know where to start looking.

Some mushrooms are delicious edibles, while others are dangerously toxic—even deadly. As discussed above, these distinctions do not follow genus classifications. Before you take the field in search of edibles, it is helpful to know which mushrooms are safe even for beginners, but it is also imperative to become familiar with the deadliest mushrooms so you know what to avoid. This book starts with two sections that offer expanded coverage on the Top Edibles and Top Toxics in our area. The rest of the book is like a catalog of mushrooms, organized by their shape and other visible features.

In this book, mushrooms are grouped by basic categories, and within each of those categories they are grouped by color. Thus, if you find a mushroom that has a distinct cap and stem, and it has gills under the cap, you would go to the section entitled Cap & Stem with Gills, starting on pg. 74 (refer to the listing of

Basic Categories on pgs. 22–23 to locate the proper category). Colors within the section are organized from light to dark, as much as possible. So if your cap-and-stem mushroom is brown, go to pg. 86, where the first of the brown cap-and-stem mushrooms is listed. Compare your specimen to the photos and pay particular attention to the details listed. With luck, you'll find a description that matches your specimen, but if not, use the scientific name of the closest match to search more complete references. Also remember to check the Top Edibles and Top Toxics sections, as well as the abbreviated Others of Note sections found at the end of each category.

TOP EDIBLES AND TOP TOXICS

These special sections highlight two categories of mushrooms you should be very familiar with before collecting anything for the table. First up is a selection of some of the top edibles in our region, chosen not only for edibility but also because these are easy to identify without fear of collecting a toxic species. Following that are the top toxic mushrooms in our area. Some are **deadly**; all will make you very sick if you ingest them. Study them until you can easily recognize them in the field. Remember that it is always best to have an experienced mushroom forager with you when you first learn about edibles—or about toxic species.

Top Edibles starts on pg. 24; Top Toxics starts on pg. 56. Each section includes expanded coverage of highlighted species, along with descriptions of lookalikes to watch out for. Some of the lookalike descriptions include references to other pages in this book; others include photos of species that aren't discussed elsewhere in the book. At the bottom of each of the lookalike photos, you'll find a band that provides information about edibility. A green band indicates that the lookalike is edible. A red band indicates that the lookalike is toxic, while a pinkish band indicates that while it may not be extremely toxic, the lookalike should not be considered edible.

Elm Caps
EDIBLE

Angel Wings
NOT RECOMMENDED

Jack O'Lantern (toxic)
TOXIC

Basic Categories

Here are the basic categories used in this book, along with the page range for each section. Notes next to each category give a brief description and also list species that are covered in the Top Edibles or Top Toxics sections. The bands next to the photos indicate the color used for each section.

CAP & STEM WITH GILLS (PGS. 74–171)
Traditional cap-and-stem shape with gills underneath the cap.

In the Edibles section: Inky Caps
In the Toxics section: Deadly Galerina, Green-Spored Lepiota, Amanitas, Brown Roll-Rim, Jack O'Lantern

CAP & STEM WITH PORES (PGS. 172–197)
Traditional cap-and-stem shape with pores underneath the cap.

In the Edibles section: King Bolete
In the Toxics section: Toxic Boletes

ATYPICAL CAPS (PGS. 198–201)
Mushrooms that have stems but do not have a traditional cap with gills or pores.

In the Edibles section: Morels, Chanterelles, Hedgehogs
In the Toxics section: False Morels: Gyromitras

SHELF WITH PORES (PGS. 202–223)
Typically growing on trees or wood as a shelf or cluster with pores underneath; lacking a distinct stem.

In the Edibles section: Chicken of the Woods, Hen of the Woods

SHELF WITH GILLS (PGS. 224–229)
Typically growing on trees or wood as a shelf or cluster with gills underneath; lacking a distinct stem.

In the Edibles section: Oyster Mushrooms

SHELF/OTHER (PGS. 230–235)
Typically growing on trees or wood as a shelf or cluster with neither pores nor gills underneath; lacking a distinct stem.

SPHERICAL MUSHROOMS (PGS. 236–243)
Rounded or ball-like mushrooms that lack a distinct stem.

In the Edibles section: Giant Puffball

CUP-SHAPED MUSHROOMS (PGS. 244–253)
Mushrooms with no distinct stem whose body consists of a cup-like or flattened structure.

CORAL AND CLUB FUNGI (PGS. 254–261)
Irregularly shaped mushrooms that look like branches, soft sticks or sea coral; generally small in stature but often growing in large groups.

MISCELLANEOUS MUSHROOMS (PGS. 262–281)
Mushrooms whose shapes fit no other category.

In the Edibles section: Cauliflower Mushrooms, Lion's Mane, Black Trumpet

FROM THE SOIL NEAR TREES · SPRING

TOP EDIBLES

Morels (several)

Morchella spp.

Morels are probably the most sought-after wild mushrooms in our area; they are so popular that they have been named the official state mushroom of Minnesota. Even novices can easily learn to identify Morels with confidence—once they find some to identify. Experienced foragers guard the locations of prized Morel spots like a treasure and have been known to park a mile or more from a favorite spot to throw off anyone who may be following them. The Morel season is very short—typically a few weeks—which adds to their mystique.

Like many other mushrooms, Morels are subject to debate about how many species there are and what they should be called; ongoing DNA studies are redefining traditional concepts and discarding long-standing species names. At the simplest, "classic" Morels can be divided into two categories: Yellow Morels and Black Morels. Half-Free Morels are another

Hollow interiors

"true Morel," but they have some significant differences in appearance (see pgs. 26–27).

HABITAT: Most Morels are found around trees, including living, dying and dead; some fruit only in areas that have recently burned. They are occasionally found in gardens and shrubbery and sometimes appear on wood chips. Morels typically grow singly or scattered but may also be found in small clusters.

DESCRIPTION: Morels have **pitted caps** that appear **honeycombed**. Caps may be conical, egg-shaped, elongated or nearly spherical. Stems have a smooth or granular texture; they are often crumbly or brittle, and there is no ring. Stems are whitish, cream-colored or yellowish. They may have a round profile in cross-section, or may be slightly flattened or irregular; they often appear creased or folded, particularly at the base, which may be slightly wider than the rest of the stem. When sliced lengthwise, both cap and stem are **completely hollow** (photo at left) with **no trace**

M. esculentoides

Gray form of
M. esculentoides

M. diminutiva

of cottony material inside. The cap and stem are seamlessly connected so that the hollow space inside is a **single, continuous cavity.** On Black Morels, there is a slight but distinct **rim at the base of the cap** (sometimes called a groove). Half-Free Morels have a **short skirt around the lower half of the cap,** but they *do not have a full, loose skirt that dangles from the top of the stem.*

Yellow Morels have ridges that are typically paler than the pits. • *M. esculentoides* (previously listed as *M. esculenta* and *M. deliciosa,* which are European species) is the most common in our area, where it is often found under dead or dying elms and living ash. It is typically yellowish but may be gray or whitish when small. The ridges are **irregularly arranged** and are **paler** than the pits. The gray form is often found at the start of the season; in addition to being dark, these early-season Morels are often smaller than the yellow form that follows, making them particularly difficult to find. *M. esculentoides* are typically 2 to 4 inches tall, but size varies quite a bit and they may reach enormous sizes at the end of the season, sometimes growing to a foot in height; older sources list this form as *M. crassipes,* a name which has been invalidated. **M. cryptica** is visually identical to *M. esculentoides* and can be identified only by microscopic examination. • *M. prava* is very similar to *M. esculentoides,* but its ridges and pits are **more irregular,** making it look somewhat **deformed or gnarled.** Total height is less than 4 inches. It may be found near conifers as well as hardwoods; it also fruits in sandy soil, making it a challenge to clean for the table. • *M. diminutiva* is typically smaller than other Yellow Morels. Caps have **long, vertical pits,** and the stems sometimes seem proportionally longer in relation to the cap than other Morels. Pits are grayish at first, soon becoming the same color as the ridges. They are found near hardwoods and have been reported under ash, oak, cherry, apple and hickory trees; farther to the east, they also fruit under tulip trees, giving them the common name of Tulip Morel.

M. angusticeps | Half-Free Morel | Half-Free Morel, split

Black Morels have **strongly vertical ridges** bisected by numerous short horizontal ridges; the ridge arrangement may look **ladder-like**. • *M. angusticeps* (previously listed as *M. elata* and *M. conica*, which are European species) is the most common Black Morel in our region. It is found under hardwoods, including ash and cherry trees; it has also been reported under poplars and pine trees. The base of the cap **hangs slightly over the stem**, creating a small rim with a groove underneath. Ridges are tan at first—sometimes nearly the same color as the pits—becoming **much darker than the pits** with maturity, often nearly black. *M. angusticeps* are typically 2 to 5 inches tall, sometimes up to 6 inches; they do not reach the gigantic proportions that Yellow Morels do at the end of the season. • *M. septentrionalis* is very similar to *M. angusticeps* but smaller, seldom reaching 3 inches in height. It is a **northern** species, found in our area only in Minnesota and the far northern parts of Wisconsin and Michigan, including the Upper Peninsula. It fruits near hardwood debris and also **directly on rotting wood**. Other differences between the two species are microscopic.

Half-Free Morels (*M. punctipes*; previously listed as *M. semilibera*, which is a European species) are true, edible Morels that have a **small cap** perched atop a stem that may be up to 6 inches tall. The **bottom half of the cap is free from the stem**; when the mushroom is halved vertically, the top half of the cap is **part of the same hollow chamber** as the stem, while the bottom half of the cap hangs free like a **short skirt-like extension**. They grow under hardwoods.

SPORE PRINT: Creamy, whitish or yellowish; spore prints are seldom taken.

SEASON: Spring.

OTHER NAMES: The scientific names are in flux and change periodically.

V. bohemica

V. bohemica, split

V. conica

COMPARE: Several mushrooms with wrinkled or pitted caps may appear in the woods during spring. • Verpas are found earlier than Morels and continue to grow during the Morel season. *Verpa bohemica* has a cap that is **wrinkled** or pitted; the

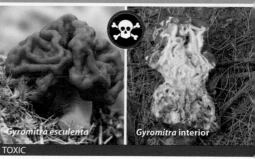

Gyromitra esculenta

Gyromitra interior

TOXIC

cap of *V. conica* is **smooth**. With both forms, the cap is attached to the stem **only at the top**; the sides **hang completely free** from the stem, which is at least **partially stuffed** with a cottony material. Verpas can cause gastrointestinal distress and are best considered inedible. • Several *Gyromitra* species (also called False Morels; pgs. 56–57) share the spring woods with Morels; they are often much larger, leading to confusion with large, end-of-season Yellow Morels. Their caps appear **wrinkled, folded or brain-like** rather than pitted, and the interiors are **stuffed with pockmarked flesh**. Colors range from reddish to brownish; stems are whitish or yellowish. Most are regarded as **toxic**; none should be eaten. • Also see **Stinkhorns** (pg. 198) and **Elfin Saddles** (pg. 200) for other mushrooms that have some similarities to Morels.

NOTES: All true Morels are edible when cooked, although Half-Free Morels are considered less desirable. Some people may have a reaction to one variety or another, so small quantities should be eaten at first.

FROM THE SOIL   SPRING THROUGH FALL

TOP EDIBLES

Inky Caps (several)
Various species

These mushrooms are common in both urban and woodland settings. While they're not as highly regarded for the table as some others in this section, they are easy to identify and a good choice for beginners.

HABITAT: Inky Caps are saprobes, getting their nutrients from decaying organic matter. They often appear in large clusters but also grow in scattered groupings.

DESCRIPTION: The most obvious feature of Inky Caps is that the gills of mature specimens dissolve, partially or completely, turning into an **inky black fluid** (photo at left). All species discussed here have a partial veil covering the gills of young specimens, and some have a universal veil; the resulting ring on the stem may be present for only a short time, often disappearing as the specimen matures. Caps of young specimens are rounded, but the edges soon flare and turn upward; as the cap opens up from the bottom, the gills and cap begin to deliquesce (dissolve) to release the spores. Gills are crowded or very closely spaced and white on young specimens; they soon turn gray or purplish-brown before turning **black** as they dissolve. Stems are **whitish and hollow**. Other features which separate the various *Coprinoid* species are microscopic.

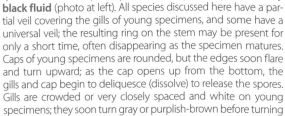

- Shaggy Manes (*Coprinus comatus*) are found in grassy areas, on wood chips, on disturbed ground and in areas with compacted soil. Caps of young specimens are shaped like an **elongated oval** and may be nearly **6 inches tall**, although they are usually shorter. They are whitish and covered with **small, elongated, shaggy scales that curl upward**; the very top of the cap is generally smooth and somewhat darker in color. Stems are 3 to 8 inches tall; when cut in half vertically, a **string-like filament** can be seen on the inside, hanging down from the top of the cap into the stem.

Shaggy Manes

green = key identification feature

- Tippler's Bane (*Coprinopsis atramentaria*; also listed as *Coprinus atramentarius*) grows on decaying roots and other woody debris that may be buried. They generally grow in **tight, dense clusters** and are

Tippler's Bane

often found at the base of stumps and dead trees. Young specimens have **egg-shaped to conical caps** up to 2 inches wide and tall; they are **pewter-gray or grayish-brown**. The surface is **silky** except at the center, which is **finely scaly** and often darker in color; **faint** grooves run upward from the edge of the cap. Stems are 3 to 5½ inches tall.

SPORE PRINT: Blackish to brownish-black.

SEASON: Tippler's Bane can usually be found starting in late spring; Shaggy Manes appear in early summer. Both types grow through fall.

OTHER NAMES: Inkies; Shaggy Mane is sometimes called Lawyer's Wig.

COMPARE: Mica Caps (pg. 100; edible) have **tawny**, conical caps that are **finely ribbed**, with no hairs, scales or overall patches; young caps are covered with **salt-like granules**. Caps may not dissolve completely. • Scaly Inky Caps (pg. 102) have tan to grayish-brown caps that are covered with **large, flaky pale patches**. Some people suffer digestive upset after eating them; like Tippler's Bane, they should not be consumed with alcohol. • Wooly Inky Cap or Hare's Foot Inkcap (*Coprinopsis lagopus* or *Coprinus lagopus*; inedible) is generally 2 inches tall or less. Young caps are **gray and covered with pale hairs**. • Fairy Inkcap (pg. 148) is less than 2 inches tall, with a ribbed cap; gills **do not liquefy**.

Wooly Inky Cap

INEDIBLE

NOTES: Collect Inky Caps for the table before the gills darken. They deteriorate very quickly after picking and must be cooked without delay. Tippler's Bane **causes severe illness if consumed within several days of drinking alcohol** (either before or after the mushrooms are eaten). Some compare the reaction to the worst hangover imaginable, or even worse.

NEAR DEAD AND DYING TREES   SPRING THROUGH LATE FALL

Cauliflower Mushrooms

Sparassis spathulata, Sparassis americana

Many books show pictures of this mushroom in a basket, on a plate, or being displayed proudly in someone's hands. The first reason is to show the impressive size that this mushroom reaches, but the second may be that hunters who find this delicacy aren't willing to show anyone exactly where in the woods they found it!

HABITAT: Cauliflower Mushrooms are saprobes, getting their nutrients from the buried roots of dying and dead trees. Found alone or in groups in mixed woods next to deciduous and coniferous trees.

DESCRIPTION: This large, brain-like **cluster** mushroom is easy to recognize. It is made up of a mass of **creamy white to tan-colored folds** growing from a **branching base**. Some describe it as looking like a pile of egg noodles. Large examples have been reported at sizes up to almost 2 feet across and weights of 50 pounds! However, most specimens are much smaller. This mushroom doesn't have gills or teeth but a **smooth surface** with very fine pores on one side of the folded flesh to release its spores. Two species are found in our area; both look similar and both are highly sought-after edibles.

S. spathulata

green = key identification feature

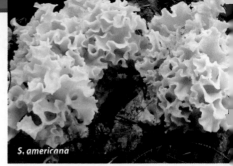
S. americana

- *S. spathulata* is typically found under **oaks**. It has an underground central base but is not deeply rooted. Individual folds have **distinct color zones or bands**; the folds are spread out and **fairly flat**.

- *S. americana* (also listed as *S. crispa*) is sometimes referred to as the Rooting Cauliflower Mushroom because it grows from a **deeply buried root** that is dark brown to black; if the root is not disturbed, it will continue to fruit in the same place from year to year. Individual folds of *S. americana* are **very curly** and **uniformly colored**, with no banding; they are more tightly packed together than the folds of *S. spathulata*. Clusters of *S. americana* are generally larger than those of *S. spathulata*. *S. americana* is found near conifers; it is less common in our area than *S. spathulata*.

SPORE PRINT: Whitish to cream-colored.

SEASON: Spring through late fall.

OTHER NAMES: Wood Cauliflower, Noodle Mushroom, Eastern Cauliflower Mushroom. *S. radicata* is sometimes listed as a synonym for *S. spathulata*, but *S. radicata* is actually a separate, closely related species found west of the Rocky Mountains.

COMPARE: Hen of the Woods and its lookalike, the **Umbrella Polypore** (pg. 55), can grow quite large like the Cauliflower Mushroom and are also delicious edibles. They are found at the base of trees (usually oak) but have **fleshy caps** with **porous**, white spore-producing surfaces underneath. • **Crown-Tipped Coral** (pg. 256) looks like a whitish cluster in the woods, but it is much **smaller** and is composed of **fine, multi-branched arms**. It is edible when young but is not considered choice.

NOTES: Though not easy to find, the Cauliflower Mushroom is quite the treat! A large specimen, however, can require lots of cleaning. Though brittle, they can be pulled apart at the base and soaked in mild saltwater to remove debris and unwanted critters. The flavor and texture of cooked Cauliflower Mushrooms are often compared to buttered noodles.

NEAR OR ON LIVE OR DEAD TREES

LATE SPRING THROUGH FALL

TOP EDIBLES

Chicken of the Woods (several)

Laetiporus spp.

Unlike other edible mushrooms that seem to use natural camouflage to hide from the eager forager, Chicken of the Woods announces its presence loudly. Its bright colors, large size and frequently elevated location make it easy to spot from a fair distance.

HABITAT: Found in association with live, dead or dying trees; these mushrooms are both saprobes and parasites. The appearance of Chicken of the Woods on a living tree is a signal that the tree has been attacked by the mushroom's parasitic mycelium (threadlike fungal filaments), which can sometimes be seen as whitish fibers in cracks in the wood. The fungus causes heart rot of the host tree.

DESCRIPTION: Three *Laetiporus* species are found in our area. All grow as a **grouping of thick, stemless fan-shaped caps**; individual caps may be up to 12 inches wide but are generally smaller. Caps are some shade of **orange to yellow-orange**, with a fair amount of variation among different groupings of the same species. They are smooth to wrinkled and may be leathery but are **not hairy**. Edges may be rounded or scalloped and range from flat to wavy. The underside of each cap is covered with **tiny pores**.

• *L. sulphureus* (also called Sulphur Shelf and *Polyporus sulphureus*) is the most well-known Chicken of the Woods. It grows directly on

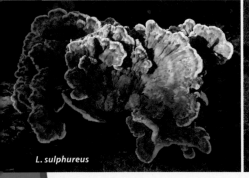

L. sulphureus

L. sulphureus, showing yellow pore surface

green = key identification feature

L. cincinnatus, showing white pore surface

deciduous wood, favoring oaks; it often grows on standing trees but also is found on stumps and downed wood. The caps are typically arranged in **tight, overlapping shelf-like layers** but may occasionally grow as a rosette. The pore surface is **bright yellow**; cap edges are often yellow.

- White-Pored Chicken of the Woods (_L. cincinnatus_; also listed as _P. cincinnatus_) has a **white** pore surface and grows as a **rosette** rather than as a cluster of overlapping shelves. _L. cincinnatus_ is not found on the sides of trees; rather, it grows **from the ground** over buried roots of oak and, occasionally, those of other deciduous trees. It is typically found at the base of the tree but may be a small distance away. It sometimes has softer, more muted colors than _L. sulphureus_. Cap edges are often white.

- _L. huroniensis_ has an appearance that is identical to _L. sulphureus_, but it grows on **hemlocks and other conifers** rather than on deciduous trees.

SPORE PRINT: White.

SEASON: Late spring through fall.

OTHER NAMES: Chicken Mushrooms.

COMPARE: Another choice edible, **Hen of the Woods** (pgs. 54–55), also grows as a cluster of caps, but its caps are **tan or gray** and thinner. • **Jack O'Lantern** (pgs. 72–73; **toxic**) is a bright orange, clustering mushroom that bears some resemblance to Chickens when glimpsed from afar, but closer inspection reveals that Jacks have **distinct stems** and **gills**. • The inedible **Orange Mock Oyster** (pg. 229) is a fan-shaped orange mushroom that grows on deciduous and coniferous trees. It has **gills** rather than pores, and its caps are **hairy**. It often grows in clusters but may be scattered.

NOTES: Chicken of the Woods has a meaty texture and a chicken-like taste. Young growth on the cap edge of _L. sulphureus_ is tender, but the older center portion becomes tough and requires stewing; many eat only the tender edges. The flesh of _L. cincinnatus_ is more tender than that of _L. sulphureus_ and the entire fruiting body is generally edible; most foragers consider it a better culinary prize than _L. sulphureus_. Chicken of the Woods, particularly older specimens, may cause digestive upset in some people.

green = key identification feature   **33**

NEAR OR ON LIVE OR DEAD TREES

LATE SPRING THROUGH EARLY WINTER

Oyster Mushrooms (several)

Pleurotus spp.

Four *Pleurotus* species in our area are variations of the traditional Oyster Mushroom; they are a choice edible that is easy to identify. All share several common characteristics. They are shelf-like mushrooms that grow in overlapping clusters on living and dead wood; their gills run down the stem, which is often so short as to appear nonexistent. Caps have a smooth upper surface and are often wavy or ruffled around the edges. They hasten decomposition of the wood on which they grow.

HABITAT: Oyster Mushrooms always **grow from wood** and are found on living trees, dying trees, or dead trees, stumps and logs; they also may grow on buried roots, appearing to grow from the soil. They may be found singly, but typically grow in clusters that may be quite large.

DESCRIPTION: The shelf-like cap is the most prominent part of any Oyster Mushroom; it is fan-shaped if growing against a standing tree but may be circular if growing upright from a fallen log or from buried roots. Edges are often wavy, scalloped or irregular. The cap is **smooth** and is **fairly meaty**, especially at the point where the gills come together on the underside. Stems may be short and stubby, or virtually

Pleurotus ostreatus

green = key identification feature

Pleurotus pulmonarius *Pleurotus populinus*

nonexistent; when present and not covered with gills, they are usually hairy near the base. Stems have **no ring**. The gills are closely spaced and run down the stem, or may simply taper down to a stem-like stub. The first three Oyster Mushrooms discussed here are similar in so many ways that it may be difficult to determine exactly which species you have found. Below are some traits that may be helpful; however, microscopic examination is necessary for absolute certainty. Happily, all are equally edible, so exact identification is not required.

- "Classic" Oyster Mushrooms (*Pleurotus ostreatus*) are up to **7 inches** across and vary in color, ranging from brownish to whitish, and pale to dark. Gills are whitish. Most commonly found on deciduous wood, they also grow on conifers and are found from spring through **early winter**. They have a sweet smell that is sometimes described as anise-like. Spores are whitish, lilac-tinged or grayish.

- *Pleurotus pulmonarius*, also called the Pale Oyster or Summer Oyster, is generally **smaller and paler** than Classic Oysters, often with a lung-like shape. They are typically less than 4 inches across. Caps and gills are white to cream-colored to tan. They are found from late spring through early fall on the wood of living and dead deciduous trees. Spores are whitish, lilac-tinged or grayish.

- The **Aspen Oyster** (*Pleurotus populinus*) is similar in size and coloration to *Pleurotus pulmonarius*, but it grows only on the wood of living and dead trees in the *Populus* genus, which includes **poplars, aspens and cottonwoods**. It is found in late spring and, occasionally, into the summer. Like Classic Oysters, it has an anise-like scent. Spores are whitish.

- The **Golden Oyster** (*Pleurotus citrinopileatus*; known in Europe as *Pleurotus cornucopiae*) is native to eastern Asia but commonly cultivated in the U.S. New to our woodlands, it is found growing gregariously, likely invasively, on dead or dying deciduous trees, from spring through fall. Large groups

Golden Oyster

of **densely clustered** caps are **bright to egg-yolk yellow**, fading to tan with age. Individual caps have a **dimple** in the center, expand out to 6 inches or more across and flatten with age. The central depression may deepen, creating nearly hollow stems, which can be up to 5 inches long and ½ inch thick; they are **multi-branched** and curve around a central, thicker base. Gills are white; spores are **pale pink**. DNA studies have begun to trace origins of the wild strains found in North America. Like the cultivated varieties, Golden Oysters are edible and seem relatively bug-resistant. They have thin flesh but dehydrating enhances the texture, which is a good thing since you may find loads.

SPORE PRINT: Most are whitish, but spore color of the Oysters described here varies, depending on species; see individual accounts.

SEASON: Late spring through early winter, depending on species.

COMPARE: Numerous mushrooms in our area have some resemblance to traditional Oyster Mushrooms. Some are edible; others are not recommended.

- The **Veiled Oyster** (*Pleurotus dryinus*) is related to the other Oyster Mushrooms, but it has some significant differences. It has a **distinct, stocky stem** up to 4 inches long that is **covered with fuzz**. Caps are up to 6 inches across or more and **densely fuzzy**. Both caps and gills are white to cream-colored, turning **yellowish** when bruised or old. There is a **partial veil** over the gills of young specimens, which breaks apart as the cap expands with age, leaving **remnants on the cap edge** and a **thin ring** on the stem; the ring disappears with age. Veiled Oysters grow from midsummer through fall

Veiled Oyster
EDIBLE

36   **green** = key identification feature

**Angel Wings
(no longer recommended)**

Stalkless Paxillus (inedible)

on the wood of living and dead oak and other deciduous trees. They are edible but not as choice as the other Oysters.

- **Angel Wings** (*Pleurocybella porrigens*) look very similar to white Oyster Mushrooms, but the cap is so thin that it is **partially translucent**; it is smaller than most white Oyster Mushrooms, generally 3½ inches across or less. Angel Wings are found from late summer through fall on dead **conifer wood**. Many sources list Angel Wings as edible, but the North American Mycological Association reports that more than a dozen deaths in 2004 were attributed to ingestion of this mushroom in Japan; it is best to regard it as inedible.

- **Stalkless Paxillus** (*Tapinella panuoides*; also listed as *Paxillus panuoides*) grows on **conifers**. Caps are shell-shaped and up to 4 inches wide, becoming narrower but still fairly broad at the base. The surface is **tan to orangish-brown**; it is downy when young. Gills are yellowish. They have **cross-veins** and are **wavy**, appearing **corrugated**; they may be forked. Its spore print is **yellowish to yellowish-brown**. It is inedible.

- **Elm Caps** (pg. 153) resemble Oyster Mushrooms but have a **distinct, thick stem** and its gills **do not run down the stem**. Caps are edible when young but the stem is tough and fibrous and is generally not eaten.

- Gills of *Lentinellus* **species** (pg. 227) have **serrated edges**; caps are **fuzzy or hairy** and up to 4 inches across. Lentinellus are too bitter to be edible.

- **Hairy Panus** (pg. 224) have **hairy caps** that are **tan to purplish** with a **rolled-under edge** and often have a distinct stem. They are bitter and tough, and considered inedible.

NOTES: Oyster Mushrooms can be cultivated fairly easily and are available in grow-it-yourself kits.

TOP EDIBLES

Chanterelles (several)
Cantharellus and *Craterellus* spp.

At first glance, Chanterelles appear to be a gilled mushroom. Closer inspection reveals that what appears to be gills are actually **blunt-edged folds or ribs**. The folds dent when pressed with a blunt object and can be teased from the cap in small sheets containing numerous folds. True gills have sharp, **knife-like edges**; individual gills break or collapse when pressed with a blunt object and don't peel away easily. The folds are a key characteristic to differentiate between the Chanterelle, a prized edible, and the **toxic** Jack O'Lantern (pgs. 72–73).

The most popular Chanterelle is the Yellow Chanterelle, generally listed as *Cantharellus cibarius*. Many mycologists believe this is a European species that doesn't appear in North America. As reported by Dr. Tom Volk, the Yellow Chanterelles found here should be divided into several new species based on DNA evidence. Research is ongoing and name changes are likely in the future. Regardless of their scientific names, all Chanterelles are edible, although some are considered less delicious than the highly prized Yellow Chanterelle.

Yellow Chanterelle

green = key identification feature

Red Chanterelle — Smooth Chanterelle — Yellow-Foot Chanterelle

HABITAT: Chanterelles grow **from the soil**, singly or in loose groups, under hard-woods (particularly oak) or conifers. The mycelium (threadlike fungal filaments) has a symbiotic relationship with the tree roots.

DESCRIPTION: With few exceptions, Chanterelles in our area have distinct, **gill-like folds** under the cap (see further description on pg. 16). The folds are often forked and **continue down the stem** for a short distance below the cap; the folds may feel waxy, and there may be a network of fine veins between the folds. Stems are fairly sturdy and have no rings. Caps are smooth on top; they are rounded with a depressed center and rolled-under edge on young specimens. As the Chanterelle ages, the cap spreads and flattens out, turning upward to form a shallow, funnel-like bowl with edges that are generally **wavy or ruffle-like**. Flesh of the stem and cap is **white**.

- **Yellow Chanterelles** (*Cantharellus cibarius*) are **deep yellow, golden, or golden-orange**. Undersides have numerous **forked** folds that are yellowish, whitish or creamy peach. Caps are 1 to 5 inches across. Stems are up to 2¼ inches tall and one-third as wide; they may be paler than the cap, particularly at the base. Cap edges may bruise darker. They have a fruity or **apricot** odor.

- **Red Chanterelles** (*Cantharellus cinnabarinus*) are **deep orange to reddish-orange**. Caps are less than 2 inches across; stems are up to 1½ inches tall.

- **Smooth Chanterelles** (*Cantharellus lateritius*) **lack the folds under the cap**, or have very faint folds. The color is similar to the Yellow Chanterelle; Smooth Chanterelle may be a bit larger. Look for it under oaks.

- **Yellow-Foot Chanterelles** (*Craterellus tubaeformis*) are similar in size to Red Chanterelles, although often taller. Caps are **brownish to olive-brown**; stems are **yellowish to orangish-tan** and gills are grayish-lilac. Folds are very thick, with many forks near the edge of the cap. *Craterellus lutescens* and *Craterellus*

Cantharellus appalachiensis

False Chanterelle (not recommended)

NOT RECOMMENDED

ignicolor are also called Yellow-Foot Chanterelle; caps are **smooth underneath or with a few wide folds near the edge**. They grow in damp areas.

- The Small Chanterelle (*Cantharellus minor*) is yellowish to orangish, with a cap that is ¼ to 1¼ inches across and a somewhat delicate stem up to 2 inches tall; it grows in mossy or damp areas.

- Caps of young *Cantharellus appalachiensis* are **brownish and rounded**. They soon become vase-shaped, turning **yellowish to brownish-yellow** but retaining a **brownish center**; they are less than 2½ inches across. Folds are yellowish; stems are pale yellowish-brown. Found in mixed woods.

SPORE PRINT: Spores of Red Chanterelles are cream-colored, often with a faint pinkish cast; all other Chanterelles listed here have pale yellow, buff-colored, cream-colored or whitish spores.

SEASON: Chanterelles in our area fruit in summer, sometimes into early fall.

OTHER NAMES: The Yellow Chanterelle is also called Golden Chanterelle. Yellow-Foot Chanterelles are also called Trumpet Chanterelles and were formerly listed in the *Cantharellus* genus.

COMPARE: Jack O'Lantern (pgs. 72–73; **toxic**) is bright orange, with **true, knife-edged gills that can be separated individually from the cap**; the gills are **unforked**. Jack O'Lanterns tend to grow in dense clusters and always **on wood**, although the wood may be buried and easy to miss. Its flesh is **orange**. • False Chanterelle (*Hygrophoropsis aurantiaca*) has **true gills**; it is **orangish-yellow** to brownish with a darker area in the center of the cap and grows from the soil or on woody debris. Its gills are orange; they are **more brightly colored than the cap and fork repeatedly**. Some sources list it as edible, while others say it causes intestinal problems.

NOTES: Most Chanterelles have a fruity aroma and a mildly peppery flavor.

Giant Puffball

Calvatia gigantea

You might mistake this round, white mushroom for a softball, a soccer ball or something larger (an alien spaceship?). Fresh, young specimens are a popular edible and the old, brown ones become a giant smoke bomb that kids like to stomp on (be careful not to inhale the spore cloud; it can cause respiratory distress).

HABITAT: Grows from the ground singly, in groups or sometimes in large circles (called fairy rings) in grassy areas or woodlands. It is common in the northern and central portions of our area, becoming less common or not present in the southern portions, where it is replaced by two other large puffballs; see the Compare section on pgs. 42–43 for more information.

DESCRIPTION: These generally **spherical, white-skinned** mushrooms are usually 8 to 12 inches across, but can grow up to 3 feet wide! They

Giant Puffball

Co-author Kathy with Giant Puffball

Interior of Puffball

get more misshapen and dented as they expand but are still attached to the ground with only a **small root-like structure**. The exterior skin encases the spore-producing flesh inside that is **smooth and pure white** when young, much like a loaf of white bread. As it ages, the skin develops scaly patches and cracks, becoming more tan in color. The interior becomes yellow, then greenish, until finally the spores are ripe brown. If untouched, it will eventually shed its outer skin to expose the mass of spores, which will be spread by the wind.

SPORE PRINT: Brown.

SEASON: Early summer through fall.

OTHER NAMES: Moon Melon, *Langermannia gigantea*, *Lycoperdon giganteum*.

COMPARE: Several other large puffballs are also found in the Upper Midwest. • The **Skull-Shaped Puffball** (*C. craniiformis*) is less spherical overall and doesn't grow as large as the Giant Puffball; it is generally less than 10 inches in diameter. The entire mushroom is covered in smooth white to tan skin and has a **narrower, goblet-like base**, making the puffball appear **skull-like**. The base doesn't produce spores and remains attached to the ground even after the ripe, **yellowish-brown** spores have been released and the rest of the puffball disintegrates. • The **Purple-Spored Puffball** (*C. cyathiformis*) is smaller than the Skull-Shaped Puffball. It is generally less than 6 inches in diameter and seems to prefer grassy areas to woodlands. Initially white throughout, it is distinguished from other puffballs when ripe by the **dark brown cracked skin** and by its **purple spore mass**, which may be visible year-round in the remaining nest-like piece that is left attached to the ground after the spores have been released and the rest of the puffball disintegrates. • Scaly Puffball (*Mycenastrum corium*) has a **thick, scaly skin** and grows to 8 inches across. It is found in grassy areas

Skull-Shaped Puffball
EDIBLE

Purple-Spored Puffball
EDIBLE

and is attached to the ground by a **strong, central root**. With age, it becomes rougher and discolors tan to brown, particularly in the cracks. The flesh is fairly firm; the skin should be peeled off before cooking. It is more common west of the Rocky Mountains, but its occurrence in our area is increasing. • Several smaller puffball species are common in our area; see pg. 236 for information.

Scaly Puffball
EDIBLE

NOTES: All the puffballs listed here are edible when they are young and the flesh is **pure, featureless white throughout**. If the flesh appears to be anything other than pure, featureless white, the puffball is too mature to eat, or it may be another species. Small puffballs growing from the ground should always be cut in half, as they can be mistaken for a number of cap-and-stem species in the button stage, including **deadly** Amanitas (pgs. 62–67), **toxic** Agaricus (pg. 82) or the egg stage of Stinkhorns (pg. 198); they may also be mistaken for **toxic** Earthballs (pg. 240). Note that the button stage of an Amanita is not featureless inside; instead, a faint outline of the developing mushroom can be seen in the interior flesh. The outline is often very subtle, as shown in the photo at left.

Split Amanita button
TOXIC

green = key identification feature   43

TOP EDIBLES

King Bolete
Boletus 'edulis'

As the name King Bolete suggests, *Boletus 'edulis'* is one of the most sought-after edible mushrooms. This is the mushroom that Europeans call the Porcini or Cep. It grows in our area but is more commonly found in large numbers and much larger sizes in the Rocky Mountains. According to experts there are most likely many different species across North America that we simply refer to as *B. edulis* (which is a European species) due to their similarities and popularity as a good edible. Additionally, there are hundreds of other distinct species of boletes in various colors, shapes and sizes, many of which are inedible or even **toxic** (see pgs. 68–70).

From above, this brown-capped mushroom looks like a typical cap-with-stem shape, but turning it over reveals a **spongy pore surface**. This is really a series of tubes that hold spores. It is the feature that most strongly defines the group of mushrooms called, in general, *boletes*, a term used to refer to many cap-and-stem mushrooms with pores.

King Bolete

green = key identification feature

HABITAT: King Boletes are mycorrhizal, growing from the soil singly or in loose groups in association with trees; they are generally found under conifers but may also grow near oaks and other deciduous trees. The mycelium (threadlike fungal filaments) has a symbiotic relationship with tree roots; because of this, Kings are often found in the same place from year to year.

Spongy pore surface

Reticulation on stem

DESCRIPTION: This stout mushroom has a large, dull brown cap, 3 to 10 inches across, that becomes almost polished in old age. When young, the rounded cap may have a flush of white that can remain as a faint edging on the outer rim as it enlarges and flattens out. Immature caps may also seem small in relation to the swollen stem, which tends to be short and bulbous on young specimens. The stem lengthens with age and may be up to 7 inches tall and 1 to 3 inches thick; it is always **white or cream-colored** with surface **reticulation** (mesh-like texture) of the **same color**. The reticulation is most prominent at the top of the stem. The stem has no ring. The interior of the stem is solid, white, and although a little firmer than the cap, is valued just as much for edibility. The interior flesh of the cap is also white. The pore surface of the King is white and **very finely textured** when young; pores are stuffed, making the surface appear nearly solid. With age the pores turn yellowish and become coarser. When handled, bruised or cut crosswise, King Boletes **do not bruise or change color**. In comparison, the flesh and pore surface of many of the other boletes stain or discolor when cut, scraped or bruised; some **toxic** varieties (pgs. 68–70) turn blue.

SPORE PRINT: The King Bolete has an **olive-brown** spore print.

SEASON: Summer, sometimes into early fall.

OTHER NAMES: Porcini, Cep, Penny Bun, Steinpilz. Other members of the *B. edulis* group in our area include *B. atkinsonii* and *B.* cf. *reticulatus*

B. variipes   **Lilac Bolete**   **Pallid Bolete**

COMPARE: Numerous mushrooms in our area look similar to the King Bolete; those listed here are edible.

• *B. variipes* is similar to the King and is considered part of the *B. edulis* group, but it has a more **grayish** tint to the brown cap, which is often finely cracked when old and dry. Like the cap, the stem is **grayish brown**, with white reticulation. Found near oaks and other hardwoods.

• **Lilac Bolete** (*B. separans*; also listed as *Xanthoconium separans*) has **purplish-brown to lilac-colored** caps that are up to 7 inches across and often **wrinkled**; caps turn brownish with age. Stems have white reticulation and are colored like a pale version of the cap; they lose much of their color with age. The pore surface is white at first, turning yellow and finally brownish; it **does not discolor** when bruised. Lilac Bolete grows near hardwoods and occasionally conifers. Bicolor Bolete (pg. 196) may be mistaken for a young Lilac Bolete, but its cap is more intensely red and it has a bright yellow pore surface that **stains blue**. If the specimen is a Lilac Bolete a drop of household ammonia turns purplish areas deep blue-green (brown areas of the cap will turn deep red); ammonia produces no change to a Bicolor Bolete.

• The **Pallid Bolete** (*B. pallidus*) is **pale overall** when young. Caps are **whitish**, becoming brownish with age; they are up to 6 inches across at maturity. The pore surface is whitish at first, becoming yellowish to greenish-yellow; it slowly bruises **dull grayish-green or bluish** when handled. Stems are whitish and smooth, with **no reticulation**; the lower half may develop faint reddish-brown streaks with age. They associate with hardwoods, particularly oak.

• The **Bluing Bolete** (*Gyroporus cyanescens*) breaks the rule for identifying toxic boletes (pg. 68)—it is edible even though its flesh and pores **stain vivid blue** when scratched, cut or bruised. Its cap is 2 to 5 inches across and its stem is less than 5 inches tall. Both cap and stem are **cream-colored**; the stem

Bluing Bolete

EDIBLE

X. purpureum

P. indecisus

EDIBLE

is **easily broken** and stuffed with cottony material, becoming hollow with age. The spore print is **light yellow**. Found near hardwoods.

- Caps of **X. purpureum** are up to 5 inches across and **reddish-brown, dark red or purplish**; they **briefly turn greenish-blue** when a drop of ammonia is applied. Stems are whitish to yellowish-brown; there is **no reticulation,** but they are often streaked or tinted reddish to brownish, especially the lower portion. The pore surface is whitish at first, turning yellowish-brown; it may bruise brownish, but not always. The spore print is **rich yellowish-brown**. This choice edible is found near oaks and other hardwoods.

- *Porphyrellus indecisus* (also listed as *Tylopilus indecisus*) has brownish caps that are up to 6¾ inches across. Stems are up to 4 inches long and roughly equal in width from top to base, although young specimens may be club-shaped. They are whitish, becoming brownish with age and handling; there is often, but not always, fine brownish reticulation at the top. The pore surface is beige, becoming **pinkish or brownish-pink** with age; it bruises **brown**. The spore print is **pinkish-brown**. Found near oak and other hardwoods. It resembles the Bitter Bolete (*T. felleus*; pg. 182) but is **mild-tasting**, not bitter.

NOTES: Both the cap and stem of the King Bolete are edible and choice. It dries well, and drying intensifies its nutty flavor. Boletes should be cut into evenly thick slices before cooking or drying; this ensures that all pieces cook at the same rate and also allows you to check for insect larvae. In the Midwest, the bugs will often beat you to this tasty find.

ON DEAD OR DYING TREES   SUMMER THROUGH FALL

Lion's Mane (several)

Hericium spp.

This beautiful waterfall-like mushroom is a delight to come upon in the woods. It often grows in large clusters, so if you are lucky enough to find it, you will probably find a lot!

HABITAT: Grows as a parasite and decomposer (called saprobic) of dying and dead deciduous trees; may be found rarely on conifers. Usually found in mixed woods on fallen maple, beech or oak logs.

DESCRIPTION: The sheer number of common names given to this mushroom helps convey its unique look. Rather than a cap or shelf, it is a **large, white mass with dangling teeth** that are actually the spore-producing structures. It can grow up to **one foot** across and is comprised of soft but brittle **white** flesh that becomes yellow or even tinged with brown when old. Three *Hericium* species grow in our region. Due to constant evolution of naming in mycology (the study of mushrooms), the scientific names of two of them have been switched with each other, so you may come across conflicting names in older references. Happily, all are edible and delicious.

H. erinaceus

• *H. erinaceus* is easy to identify because it has teeth up to **2 inches long**. The teeth grow from an **unbranching central base**, like a white pom pom. It is commonly cultivated, dried and sold in Asian grocery stores as Monkey Head Mushroom.

green = key identification feature

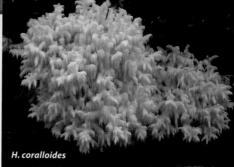

H. americanum

H. coralloides

- *H. americanum* (formerly listed as *H. coralloides*) has **numerous branches** growing from the central base. Its teeth are shorter than those of *H. erinaceus*, generally about 1 inch long or less; they create a tufted appearance.

- *H. coralloides* (formerly listed as *H. ramosum*) resembles coral due to its more **loosely branching** habit and teeth that are ½ **inch long or less**.

SPORE PRINT: White.

SEASON: Summer through fall.

OTHER NAMES: Bear's Head Tooth Fungus, Monkey's Head, Icicle Mushroom, Pom Pom Mushroom, Satyr's Beard, Bearded Hedgehog, Comb Tooth, Waterfall Hydnum.

COMPARE: Crown-Tipped Coral (pg. 256) grows on fallen logs. It has a more **upright, loose** structure and **does not have teeth**. The branches are white or yellowish and somewhat translucent. Crown-Tipped Coral is edible when young and has a peppery flavor but develops a tough texture with age. • **Northern Tooth** (pg. 231) is similar in size, habitat and color to Lion's Mane and even has spore-bearing teeth. However, those teeth are found on the underside of **large, rough, overlapping shelves**. It is not edible due to its tough texture and bitter flavor.

NOTES: All Hericium are sought-after edibles, but the Pom Pom version is said to taste the best. They are lovely when sliced and cooked, with a flavor and texture that is sometimes compared to lobster. It is best when young and fresh, because it gets sour or bitter tasting when old. It is popular in Chinese cooking and is also reported to have medicinal properties.

TOP EDIBLES

Black Trumpet

Craterellus fallax

Shaped like a lily blossom, this fragrant mushroom is often found while looking for Chanterelles (pgs. 38–40). However, unlike the brightly colored Chanterelles that seem to want to be found, this lovely edible mushroom could be right under your feet and you might not even notice it!

HABITAT: Grows **from the ground**, singly or more often in tight clusters, near living conifers and hardwoods. They are particularly fond of mossy areas. The mycelium (threadlike fungal filaments) are thought to have a symbiotic relationship with tree roots (mycorrhizal).

DESCRIPTION: These **thin, funnel-shaped** mushrooms are hard to see simply because of their color. Ranging from **gray to brown to black**, they don't stand out against the soil, unless you happen to find a nice clump on a bright green patch of moss. They can also be quite small, ranging from 1 to 3 inches across but may grow prolifically and over large expanses. The edges of these delicate funnels are rolled under when young but become wavy as they grow and may get darker along the edges. Stems are less than 4 inches tall and are **hollow** like a true funnel but may be tightly pinched at the bottom, especially when

Black Trumpets

green = key identification feature

Brownish form

Fragrant Black Trumpet
EDIBLE

growing in a tight cluster. The spore-producing surface on the exterior has **no gills**; it is smooth or slightly wrinkled, ranging in color from **very light gray to brown to charcoal or even jet-black when wet**. Black Trumpets have a distinctly **fruity scent**, like plums or prunes.

SPORE PRINT: Pale pinkish-orange to buffy yellow.

SEASON: Summer through fall.

OTHER NAMES: Horn of Plenty, Black Chanterelle, Trumpet of Death (based on the color only), *Craterellus cornucopioides* (see NOTES below).

COMPARE: Devil's Urn (pg. 244) could be confused with Black Trumpets, but it grows **on wood** in **early spring**. It is generally regarded as inedible and is not collected for the table. • The **Fragrant Black Trumpet** (*Craterellus foetidus*) is **thicker** and the bottom part of the stem is **solid**. It also has **distinct veins**, much like a Chanterelle (pgs. 38–40), and the exterior is light gray with a pink to purple tinge. It is reported to have a much stronger aroma than other Black Trumpets and is equally edible and delicious. • *Cantharellus cinereus* (also listed as *Craterellus cinereus*) is extremely rare but has an **almost white exterior** with prominent ridges and a strong, sweet smell like the Fragrant Black Trumpet. It is edible but some say it is less delicious than the Black Trumpet. • **Hairy Rubber Cup** (pg. 244) can found in the same season and habitat as Black Trumpets, but it grows **on wood**. Very mature species can have a wrinkled, black, vase-shaped exterior, but the interior is **light brown and solid**, with a **rubbery texture**. (Young examples are cup-shaped and look nothing like a trumpet.) Hairy Rubber Cup is inedible.

NOTES: The Black Trumpet found in North America has long been listed as *Craterellus cornucopioides*, but that is a European species with **white** spores. Black Trumpets are often dehydrated, which further enhances their fruity aroma and flavor.

TOP EDIBLES

Hedgehogs

Hydnum repandum, Hydnum umbilicatum

At first glance, these mushrooms look like many other cap-and-stem species. When the mushroom is turned over, however, the difference becomes clear: instead of gills or pores, the underside of the cap is covered with **distinct spines or teeth**. There are two similar species; both are edible and delicious.

HABITAT: Growing from the ground, singly or in groups, near living trees; the mycelium (threadlike fungal filaments) has a symbiotic relationship with tree roots (mycorrhizal).

DESCRIPTION: Two closely related mushrooms are commonly called Hedgehogs. Both have a **bristly-looking pore surface** under the caps, consisting of spore-bearing spines or teeth.

• *Hydnum repandum* is the larger of the two, with **cream to tan to apricot** caps that are 2 to **7 inches** wide. The edge of the cap is rolled under when young, becoming flattened and more lobed and wavy as it grows, a bit like Chanterelles (pgs. 38–40). The thick **white** stem is often **off-center** and is less than 4 inches tall;

Hydnum repandum

green = key identification feature

the **cream-colored teeth** may run partway down it. The stem and teeth **bruise orangish-brown** when handled, and the whitish interior flesh may **discolor yellow** when cut. It prefers deciduous trees, especially oak, but may be found near conifers.

Hydnum umbilicatum

• *Hydnum umbilicatum* is much smaller and prefers a **boggy pine habitat**. It generally has a **darker orangish** cap that is 2 inches wide or less and is **sunken in the center**, lending it the common name of Belly Button Mushroom. The whitish flesh **does not discolor** when cut. The stem is thinner and **more centrally located** and the teeth are darker than those of *Hydnum repandum*.

SPORE PRINT: White to cream.

SEASON: Late summer through fall.

OTHER NAMES: Sweet Tooth (usually applied to *Hydnum umbilicatum*), Wood Hedgehog, *Dentinum repandum*.

COMPARE: The inedible **Orange Hydnellum** (pg. 262) is usually found under conifers. Its caps are bumpy, **clustered** and often fused; they are orange to brownish with a pale edge, darkening with age. Its **brown teeth**, stocky **brown** stem that is less than 3 inches tall and **brown** spore print easily distinguish it from the edible Hedgehogs. • The inedible **Drab Tooth** (*Phellodon fuligineo-ulbus*; also listed as *Bankera fuligineoalba*) is similar to *Hydnum repandum* in cap color and size, but it is rare and found only under **pines**. The teeth and upper part of the stem are white; the bottom part of the stem is **dark brown**. It is sometimes called Blushing Fenugreek Tooth because dry specimens may smell like fenugreek (similar to curry). • Other *Hydnellum* **species** (pg. 262) are similar only because of the presence of teeth under their oddly shaped caps.

NOTES: A favorite and easily distinguished edible, Hedgehogs are closely related to Chanterelles and are often found in the same locations and at the same time. Hedgehogs have a lightly fruity aroma and peppery taste and unlike many good edibles, insects seem to leave them alone.

NEAR LIVE OR DEAD TREES

LATE SUMMER THROUGH LATE FALL

TOP EDIBLES

Hen of the Woods

Grifola frondosa

The discovery of a large Hen of the Woods is a thrill for any mushroom seeker. Not only do the clusters sometimes reach enormous proportions—2 feet across is possible, or even bigger—but the mushrooms have a firm texture and meaty taste that is highly prized. They are also in high demand for medicinal uses in Japan, Korea and China.

HABITAT: Hens grow in clusters **at or near the base of trees**; they are generally found under oak but also reported under maple and other species. Trees may be living or dead. Several clusters may grow around the same tree or on nearby trees.

DESCRIPTION: Hen of the Woods grows as a **tight cluster or rosette** of **many individual fan-shaped caps** arising from a central fleshy base, similar to a cauliflower. The upper surface of the caps may be

Several Hen of the Woods clusters

tan, gray, cream-colored or white; the texture is **smooth to slightly velvety**. Individual caps are **1 to 3 inches across** and may have subtle streaks radiating from the center, or may appear slightly mottled; edges sometimes have a darker band. The undersides are white to cream-colored and covered with **small pores** that descend the base of each cap towards the central base; individual caps have no actual stem. The flesh of both the caps and the base is firm but tender on fresh specimens; older specimens become tough, especially the central base.

SPORE PRINT: White.

green = key identification feature

Gray cluster

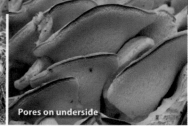
Pores on underside

SEASON: Early to late fall; sometimes found in late summer.

OTHER NAMES: Maitake, Sheepshead, Ram's Head, *Polyporus frondosus*.

COMPARE: Other clustering shelf-like mushrooms are found in our area near deciduous trees; here is how to distinguish them. • **Black-Staining Polypore** (*Meripilus sumstinei*; also listed as *M. giganteus*, which is a European species) has caps that may grow up to **12 inches wide**, although they are often smaller. Caps are grayish to drab yellowish and may appear banded or ringed. They are thicker than Hens, especially towards the center, with a **fibrous, tough texture**; when a cap is pulled apart, **thin fibers may be visible**. Pores are **white**; caps slowly **bruise brownish to blackish** when handled. Stems are short and stubby and generally off-center. Black-Staining Polypore may be found near beech trees in the eastern part of our area. Young specimens are generally regarded as edible although reports of its flavor range from mild to bitter or sour, and some people suffer digestive problems after eating it. • **Umbrella Polypore** (*P. umbellatus*) has **circular** caps; each cap has a **central stem** that joins with others in the cluster to form a large, thick, central stalk. Umbrella Polypore is less common than Hen of the Woods and its clusters are smaller, but it is also a delicious edible. • **Chicken of the Woods** (pgs. 32-33) is **bright yellowish to orangish**, and its lobes are larger and thicker; it is a delicious edible when young. • **Berkeley's Polypore** (pg. 213) has large, whitish caps up to **10 inches** across; they are dry in texture and produce milky sap when squeezed. Although edible when found in a young, finger-like growth stage, developed caps are bitter and inedible.

NOTES: Hen of the Woods clusters grow around anything they encounter, and it's not uncommon to find twigs, leaves or other debris embedded in the cluster. Bugs also burrow into the clusters; a soak in a mild saltwater solution should dislodge these unwanted inhabitants. Hen of the Woods typically appears in the same location year after year.

SPRING

TOP TOXICS

False Morels: Gyromitras (several)

Gyromitra spp.

Gyromitras are often found in the spring woods by people seeking Morels (pgs. 24–27). At first glance, the two mushrooms can be confused, but closer inspection reveals some significant differences.

HABITAT: Gyromitras grow singly or scattered from the ground in forests.

DESCRIPTION: At a quick glance, the Gyromitras discussed here look lumpy, with a brain-like, folded or wrinkled texture. All have **pale, chambered flesh inside**. Stems are white to pale tan.

• **Big Red** (*G. caroliniana*; found near deciduous trees) is 2 to **7 inches** tall and wide, with a **reddish, coarsely wrinkled** cap that may appear to have vertical ridges. The stem is **stocky**, with a **highly ribbed** texture.

• **Conifer False Morel** (*G. esculenta*; found primarily near conifers) is up to 4 inches tall and wide. Its **brownish cap** is covered with **rounded, brain-like wrinkles**. Its medium-width stem may be smooth or creased.

• **Gabled False Morel** (*G. brunnea*; found near deciduous trees) is up to 4 inches tall and wide, with **a tan to reddish-brown** cap composed of **flattened, wavy folds** that appear **seamed**; its stem is short and stocky.

Big Red

Conifer False Morel

green = key identification feature

• **Bull-Nose False Morel** (*G. korfii*; found in mixed woods) is tan with a **wrinkled or wavy** texture; it is generally less than 3 inches tall and wide. The cap hangs over the stem so much that the mushroom may appear **stemless**.

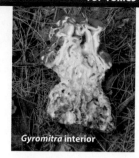

Gyromitra interior

SPORE PRINT: Spore color is not an identifying factor with Gyromitras.

SEASON: Spring.

OTHER NAMES: False Morel.

COMPARE: Morels (pgs. 24–27) may appear similar at first glance, but their caps are **pitted and ridged** and the insides are **completely hollow**. • Several *Gyromitra* species appear cup-like and resemble *Peziza* (pg. 246) • The **Saddle-Shaped False Morel** (pg. 200) appears in **late summer and fall**, fruiting on conifer wood or woody humus. The brownish caps are usually **saddle-shaped**.

NOTES: Although some people eat Big Reds and Conifer False Morels after boiling them in several changes of water, all Gyromitras contain toxic compounds that can cause severe illness or death. The toxic effects may be cumulative, and even exposure to the steam released from cooking is dangerous. Gyromitras should be considered inedible and possibly **toxic**.

Gabled False Morel

Bull-Nose False Morel

ON DECAYING WOOD

SPRING THROUGH FALL

TOP TOXICS

Deadly Galerina
Galerina marginata

This pretty little mushroom prefers cool weather; it typically graces the woods in spring, then again in fall. Unfortunately, it is one of the most **toxic** mushrooms around. It contains amatoxins, the same deadly poisons found in Amanitas; for more information on this toxin, see pg. 63.

HABITAT: Deadly Galerina are saprobes, getting their nutrients from dead wood. They grow in **clusters** on decaying deciduous and coniferous wood; they are often found on rotting logs that are mossy.

DESCRIPTION: Deadly Galerina are small to medium mushrooms, with caps that are generally 1½ inches wide or less; large specimens may be up to 3 inches across. The caps are **rust-colored, tawny or brownish** with a tacky surface, fading and becoming paler with age or upon drying; they may feel slimy in damp weather. They are rounded or bell-shaped when young, opening up and becoming fairly flat with maturity. Stems are slender and generally 2 to 3 inches long; they are fairly equal in width from top to bottom but often curve as they emerge from a rotting log or from a cluster. They are pale gray to brownish; the lower portion of the stem may be darker and somewhat shaggy. White

green = key identification feature

Yellowish gills, skirt-like ring

Velvet Foot (pg. 130)
EDIBLE

mycelium (threadlike fungal filaments) can sometimes be seen where the stem grows out of the wood. A **fragile, short skirt-like ring** is present on the upper half of the stem of young specimens. The ring is whitish at first, turning **brown** as it catches falling spores. It often disintegrates, leaving behind a **thin, collar-like ring zone**; the ring may be fairly obvious or may disappear completely. Gills are **honey-colored** at first, becoming **rust-colored** as the spores develop; they are attached to the stem and closely spaced.

SPORE PRINT: Rust-colored.

SEASON: Deadly Galerina are most common in spring and fall but may appear in summer during periods of cool weather.

OTHER NAMES: Autumn Galerina, *G. autumnalis*.

COMPARE: Velvet Foot (pg. 130) is an edible orangish mushroom that thrives in the same habitat and season as Deadly Galerina, but it produces a **white** spore print. Velvet Foot stems have **no ring**, and they turn **dark brown to blackish** with age. Its caps are slimy. Great care must be taken to distinguish between the two species when collecting Velvet Foot for the table, as young Velvet Foot look nearly identical to Deadly Galerina. • **Honey Mushrooms** (pg. 110) are yellowish to brownish, and are larger and **beefier** than Deadly Galerina; they have a **sturdy ring** on the stem and a **white** spore print. • Various **Little Brown Mushrooms** (pg. 112) may resemble Deadly Galerina; the resemblance of LBMs to a species as dangerous as Deadly Galerina should be enough to dissuade anyone from eating most small, brownish mushrooms.

NOTES: Both Deadly Galerina and Velvet Foot are often found by Morel hunters in the spring. Careless collectors of Honey Mushrooms and Velvet Foot have been poisoned by failing to inspect every mushroom.

FROM THE SOIL

EARLY SUMMER THROUGH FALL

Green-Spored Lepiota

Chlorophyllum molybdites

This mushroom is very common in urban areas, where it pops up in even the most well-manicured lawns starting in early summer. It's easy to spot, even from a distance, as young specimens look like elevated white balls on the lawn; small specimens look like golf balls, while larger ones are the size of softballs. Unfortunately, according to a 2005 report from the North American Mycological Association, this **toxic** species is responsible for almost as many poisonings (caused by positively identified mushroom species) as the top two *Amanita* species combined. Symptoms include intense vomiting and other severe gastrointestinal problems one to three hours after ingestion.

HABITAT: Found in grassy areas such as lawns and meadows. Grows singly or scattered; may also grow in a ring.

DESCRIPTION: A **sturdy-looking medium to large** mushroom that is whitish overall. Young specimens have a spherical or egg-shaped cap that is white to cream-colored and typically 1½ to 2½ inches wide. The cap expands dramatically as it opens up, becoming softly rounded

green = key identification feature

Young specimens

to flattened, sometimes with upturned edges; it is typically **6 to 9 inches** across when mature but may be larger. Mature caps have **large buff to brownish patches** at the top and smaller scales around the bottom. The stem is whitish to tan, sturdy and typically 4 to 8 inches long; it is typically smooth but may have a few small scales. Once the cap opens, there is a **double ring** near the top of the stem that may disappear on old specimens. The base may be somewhat enlarged but is not bulbous. Gills are closely spaced and **not attached** to the stem; they are white at first, turning **grayish-green** with age.

Mature gills

SPORE PRINT: Greenish to dull olive.

SEASON: Early summer through fall.

OTHER NAMES: Green Gills, *Lepiota morgani*.

COMPARE: Species listed in this section are very similar to Green-Spored Lepiota, but all have **white** spore prints. • Shaggy Parasol (pg. 78) is more **coarsely scaled**; young caps and the patches on mature caps are typically **brown**. • American Parasol (pg. 78) is **smaller** than Green-Spored Lepiota; its cap is covered with small **rust-colored scales**. • *Macrolepiota procera* (pg. 78) has a **narrow, scaly**

Greenish spore print

stem; the cap has a dark, **nipple-like bump** in the center. • Many **toxic Amanita species** (pgs. 62–67) have patchy caps and swollen bases; some have a **cup** at the stem base.

NOTES: Other than **toxic** *Amanita* species, the lookalikes listed above are sometimes collected for the table by experts, but this is strongly advised against due to the difficulty of positive identification.

Amanitas (numerous)

Amanita spp.

It's probably safe to say that if you asked most people to name just one poisonous mushroom, they would mention the Amanita, although each person might have a different picture in their mind as to what this dastardly fungus looks like. Many people would think of the delicate, all-white Destroying Angel, with its skirt-like ring on the stem and its fragile cup at the base. Others might conjure up an image of the Fly Agaric, with its cheerful, brightly colored cap dotted with numerous small but thick white patches.

The Amanita genus is a large, diverse group of mushrooms, encompassing hundreds of species in a wide palette of colors. The species discussed in this book have caps with gills underneath and stems that are centered under the caps; many other key characteristics are microscopic. Common traits shared by many—but not all—are the presence of a ring on the stem and a fragile, cup-like structure called a ***volva*** around the base of the stem. Many also have patches on the caps. All three of these characteristics are remnants of a veil, a thin membrane that covers all or part of the developing mushroom.

All Amanitas start their lives encased in a ***universal veil***, a thin membrane that surrounds the developing mushroom entirely, making it resemble a small, rough-skinned egg; this is often referred to as the ***egg stage***. As the mushroom grows, it breaks through the universal veil. The volva is

Amanitas, from egg to button stage (different species shown)

Egg stage

Emerging from veil

Button stage

green = key identification feature

the part of the universal veil surrounding the base of the stem after the mushroom has emerged from the egg-like sac; it is often necessary to dig around the base to uncover evidence of the volva, which may be covered by dirt and sometimes has disintegrated entirely. The patches on top of the cap, when present, are another remnant of the universal veil; patches may be thick, wart-like and persistent, or thin, insubstantial and easily washed away by rain.

Some Amanitas also have a *partial veil*, a thin membrane attached to both the stem and the lower edge of the young, unopened cap. As the cap expands, the partial veil stretches to cover the gills, finally breaking away from the cap when it becomes too wide. The partial veil remnant often remains attached to the stem under the cap, hanging down and appearing skirt-like or ring-like; fragments may also hang like broken tissue from the edges of the cap.

Skirt like veil remnant

Some Amanitas are notorious because they contain *amatoxins*, extremely poisonous substances that cause liver and kidney failure and, often, death; the fatality rate for this type of poisoning, according to the North American Mycological Association, is as high as 50% unless prompt, often radical treatment is effected. Other Amanitas have no amatoxins but contain other poisonous substances that cause failure of the nervous system, severe gastric problems or psychosis. A few lack any toxins and are, surprisingly, edible; however, due to the possibility of confusion with toxic species, **no Amanita should be eaten** by any but the most experienced of foragers—and even then, it is risky business that is best avoided.

HABITAT: All Amanitas grow **from the ground**. Most are found near living trees; the mycelium (threadlike fungal filaments) has a symbiotic relationship with tree roots (mycorrhizal). They grow singly, scattered or in loose groups; with one exception, the species here grow in mixed woods, near oaks and conifers.

DESCRIPTION: Although there are many differences in appearance between the numerous *Amanita* species, all share some common aspects. Young Amanitas at the button stage have rounded or egg-shaped caps that are generally 1 to 1½ inches across. As the specimen matures, the cap opens up like an umbrella, becoming wider and flatter; mature specimens of the species discussed here are generally 3 to 6 inches wide. The surface texture of the cap varies depending on species. Stems are stocky on young specimens, becoming moderately sturdy to slender; all of the toxic species discussed here have a ring or skirt on the stem, although it may deteriorate or fall off with age. All Amanitas have

Destroying Angel | False Death Cap

some remnant of the universal veil at the base; it can be cup-like and quite obvious, but it is sometimes buried or broken up. Gills are closely spaced and generally free from the stem or just attached; they are typically white.

- The **Destroying Angel** (*A. bisporigera*) contains amatoxins (pg. 63) and is one of the most deadly mushrooms known; *ingestion of a single cap can kill an adult*. This graceful-looking mushroom is common in our area; it grows near deciduous trees, primarily oak. It is typically **pure white** overall but may be pale ivory; the center of the cap may be slightly darker. The cap has a smooth, silky texture; very rarely there may be a patch of veil remnant on the cap. Stems may be smooth or slightly shaggy. A **delicate, skirt-like ring** is present near the top of the stem. A cup-like volva surrounds the base, which is often bulbous or swollen; you may need to dig in the dirt to see these characteristics. Two related species, *A. virosa* and *A. verna*, are also referred to by the same common name; other than slight variations in size, they are inseparable from *A. bisporigera* without aid of a microscope. Some mycologists believe they are European species that do not appear occur in the United States.

- **False Death Cap** (*A. 'citrina'* and *A. citrina* f. *lavendula*; regarded by some mycologists as a group of related species) is generally regarded as **toxic**; depending on the color of the specimen, it may also be confused with the true Death Cap (*A. phalloides*), a **deadly** mushroom that is found in our area only in the far eastern portion. Caps of False Death Cap may be whitish-yellow, pale greenish-yellow or lemon-yellow. They are adorned with soft, thick patches that range from whitish to buff to brownish. Stems are tall, slender and whitish, often with scattered hairs on the lower part; the base is bulbous and **marshmallow-like** in appearance. A thin, skirt-like ring is generally present towards the top of the stem. Some say that it smells like raw potatoes.

Cleft-Foot Amanita   **Fly Agaric**

- Cleft-Foot Amanita (*A. brunnescens*) is another **toxic** species that has a variable cap color. Typically brownish, it fades with age to gray or even white, but may be darker in the center with a slight hump; it grows up to 6 inches across and typically has scattered pale wart-like patches. Stems are up to 5 inches tall and about a half inch thick and tapered. The **distinctly abrupt bulb** at the base of the stem, which may be vertically split in one or more places, helps distinguish this species along with the **reddish-brown bruising** of the stem and gills. There may be veil remnants on the cap edge, but the skirt-like ring disappears quickly and is usually only seen on young specimens.

- Fly Agaric (*A. muscaria*) is **toxic** but not generally lethal; among other unpleasant symptoms, including delirium, it causes a coma-like condition that may last for hours. One of the loveliest of Amanitas, its cap, which may be up to **10 inches wide**, is heavily speckled with **buff-colored wart-like patches**; cap edges may be faintly ribbed. Caps of specimens found in the Midwest (called var. *guessowii*) are **yellowish to orangish**; in the Western United States and in Europe caps are bright red. Stems are buff colored with a scaly texture that appears banded, particularly near the base. A thin, skirt-like ring is generally present near the top of the stem. A **white** version, called var. *alba*, is much less common. It has the same features as the colored varieties, with tan to white patches, but the stem may **bruise yellow to brown** when handled.

- Yellow Patches (*A. flavoconia*, also called Yellow Dust Amanita) is a lovely mushroom that is common in our area. Toxicity is unknown, but is so similar to *A. muscaria* it should not be ingested. It has **bright yellow to orangish** caps that are adorned with **yellow patches** when young, but they typically, fall off fairy quickly, leaving a **smooth, slightly sticky** surface. Mature caps are up to 3 inches wide and fairy flat, but may have a small raised knob in the center and

Yellow Patches

faint grooves along the edges. Thin stems are up to 4 inches tall and yellow to whitish with a slightly bulbous base; the base, and often the lower part of the stem, is roughened with small, **scruffy yellow patches**. A delicate, pale yellow skirt-like ring is present on the upper part of the stem.

- **Frost's Amanita** (*A. frostiana*) looks similar to Yellow Patches, but is much less common. Caps are heavily dotted with **small, cottony wart-like patches** that are pale yellow; edges are **distinctly ribbed**. The top of the bulb-like base has a **collar of yellowish, cottony material**.

- The 'Pantherina Group' in our area includes **toxic** species *A. velatipes* and *A. multisquamosa*. Both have caps that are **smooth or slighty sticky** when wet and vary in color from whitish to tan to brown, usually **darker in the center with plentiful white warts**. They are often called panthers because of this spotted appearance. The true *A. pantherina* is considered a West Coast species; research is needed to determine the proper name for the brown-capped versions found in our area. They are also called "Booted Amanitas", referring to the **collar or defined rim** on the bulb at the base of the stem. *A. velatipes*

is more common in the East, but can be also be found in sandy soils in the Midwest. Caps are up to **7 inches** across and the warts appear in **concentric circles**. Stems are tapered, less than 1 inch thick and up to 7 inches tall. *A. multisquamosa* is smaller; caps are typically 4 inches across or less. Elegant, tapered stems are less than ½ thick and up to 5½ inches tall. Both species have a ring on the stem, often flared upward. Placement is high on the stem for *A. multisquamosa*, varied in location for *A. velatipes*.

A. multisquamosa

- *A. russuloides*, the Russula-like Amanita, is also considered "booted" with a small but bulbous base that may have a **collar-like edge**. It is **toxic** but not lethal. It is a smaller mushroom whose cap is less than 4 inches across, with ribbed edges. Cap color is **pale yellow, fading to tan or cream**; caps are slightly sticky, especially when wet.

A. russuloides

A **few, scattered whitish patches** are often present on the cap, but may be washed away by rains. The stem is whitish or cream-colored and generally smooth; the ring is very fragile and disappears quickly, so may not be present. Previously referred to as a Gemmed Amanita (*A. gemmata*), a variety that is now considered a West Coast and European species only. *A. russuloides* is likely part of a group that will have additional name changes in the future.

SPORE PRINT: White.

SEASON: Summer through fall.

OTHER NAMES: Most Amanitas are called by more than one common name; refer to the scientific names when researching or discussing them.

COMPARE: Grisettes (pg. 104) are non-toxic Amanitas. Their cap edges are **distinctly ribbed** and the stems have **no rings**. • Puffballs (pgs. 41–43, 236) resemble the egg stage of the Amanita; for this reason, all small puffballs collected for the table should be cut in half and inspected as described on pg. 43 to ensure that the specimen it is not an Amanita egg. • Smooth Volvariella (pg. 149) have a volva at the base of the stem, but they have **no rings** on the stems and their spore print is **pink to brownish-pink**. • *Agaricus* species (pg. 82) have **distinct rings** on the stems, but they lack the cup-like volva at the base of the stem, and their spore prints are some shade of **dark brown**. • Green-Spored Lepiota (pgs. 60–61; **toxic**) is a white mushroom that has shaggy scales on the cap and a ring on the stem, but it has no volva at the base of the stem; the spore print is **greenish**.

NOTES: Sadly, it is not uncommon to hear of a family or group who has come to America from another country and picked mushrooms that resemble edible species of their homeland—only to discover, too late, that toxic Amanita species resemble familiar favorites from home. Making a spore print before consuming mushrooms prevents many tragedies.

Toxic Boletes (numerous)

Boletus spp.

Like the edible King Bolete (pgs. 44–47), the boletes discussed here look like a typical cap-with-stem shape but reveal a **spongy pore surface** when turned over. Some of the most brightly colored boletes are **toxic** and cause severe gastrointestinal distress if eaten. Others are good edibles but are virtually impossible to distinguish from the toxic ones without a microscope. In general, the easiest way to identify some of the most toxic varieties is by the color of the cap and pore surface and by the tendency of the flesh to **stain or bruise blue**. There are, however, exceptions to this rule; the most dramatic is the edible and brilliantly staining Bluing Bolete discussed on pgs. 46–47.

HABITAT: Boletes grow **from the soil** and humus, singly or in loose groups, in mixed woods. Most have a symbiotic relationship with trees.

DESCRIPTION: The boletes discussed here have a cap that is reddish, brownish or yellowish and a **bright pore surface** (ranging from yellow to orange to red); some or all parts **stain blue** when cut or bruised. Some edible and even choice varieties, including Bicolor Bolete (pg. 196), fall into this broad group; because of difficulty in identifying them, however, they should not be collected for the table by any but the most experienced foragers.

green = key identification feature

Red Mouth Boletes

- Boletes with an **orangish to red pore surface** are often called **Red Mouth Boletes**. They are often referred to as the *Boletus subvelutipes* group, which is poorly defined in North America; names used are often European species that may not occur here. Members of this species group share some characteristics. They are medium-sized, with brownish (or yellowish-brown) caps that typically have **yellow** edges. Stems have no reticulation and are frequently yellow but may be colored like the cap; stem bases are hairy or velvety. All parts **bruise blue**, including the yellow flesh, which **instantly stains blue** when cut. Red Mouth Boletes are found under hardwoods.

- The **Brick-Cap Bolete** (*Boletus sensibilis*) grows in mixed deciduous woods. It has a **brick-red** cap up to **6 inches** across on a **smooth** stem that is 5 inches tall or less; the cap color may fade to brown with age. The stem is **yellowish**, often tinged with red on the lower part. The pore surface and interior flesh are **bright yellow** and **instantly stain blue** when bruised or cut. It is said to have a distinct curry smell. The similar *Boletus pseudosensibilis* **does not smell like curry** or fenugreek.

Brick-Cap Bolete

SPORE PRINT: Olive-brown.

SEASON: Summer through fall.

OTHER NAMES: Two-Color Boletes.

Frost's Bolete

COMPARE: Some boletes with red caps and bright pore surfaces are generally regarded as edible, but are not recommended for novices due to possible confusion with **toxic** species. • Frost's Bolete (*Butyriboletus frostii*; formerly listed as *Boletus frostii* and also called the Apple Bolete) has a deep red cap, striking **red pore surface** and **deeply textured red stem**. Caps are up to 6 inches wide, with **yellow flesh** inside that **quickly bruises blue** when cut. Many sources list this as edible but not recommended. • Smaller species with features similar to the Brick-Cap include **Sulfur Bolete** (*Hortiboletus campestris* or *Boletus campestris*), *H. rubellus* and the *Boletus fraternus* group, which are reportedly edible but not choice. These have caps that are less than 2 inches across and are typically a deeper **rose to pinkish red**; they can be so similar to small Brick-Caps that even experts say they should be avoided. • The **Peppery Bolete** (*Chalciporus piperatus* or *Boletus piperatus*) has a **rust-red cap and pore surface** when young; with age the cap fades to tan. The pore surface bruises **brown**. Flesh inside the stem is **bright yellow**; cap flesh is yellowish to pinkish. It is edible when properly identified and well cooked, but has a very peppery flavor. • Also see **Bluing Bolete** (pgs. 46–47) and **Bicolor Bolete** (pg. 196; see Note below) for other blue-staining boletes that have reddish to brownish caps and colorful pores; these are regarded as edible and choice if properly identified. Note: Bicolor Bolete is most likely to be confused with Brick-Cap, but the interior flesh of the Bicolor Bolete stains blue **slowly and faintly if at all**.

NOTES: Adding to the uncertainty when attempting to identify toxic boletes, there is a good deal of variety among specimens depending on geography and growing conditions. Though the many names and descriptions discussed here get confusing, the key point is simple: Boletes with **red, orange or yellow pore surfaces that bruise blue** should be not be eaten. That may cause you to skip a potentially edible variety, but you will also avoid getting sick. There are no known deadly bolete species, but the gastrointestinal distress can be quite severe. They are beautiful to photograph and excellent subjects to hone your species identification skills.

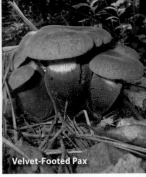

Brown Roll-Rim | **Velvet-Footed Pax**

Brown Roll-Rim

Paxillus involutus

This mycorrhizal mushroom is named for its **rolled-under cap edges**, which are very pronounced on young specimens. Caps are 2 to 6 inches wide and yellowish-brown to brownish. They are finely hairy when young, becoming become smooth with age; they may be sticky when moist. Brownish spots are often present, and there may be subtle concentric rings. Stems are moderately thick, typically **shorter than the cap's width** and colored like the cap. There is no ring. Gills are cream-colored when young, browning with age; they are **closely spaced to crowded** and run down the stem. Near the stem they are often forked, forming **small, angular pockets.** The gills can be **separated from the cap** in small sheets by teasing the edge next to the stem. All parts **bruise brown**. It grows in summer and fall from the ground near hardwoods (particularly birch) and conifers in urban parks and natural wooded areas, fruiting singly or in groups. Spores are yellowish-brown to rust-brown.

COMPARE: Spring Paxillus (*P. vernalis*) is similar but larger, with caps up to **7¼ inches** wide. Its spore print is a **darker brown**. Other differences are microscopic. • Brownish *Lactarius* species (pg. 120) have some similarities, but gills produce **milky fluid** when cut. • **Velvet-Footed Pax** (pg. 164) fruits on rotting conifer wood. Stems are usually attached off-center and covered with a brownish to blackish wooly coating.

NOTES: Brown Roll-Rim can cause Immune Hemolytic Anemia, an auto-immune disease that is life-threatening.

green = key identification feature   71

ON DECAYING WOOD

SUMMER THROUGH
LATE FALL

TOP TOXICS

Jack O'Lantern
Omphalotus illudens

These stunning mushrooms have an appearance that's similar to the highly edible Chanterelle (pgs. 38–40). Unfortunately, Jacks are not simply inedible; according to the North American Mycological Association they contain muscarine and other potent toxins that cause severe gastrointestinal distress, breathing difficulties, visual disturbances, decreased blood pressure and irregular pulse.

Luckily it's fairly easy to distinguish Jack O'Lanterns from Chanterelles. A key difference is that Jacks have **true, knife-edged gills that can be separated individually from the cap**. Chanterelles, in contrast, have folds or ribs rather than gills; the folds are actually just a textural feature of the cap and stem and can be separated **in a sheet** but not individually. The flesh of Chanterelles is **whitish** throughout.

HABITAT: Always grows from decaying wood, although they may appear to be growing directly from the ground if the wood is buried (as seen on pg. 73, bottom right). Often found at the base of trees.

DESCRIPTION: Bright orange mushrooms with **sharp, thin gills that run partway down the stems**; gills are **unforked** and closely spaced. Jacks almost always grow in **dense clusters** rather than individually. Caps of mature specimens are 3 to 7½ inches wide; stems are up to 8 inches tall and are generally curved at the base. Flesh is evenly **orange** throughout. The cap is smooth above, turning upward as the specimens age.

SPORE PRINT: Cream-colored to pale yellow.

SEASON: Summer through late fall.

OTHER NAMES: Also referred to as *O. olearius*.

COMPARE: As noted above, Jacks resemble edible Chanterelles. They also could be confused with the False Chanterelle (pg. 40), but False Chanterelles have **forked gills**; the cap surface and stems are more brownish than orange.

NOTES: Jack O'Lanterns get their name not only from the bright orange color but also because the gills of fresh specimens can produce a slight greenish glow in complete darkness.

green = key identification feature

Young specimens
growing on hidden roots

SPRING THROUGH FALL

Tiny Fragile Mushrooms (numerous)
Various species

HABITAT: Tiny fragile mushrooms of various types grow in an array of habitats, including woodlands and fields, on dead wood and on debris. They typically grow in scattered groups but may be found singly or in clusters.

DESCRIPTION: Tiny mushrooms are very common but are so small that they are often overlooked unless they are brightly colored and/or growing in a large cluster. The mushrooms included here have **long, thin stems**. Caps are **fragile** and rounded or conical; they are generally less than 1 inch wide at maturity, and many are less than ½ inch wide. Microscopic examination is required to identify many species; indeed, a hand lens is needed to properly examine them in the field. • *Marasmius* species have **tough** stems that may be wiry. They are found during or after periods of **wet weather**, growing from decaying organic matter on the ground. *Marasmius* can withstand periods of dry weather, shriveling and going dormant for weeks. They are revived by rain, returning to fresh condition and resuming spore production; they are sometimes referred to as Resurrection Fungi. • Many *Mycena* species are also tiny and fragile, but their stems are **brittle** rather than tough or wiry. They may be brightly or subtly colored, or have brownish hues like those on pg. 96. • *Parasola, Conocybe,* and some *Coprinus* and *Entoloma* also fall into the tiny, fragile category (some *Coprinus* and *Entoloma* are larger and easier to identify; these appear elsewhere in this book).

SPORE PRINT: If you want to try to place your tiny fragile mushrooms into a genus, the first step is making a spore print. Here are some generalizations to get you started. *Marasmius* and *Mycena* have white spores. *Conocybe* have rust-brown spores. *Coprinus* and *Parasola* have dark brown to blackish spores. *Entoloma* have salmon-pink or brownish spores.

SEASON: Spring through fall, depending on species.

COMPARE: See also Little Brown Mushrooms (pg. 112), Yellow-Orange Waxy Caps (pg. 122), Red Waxy Caps (pg. 132), Fuzzy Foot (pg. 124) and Fairy Inkcap (pg. 148) for other small mushrooms.

NOTES: These tiny mushrooms are too small to eat, and it's unknown if they are edible.

Marasmius rotula

Mycena subcaerulea

Parasola plicatilis

Conocybe apala

FROM DECAYING GROUND DEBRIS

SUMMER THROUGH FALL

Sweetbread Mushroom

Clitopilus prunulus

HABITAT: Growing from the ground, **singly, scattered** or in **small groups**, in open deciduous and coniferous woodlands and grassy areas. They are saprobes, obtaining nutrients from decaying or dead organic matter that may be underground.

DESCRIPTION: Although young Sweetbread Mushrooms resemble any number of whitish cap-and-stem mushrooms, developed specimens have caps that characteristically appear **wavy or lobed**; the edge is turned under and is often frilly. Caps are 1¼ to 4½ inches across with a **suede-like or felt-like** texture. The cap and stem are both cream-colored to dirty white. Stems are up to 3¼ inches tall and may have a slightly swollen base; the cap is often attached to the stem slightly **off-center**. The stem has no ring. Several specimens may grow together from a common base. The gills are very closely spaced and **run down the stem for a short distance**; they are creamy white at first, turning **pale pink** with age. Sweetbread Mushrooms have a fragrance that has been compared to the **scent of grain, flour and unbaked yeast bread**.

SPORE PRINT: Pinkish-buff to salmon-colored.

SEASON: Summer through fall.

OTHER NAMES: The Miller, due to its grain-like or floury fragrance. Some guides list *Clitopilus orcellus* as a distinct species separated from *Clitopilus prunulus* by its sticky cap, while other guides consider it a variant of *Clitopilus prunulus*.

COMPARE: Several other species are whitish, with gills that run down the stem and other characteristics similar to the Sweetbread. • *Lepista subconnexa* (also listed as *Clitocybe subconnexa*) grows in **tight clusters**; its spores are **pinkish to whitish**. The **smooth white** stems may have a bit of a **sheen**. The gills may run down the stem slightly, or may be simply attached to the cap. • **The Sweater** (pg. 151) is a **toxic** Clitocybe that is much smaller than the Sweetbread; its spore print is **white**. • **Aborting Entoloma** (pg. 108) resembles the Sweetbread; it has **cucumber-like** odor. Other *Entoloma* species may also resemble the Sweetbread; some, such as *E. sinuatum*, are **toxic** and none should be eaten.

NOTES: Sweetbread Mushrooms and *Lepista subconnexa* are edible but not recommended for amateurs due to the possibility of confusing them with **toxic** species.

Sweetbread Mushroom

L. subconnexa

Parasol Mushrooms
Various species

ON DECAYING WOOD
AND WOODY DEBRIS

SUMMER
THROUGH FALL

HABITAT: These saprobes are found growing singly, scattered or in groups. Exact habitat type varies somewhat with each species; see information below.

DESCRIPTION: The term Parasol Mushroom is applied to several mushrooms with similar features. All are **fairly large**; caps are **strongly rounded** when young, becoming broadly convex or nearly flat. Young caps are smooth; the surface **soon develops scales except for a central disc**, which remains smooth and is colored like the scales. Gills are **free from the stem** and white when young; stems are whitish to brownish with whitish rings. • **Shaggy Parasol** (*Chlorophyllum rhacodes*; formerly *Macrolepiota rachodes*, *Lepiota rachodes*) is found in disturbed areas, including gardens and roadsides. It is up to 6 inches wide and 8 inches tall. Mature specimens have **coarse, shaggy** scales with **brownish edges**. The stem is club-like, with a thick ring that is **double-edged** and **movable**. • **American Parasol** (*Leucoagaricus americanus*; formerly *Lepiota americana*) grows on wood chips and disturbed sites, often in urban areas. It is up to 5½ inches wide and tall. The cap has **small, rust-colored scales** circling a **softly pointed** center. Its stem is widest below the midpoint, often narrowing at both ends; it **bruises yellow, then turns reddish**, when rubbed. • **Sharp-Scaled Parasol** (*Lepiota aspera*; also listed as *Lepiota acutesquamosa*) grows in areas with hardwood leaf litter and debris. Its cap is less than 4 inches wide, with a shallow bump surrounded by **small, pyramid-shaped scales** that are orangish-brown to dark brown. A **cobwebby veil** covers young gills, leaving a flimsy ring. The stem is less than 3 inches tall and of even width.

SPORE PRINT: White.

SEASON: Summer through fall; Shaggy Parasols appear a bit earlier, in spring.

OTHER NAMES: See above; there have been many genus changes in this group.

COMPARE: Green-Spored Lepiota (pgs. 60–61; **toxic**) resembles Shaggy Parasol but its patches are **tan**; it has **greenish** spores and gills that turn **grayish-green** with age. • *Macrolepiota procera* is a European species; this name is used for several related but different species that grow here. Caps have a **nipple-like bump** in the center; stems are **narrow** and **scaly**.

NOTES: Shaggy Parasol and American Parasol are edible, but for experts only as there are several **toxic** lookalikes.

Shaggy Parasol

American Parasol

Sharp-Scaled Parasol

FROM THE SOIL NEAR LIVE TREES

SUMMER THROUGH LATE FALL

Whitish Milk Caps

Lactarius and *Lactifluus* spp.

HABITAT: These mycorrhizal mushrooms grow from the soil near oak and other hardwoods; some associate with conifers. Found scattered or in large groups.

DESCRIPTION: All Milk Caps produce **milky latex when cut**. Species listed in this paragraph are whitish to cream-colored and sturdy, with thick stems that are **not pitted**; caps are often shallowly depressed in the center. Most turn yellowish to brownish with age, sometimes becoming blotchy. Gills are attached to the stem or run slightly down it; they are white to cream-colored, producing white milk when cut. Stems have no ring. • **Deceptive Milky** (*Lactifluus deceptivus*) is up to **10 inches** wide and 4 inches tall, although most specimens are smaller. Caps of young specimens have **cottony**, rolled-under edges that may **partially cover the gills**. With age, the cap flattens out, becoming **scaly** or patchy and developing yellowish to brownish blotches. Gills are **moderately closely spaced** and often develop brown spots or streaks. The latex **remains white**, but stains the flesh and gills **brownish**. • **Peppery Milky** (*Lactarius piperatus* and *Lactarius glaucescens*) are typically 2 to 4 inches across and 3 inches tall. Both have **smooth** caps with **very crowded gills** that fork frequently; they produce **abundant** latex. *Lactarius piperatus* latex remains white or turns slightly yellowish, while latex of *Lactarius glaucescens* turns slowly **green**. • *Lactifluus luteolus* is up to 3 inches wide; it has a **fishy** smell and **sticky, abundant** latex that stains the cap, stem and gills (and fingers) brown. • *Lactifluus subvellereus* var. *subdistans* is up to 6 inches wide and less than 2 inches tall, with a **velvety** cap and stem. Gills are **fairly widely spaced**; they bruise brownish, and the latex turns yellowish very slowly.

SPORE PRINT: White, cream-colored or buff.

SEASON: Summer through late fall.

OTHER NAMES: The species listed as *Lactifluus* above were formerly included in the *Lactarius* genus; some references still list them that way.

COMPARE: *Lactarius maculatipes* has a whitish to yellowish cap with **faint zones** of color; its stem is **pitted**. The latex turns yellow quickly. • *Russula brevipes* resembles Deceptive Milky but **does not produce latex** when cut.

NOTES: *Lactifluus luteolus* has a mild taste, but the other Milk Caps above are bitter or hot and are not eaten; some sources list *Lactarius glaucescens* as toxic.

Deceptive Milky

Peppery Milky

FROM THE SOIL IN GRASSY AREAS

LATE SUMMER THROUGH EARLY FALL

Meadow Mushroom
Agaricus campestris

HABITAT: Growing singly, in groups or rings in **grassy areas such as meadows, fields and lawns**. They are saprobes, feeding on decaying organic matter.

DESCRIPTION: Looks like the related grocery-store Button Mushroom (*A. bisporus*). When young, the Meadow Mushroom has a **veil over the gills** and a smooth, rounded cap that is whitish to grayish-brown. With age, the cap expands and pulls the veil apart, leaving a **thin ring** on the stem; the mature cap is up to 4 inches wide, and the ring may disappear with age. The stem is stubby and up to 2½ inches tall; it may taper slightly at the base. Gills are closely spaced and **pink** at first, maturing to brownish-black; they are not attached to the stem.

SPORE PRINT: Blackish-brown or dark purplish-brown.

SEASON: Late summer through early fall.

OTHER NAMES: Field Mushroom, Pink Bottom.

COMPARE: Caps of **Wood Mushroom** (*A. sylvicola*) and **Horse Mushroom** (*A. fissuratus*; also listed as *A. arvensis*) slowly **turn yellowish when rubbed**; they have a **sweet, almond-like odor**. The moderately sized stems have a **large, skirt-like ring**. Gills are **white** at first but soon turn pink, then brown. Wood Mushroom inhabits **forested areas**; caps are up to 4½ inches wide. Horse Mushroom is found in grassy areas; caps are up to **8 inches wide** and the veil (and, later, the underside of the ring) has a **cog-wheeled** appearance. • **Spring Agaricus** (*A. bitorquis*; also called Pavement Mushroom) is up to 4 inches wide with a short, **stubby** stem and firm texture. The ring often appears **band-like** and **double-edged**. It grows in **hard-packed soil**; often just its cap pokes through the surface. • The cap of **Eastern Flat-Topped Agaricus** (*A. placomyces*) is up to 5½ inches wide and covered with **dark fibers** that are **concentrated at the center**, giving it a bull's-eye appearance. The stem is about 4 inches tall; its base **turns bright yellow when cut**. This species smells like coal tar.

NOTES: Spring Agaricus is a choice edible; Meadow Mushrooms are also tasty. Wood Mushrooms and Horse Mushrooms are edible, but may cause intestinal problems. Eastern Flat-Topped Agaricus is inedible. Be cautious when collecting *Agaricus* to eat; **toxic** Amanitas (pgs. 62-67) may look similar but have **white spores**. Also watch out for **toxic** Yellow-Foot Agaricus (*A. xanthodermus*); its cap bruises yellow and its **stem base turns yellow when cut**. It smells like **tar**.

Meadow Mushroom

Wood Mushroom

Spring Agaricus

Eastern Flat-Topped Agaricus

ON DECAYING WOOD
SUMMER THROUGH LATE FALL

Decorated Mop
Tricholomopsis decora

HABITAT: Decorated Mop is a saprobe that is found **on dead or dying conifer wood**, including trees, logs and stumps; it fruits singly or in scattered groupings.

DESCRIPTION: This species is typically **deep golden yellow overall**, but may be tan or yellowish-brown. Caps are generally 2 to 3 inches wide at maturity, occasionally larger; they are **covered with tiny brown scales** that are concentrated in the center. The surface is **moist**, particularly on young specimens, but is not sticky or slimy. Stems are generally 2 to 3 inches tall but will be longer on larger specimens. They may be smooth or dotted with fine scales or hairs; there is no ring. The golden-yellow gills are closely spaced and attached to the stem.

SPORE PRINT: White.

SEASON: Summer through late fall.

OTHER NAMES: According to Dr. Michael Kuo (mushroomexpert.com), other members of the *Tricholomopsis* genus share many similarities and may form a "species cluster" with *Tricholomopsis decora*; these include *Tricholomopsis sulfureoides*, *Tricholomopsis thompsoniana* and *Tricholomopsis bella*.

COMPARE: Several similar-appearing mushrooms are mycorrhizal, growing **from the ground. • Man on Horseback** (*Tricholoma equestre* or *Tricholoma flavovirens*) is about the same size; it associates with **pines** and may be found into early winter. It has a yellow cap with dark fibers in the center, yellow gills and a **whitish to pale yellowish** stem that becomes more yellow towards the base. • *Tricholoma odorum* may be a bit smaller; it associates with **hardwoods**. It has a **strong, foul, tar-like odor**. The cap is **pale yellowish-green** on young specimens, becoming yellowish-buff to tan with age. The surface is **dry** and **lacks scales or fibers**. • *Tricholoma subsejunctum* is slightly larger; it associates with both conifers and hardwoods. The cap, which is **tacky** when moist, is greenish-yellow and streaked with **dark fibers radiating** from the center. Gills are whitish at first, tuning yellow at the cap edge or overall. Stems may have a bulbous base. It is listed in some sources as *Tricholoma sejunctum*, but that is a European species that grows only with hardwoods. • Yellow Swamp Russula (pg. 156) has **waxy or sticky** yellow caps with a white stem and gills.

NOTES: All species listed here should be regarded as inedible; some have caused illness and are listed in some references as somewhat poisonous.

Decorated Mop

Man on Horseback

Tricholoma odorum

Tricholoma subsejunctum

Decorated Pholiota
Leucopholiota decorosa

ON DECAYING WOOD AND WOODY DEBRIS

LATE SUMMER THROUGH LATE FALL

HABITAT: Decorated Pholiota is a saprobe, feeding on decaying wood. It grows most commonly in beech-maple forests, often on rotting logs and stumps, **especially of sugar maple**. It occurs singly, scattered, or in small clusters.

DESCRIPTION: This attractive mushroom has a cap that is tan to brown due to a **dense covering of pointed tan to rusty brown scales**. The cap edge is hairy and rolled inward. Caps are 1 to 3 inches wide and convex to nearly flat at maturity. The cap flesh is white and does not change color when bruised. Stems are 1 to 3 inches tall and ½ inch wide. They are usually slightly enlarged at the base, but may be nearly equal from top to bottom. The tops of the stems are smooth and white. There is a dense covering of rusty brown scales and hairs from the bottom up to a **flaring, shaggy ring zone**. Gills are closely spaced and white. They are slightly notched at the stem and their edges are uneven.

SPORE PRINT: White.

SEASON: Decorated Pholiota is most common in September and October.

OTHER NAMES: *Armillaria decorosa*.

COMPARE: *Pholiota* species, especially *P. squarrosa* and *P. squarrosoides*, have scaly caps, but produce **brown** spore prints. • Both *P. squarrosa* and *P. squarrosoides* are called Scaly Pholiota. They grow in **dense clusters** with caps growing up to **4 inches** across. Cap color is **pale yellow to tan** with spiky brown scales that are **more densely arranged towards the center**. *P. squarrosa* has **dry** caps. Its white gills turn **greenish** before turning brownish from the spores; it often has an odor of **garlic or radishes**. Nearly identical, *P. squarrosoides* has **sticky** caps in damp weather and gills do not have a greenish stage before turning brown. • Golden Pholiota (pg. 157) caps tend to be **more yellowish overall**, with a **slimy or tacky** texture. • Destructive Pholiota (*P. populnea* or *Hemipholiota populnea*; formerly *P. destruens*) has firm, yellowish-brown caps decorated with **cottony scales** that are **whitish to buff**; veil remnants may also be present on the cap edge. Caps may be up to **10 inches** across, but are typically smaller; they are tacky when fresh and moist, becoming dry with age. They have thick, solid stems but are able to emerge from small cracks in decaying wood.

NOTES: None of the Pholiota species listed here should be eaten. Destructive Pholiota is considered edible by some, but it is bitter and is usually not eaten.

Decorated Pholiota

P. squarrosoides

Destructive Pholiota

Fieldcaps
Agrocybe spp.

FROM WOODY DEBRIS OR GRASS

SPRING THROUGH FALL

HABITAT: These saprobes grow singly or in groups; habitat varies depending on species (see below).

DESCRIPTION: Fieldcaps have rounded caps that expand and flatten with age. Gills are **closely spaced** and attached to the stem or slightly separated from it. They are pale on young specimens and covered by a **partial veil**; ragged veil remnants often hang from the cap edge. As spores develop, the gills turn **brown**. • The *A. praecox* group includes several *Agrocybe* species that require a microscope for positive identification, although habitat may provide a clue. Many sources use the name *A. praecox* to refer to **Spring Fieldcap**, the most common of the group. It is found on **woody debris**, especially in spring. Caps are smooth and **creamy to buff**, often with a slightly raised center; they are up to **4 inches** wide when mature and may develop shallow cracks in dry weather. Stems are up to 4 inches tall and colored like the cap, darkening with age. There may be a **thin ring**, but it may be incomplete or missing. Whitish mycelium (root-like fungal filaments) cling to the stem base. Group member *A. molesta* (also called *A. dura*) grows in **grassy areas**. • **Maple Agrocybe** (*A. acericola*) may be included in the *A. praecox* group, but some sources consider it separate. It has a yellowish-brown to tan cap 1¼ to 3½ inches wide; its ring is **pronounced and persistent**. It grows from summer through **fall** on woody debris and decayed logs. • **Common Fieldcap** (*A. pediades*; not part of the *A. praecox* group) has a yellowish-brown cap less than 1½ **inches** wide and a **thin** stem less than 2 inches tall; there is **no ring**. Found in summer in grassy areas.

SPORE PRINT: Brown to dark brown.

SEASON: Spring to fall, depending on species.

OTHER NAMES: Spring Fieldcap is also called Spring Agrocybe.

COMPARE: "Fairy Ring Fungus" (pg. 160) grows in grass; its gills are **widely spaced** and its spore print is **white**. • Caps of **Pale Brittlestem** (pg. 159) often have wrinkles from the center to the cap edges. The spore print is **purplish-brown**.

NOTES: *Agrocybe* species are hard to identify with certainty; some listed above are edible but are best passed by as they are small and easily mistaken for inedible species. *Agrocybe aegerita* is a species sold in grow-it-yourself kits, sometimes called Chestnut Mushroom or Velvet Pioppino.

Spring Fieldcap

Cracked Cap

Maple Agrocybe

Common Fieldcap

Common Laccaria

Laccaria laccata

HABITAT: This mycorrhizal species is found growing from the ground, scattered or in groups, near deciduous trees and conifers; often found in leaf litter.

DESCRIPTION: Common Laccaria can be difficult to identify without resorting to microscopic analysis, as the color changes throughout the life of the mushroom and is also affected by the weather. They appear in various brownish colors, ranging from reddish- or orangish-brown to tan to nearly white. Caps are smooth to finely scaly and may have a slightly translucent skin; the center is sometimes slightly depressed but may also be raised. Caps of young specimens are small and rounded, sometimes appearing softly folded around the edge. As the mushroom matures, the cap enlarges and flattens out, often flaring upwards to form a shallow bowl; it is up to 2 inches wide at maturity and may have wavy or frilly edges that are often split. Gills are **pinkish to tan, thick and widely spaced**. They are attached to the stem and may run down the stem for a short distance; additional short gills are attached around the edge of the cap. Stems are somewhat slender, up to 4 inches long and often somewhat twisted or curved; they are dry and fibrous with fine hairs or scales on the surface and are typically a **darker shade of the cap color**. The stem has no ring.

SPORE PRINT: White.

SEASON: Spring through fall.

OTHER NAMES: Deceiver, *L. laccata* var. *pallidifolia*.

COMPARE: *L. proxima* appears very similar; a microscope is needed for positive identification. It may be slightly darker, with a thicker stem; it grows strictly under pines. • *L. longipes* has caps that may be over 3 inches across and a **slender stem** that may be nearly **6 inches** long; both cap and stem are orangish-brown. It is found during fall in **sphagnum bogs** in the Great Lakes area. • Fringed Twiglet (*Tubaria furfuracea*) is similar in stature and overall appearance, but it is a saprobe that is found **on woody debris** such as wood chips. Its spore print is **tan to light brown**. • Many **toxic** Cortinarius are brownish (pg. 116) or orangish (pg. 126), but young specimens have a **cobwebby veil** over the gills; the spore print of mature specimens is **rust-brown**.

NOTES: Common Laccaria are edible but not recommended for amateurs due to the difficulty in identifying them.

Common Laccaria

Fringed Twiglet

ON DECAYING WOOD   SPRING THROUGH FALL

Deer Mushroom
Pluteus cervinus

HABITAT: These saprobes appear singly or scattered in deciduous, coniferous and mixed woodlands where they grow from rotten logs, sawdust piles, wood chips, decaying roots and other woody debris that may be underground.

DESCRIPTION: The cap of this very common mushroom is **brownish**, ranging from pale tan to brownish-gray to dark brown; it is smooth and often streaked with **darker fibers radiating from the center**. It is tacky when moist and has a **sheen** when dry. Bell-shaped when young, it expands to become broadly convex or flat, up to 5 inches across, retaining a bump in the center. The slender stem, which is up to 4 inches tall, is **white** to grayish and may be streaked with dark fibers. There is no ring on the stem and no cup around the base. Closely spaced gills are **not attached to the stem**, including some short gills; they are white at first, turning pale salmon-pink with age.

SPORE PRINT: Salmon-pink.

SEASON: Spring through fall; found shortly after Morel season until the snow flies.

OTHER NAMES: Fawn Mushroom, *P. atricapillus*. Mycologists now believe that *P. cervinus* is part of a group of similar species; additional research is needed.

COMPARE: Other Pluteus with pink spores and similar growth habits are found in our area. • White-Gilled Pluteus (*P. petasatus*) often grows in **clusters** from buried wood; its cap may be slightly larger than the Deer Mushroom and is **white** with a **brownish center**. • Pleated Pluteus (*P. longistriatus*) has **ribbing** around the bottom half to two-thirds of the cap, which is about 2 inches wide. The top half is brownish, becoming **paler gray** around the edges; the stem is whitish with gray fibers. • The cap of *P. romellii* is less than 2 inches across and slightly **wrinkled**, with a dull surface that is **brown to olive-brown** and often darker in the center. The thin stem is 1 to 2 inches tall and **yellow to greenish-yellow** when young, fading with age. Gills are **pale yellow to cream-colored** on young specimens. • Black-Edged Pluteus (*P. atromarginatus*) has a dark brown to **black** cap up to 4 inches wide that is streaked with small black fibers and may feel velvety. The gills are white with **black or dark gray edges**; the stem is covered with dark fibers. • Members of the *Volvariella* genus (pg. 149) are similar to *Pluteus* species, but they have a **cup** around the base of the stem.

NOTES: The Pluteus listed here are edible but unremarkable in taste.

Deer Mushroom

White-Gilled Pluteus

Pleated Pluteus

FROM DECAYING GROUND DEBRIS

SPRING THROUGH FALL

Oak Collybia
Gymnopus dryophilus

HABITAT: These saprobes grow from ground debris or twigs in deciduous, coniferous or mixed forests. They may be found singly, scattered, in small groups or tight clusters; several individual specimens may grow from a fused base.

DESCRIPTION: This common mushroom has a smooth **tawny to reddish-brown** cap that turns **tan, orangish-tan or buff** as the specimen matures. The cap is generally ½ to 1½ inches wide, although it may be up to 2½ inches wide on mature specimens. It is rounded at first, opening up and becoming flat or developing a wavy top as it matures. The edge of the cap is often wavy and sometimes lighter in color. The stem, which may be whitish, buff-colored or the same color as the cap, is up to 3½ inches tall and may be slightly flared at the base; it is smooth, brittle and hollow, and there may be **white rhizomorphs** (cord-like strands) at the base. The stem has no ring. Gills are **white** and closely spaced; they may be attached to the stem or free from it.

SPORE PRINT: White to pale yellowish-white.

SEASON: Spring through fall.

OTHER NAMES: Oak-Loving Collybia, *Collybia dryophila*.

COMPARE: Buttery Collybia (*Rhodocollybia butyracea*; also listed as *Collybia butyracea*) has a reddish-brown to orangish-brown cap that feels **buttery** when moist. Its stems are usually **thicker** than those of Oak Collybia and often wider at the base, looking rather like an inverted baseball bat. Its spore print is whitish to **pinkish** and its gills may have **jagged edges**. Buttery Collybia grows near conifers from late summer through fall. • Clustered Collybia (*Connopus acervatus*; also called *G. acervatus* and *Collybia acervata*) is similar but has more reddish tones; its stem is reddish-brown and may be up to **4½ inches tall**. It grows in **tight, dense clusters** on conifer logs and decaying wood. • *G. dichrous* is similar in size and coloration to Oak Collybia, but its caps often become **wrinkled**, with **fine ribbing** around the edges. They **shrivel in dry weather,** often splitting at the cap edge, but are revived by rain.

NOTES: Some sources list Oak Collybia as edible but suggest discarding the stalk due to its tough texture; others recommend against eating it altogether. Oak Collybia is sometimes attacked by Collybia Jelly (pg. 270), a fungus that causes white growths on the cap.

Oak Collybia

Buttery Collybia

Clustered Collybia

Tan to Grayish Mycena (several)

Mycena spp.

HABITAT: Most *Mycena* species grow from decaying organic material, either on ground litter or on dead trees and stumps; a few grow from the bark of live trees. They often grow in large numbers.

DESCRIPTION: Mycena are small to tiny mushrooms in the *Mycenoid* group; most have caps less than 1½ inches wide at maturity. Caps are typically conical or softly rounded. Stems of most are thin and have a **soft or fragile** texture; there is no ring. Gills of many Mycena are darker on the edge than on the inner sides. Microscopic examination is required to identify most species; a hand lens is helpful to examine them in the field. • **Common Mycena** (*M. galericulata*) grows on decayed hardwood logs and stumps; it may also grow from buried hardwood, appearing terrestrial. It is one of the larger Mycena; its cap is up to 2¼ inches wide and **tan to grayish-brown**, with faint ribs running from the center to the edge. The stem is up to 3½ inches tall and is whitish at the top, becoming tan to brownish in the lower half. Gills are attached to the stem and fairly widely spaced; they are white at first, developing pinkish tones with age. Common Mycena does not have a distinctive odor. • **Clustered Bonnet** (*M. inclinata*) is similar to Common Mycena and also grows on decayed hardwood, but its cap edges are **scalloped or toothy**. The stem is whitish at the top, yellowish in the middle and **reddish-brown** at the base. Clustered Bonnet has a **rancid** odor. • *M. leptocephala* grows **from the ground** on debris under conifers. Caps and stems are **grayish-brown to blackish** when young, fading with age; caps often appear to have stripes running from the center to the edge. Gills are white to gray and fairly widely spaced. *M. leptocephala* has a **bleach-like** odor.

SPORE PRINT: White.

SEASON: Spring through fall, depending on species.

OTHER NAMES: The *Mycenoid* group also includes *Hydropus*, *Rickenella* and others; as noted, a microscope is often needed for exact identification.

COMPARE: Bleeding Mycena (pg. 138) and several *Mycena* species are **pinkish to purplish** when fresh, becoming tan in age. • See also Tiny Fragile Mushrooms (pg. 74), Little Brown Mushrooms (pg. 112) for more small to tiny mushrooms.

NOTES: Most of these dainty mushrooms are not considered edible and are too small to be of culinary value; most enthusiasts simply photograph them.

Common Mycena

Clustered Bonnet

Clustered Bonnet stems

M. leptocephala

Rooting Collybia
Hymenopellis megalospora

HABITAT: Rooting Collybia are saprobes, getting their nutrients from decaying woody deciduous debris that is usually buried; they are often found in lawns near buried stump remnants. They grow singly or scattered.

DESCRIPTION: These tall, slender-stemmed mushrooms have a **distinct root** that is often 3 to 5 inches long, or even longer. The root is thick near the soil but becomes quite thin; it is necessary to dig around the base of the stem to extract the root, so it is often missed and the thinner portion usually breaks off. Caps of mature specimens are up to 3 inches wide; they feel chamois-like when dry, becoming slimy when wet. Colors range from whitish to tan to buff. The center has a slightly darker **knob** that is frequently surrounded by a **puckered** area that may appear sunken; the cap may become fairly flat with age but the knob will still be present. The slender stems are up to 5 inches tall and may be slightly twisted. They are whitish and silky, often with fine band-like patterning; there is no ring. Gills are attached to the stem; they are white and **moderately widely spaced**. Gill edges may be **ruffled** near the cap edge.

SPORE PRINT: White.

SEASON: Spring through fall.

OTHER NAMES: Formerly listed as *Xerula megalospora*. *Collybia radicata* is sometimes used as a synonym, while other sources list this as a separate species.

COMPARE: There are several other *Hymenopellis* species; a microscope is needed for positive identification. The most common is *H. furfuracea* (formerly listed as *X. furfuracea*), which has a **smoky brownish** cap up to 4¾ **inches** wide and a **hairy** stem that is brownish on the lower half. • *Melanoleuca* have a knobbed cap and most have a slender stem but **no root**; gills are **crowded**. Yellow-White Melanoleuca (*M. alboflavida*) has a whitish to buff cap up to 4 inches wide and a stem up to 6 inches tall. Changeable Melanoleuca (*M. melaleuca*) has a **brownish** cap up to 3 inches wide and a stem up to 3 inches tall. • Twisted-Stalked Entoloma (*Entoloma strictius*; **toxic**) has a tall, slender stem and a knobbed **grayish-brown** cap; its spore print is **salmon-pink** and it has **no root**.

NOTES: The *Hymenopellis* and *Melanoleuca* species discussed here are edible but for experts only, due to possible confusion with **toxic** *Entoloma* species.

Collybia roots

Rooting Collybia

Ruffled gills

Yellow-White Melanoleuca

FROM DECAYING GROUND DEBRIS

SPRING THROUGH FALL

Mica Cap

Coprinellus micaceus

HABITAT: Mica Caps are saprobes, getting nutrients from decaying roots and other woody debris that may be underground. They are found in woodlands and urban parks. They generally grow in **tight, dense clusters** and are frequently found at the base of stumps and dead or dying trees.

DESCRIPTION: Young Mica Caps have **hollow egg-shaped to conical caps**, generally ¾ to 1½ inches wide, that are covered with **small but prominent glistening salt-like granules** which may be washed away by rain. Thin grooves run from near the top of the cap to the edges. Caps are **honey-colored to tawny**; they may be patchy at the top depending on the weather. As the specimen matures, the cap turns brown and opens up, splitting around the edges; old specimens have flared, upturned edges. Stems are 1 to 3 inches tall; they are hollow and white with a fine, silky texture. There may be a faint ring remnant near the base. Gills are closely spaced and whitish on young specimens; they become brownish and turn **black or sooty gray,** finally **partially dissolving** into an inky fluid.

SPORE PRINT: Black.

SEASON: Most common in spring but may be present through fall.

OTHER NAMES: Glistening Inky Cap, *Coprinus micaceus*.

COMPARE: Domestic Inky Cap (*Coprinellus domesticus*) and **Orange-Mat Coprinus** (*Coprinellus radians*, a related species distinguished by microscopic features) are a bit larger overall; the granules are larger and more scale-like and may be concentrated towards the top of the cap. More significantly, these two mushrooms produce a **shaggy orange carpet-like mat** of mycelium (threadlike fungal filaments) over the substrate on which they grow; the mat may appear before the mushroom develops. These two mushrooms may grow indoors on damp flooring. • **Tippler's Bane** (pg. 29) is larger, **lacks the granules** and is **grayish.** • **Fairy Inkcap** (pg. 148) is **much smaller** and lacks the granules.

NOTES: Mica Caps are edible when young but should be cooked soon after harvesting to prevent them from deteriorating. They are soft with a mild flavor. Like Tippler's Bane, Mica Caps are edible, but some people report adverse reactions when consuming them with alcohol; see pg. 29 for more information. Most sources list *C. domesticus* and *C. radians* as inedible.

Mica Caps

Old Mica Caps

Domestic Inky Cap

ON DECAYING WOOD · SPRING THROUGH FALL

Scaly Inky Cap

Coprinopsis variegata

HABITAT: Scaly Inky Caps are saprobes, getting nutrients from decaying woody debris. They grow in woodlands and urban parks, often on rotting deciduous logs; they also appear on wood chips, at the base of dead trees and on decaying roots or stumps that may be buried. In urban areas they often grow in a circular clump where trees have been removed.

DESCRIPTION: Appearances of Scaly Inky Caps may vary depending on habitat, but all share similar traits. Caps are tan, grayish-brown or grayish and covered with **large, flaky white to tan patches** that vary in size from group to group. The centers are often darker, providing additional contrast to the pale patches. Caps are 1 to 3 inches wide and up to 3 inches tall; they are hollow and egg-shaped when young, becoming bell-shaped. As the specimens mature, the edges flare out, rolling upward at the edges; the caps become **darker, broad and fairly flat**. Stems are whitish and 2 to 4 inches tall, with a felt-like surface; they are hollow inside. Ring remnants may be present on the stem but are often absent. Gills are crowded; they are whitish on young specimens, becoming grayish before turning black and **beginning to dissolve** into a gooey substance. Unlike some other Inky Caps (pgs. 28–29), the gills **may not dissolve completely**.

SPORE PRINT: Blackish.

SEASON: Spring through fall.

OTHER NAMES: *Coprinus quadrifidus*.

COMPARE: Mica Caps (pg. 100) are similar, but caps of young, fresh specimens are covered with **small glistening granules** rather than patches; the surface is **finely ribbed**. · Shaggy Mane (pg. 28) is related, but it is **whitish**; its cap is elongated and covered with **shaggy scales**.

NOTES: Generally regarded as edible, although the flavor is disagreeable in some collections; they deteriorate quickly after picking and must be cooked promptly. They cause digestive upset in some people; like Tippler's Bane (pg. 29), Scaly Inky Caps cause illness if consumed within several days of drinking alcohol (either before or after the mushrooms are eaten).

FROM THE SOIL NEAR LIVE TREES

SPRING THROUGH FALL

Grisettes (several)

Amanita vaginata group

HABITAT: Grisettes are mycorrhizal, growing from the soil in association with living trees, often in grassy areas. Species discussed here grow singly or scattered, near both conifers and hardwoods. They are common in urban areas.

DESCRIPTION: Grisettes are a section (sub-group) of the *Amanita* genus. Key features in this group are distinct **ribbing on the cap margin**, the presence of a **volva** (a sac-like cup at the base of the stem), **scattered or no patches** on the cap and the **lack of a ring** on the stem. Over 200 members of this group have been described; each is genetically distinct. Caps are typically 2 to 4 inches wide but may be wider; cap color may be white, gray, brown or tan, and the surface is often shiny or greasy. Stems are 4 to 8 inches tall and whitish; they may be smooth or somewhat scaly. The volva may be obvious, or may be fragile and easy to miss (dig carefully in the dirt around the stem base to search for it). Gills are **closely spaced** and **white** when fresh; they are free from the stem or barely attached. Flesh is white. The names here may be applied to specimens with slight variations; European versions may differ from American collections. • *A.'vaginata'* is a somewhat generic name used to refer to the Grisette that exemplifies the group. Caps are grayish-brown to gray; the volva is prominent, cupping the stem base loosely. *A. vaginata* var. *alba* is a variation that is **white overall**. • *A. fulva*, often called **Tawny Grisette**, has a **fawn-brown to tan** cap; the volva is prominent and loose. • *A. populiphila* grows near **poplars**, particularly cottonwoods. Its cap is white, creamy or tan, becoming yellowish. The volva is **very fragile** and often **not noticed**. • *A. ceciliae* has **gray wart-like patches** on a **brown** cap. The volva is broken into **patches or flakes**.

SPORE PRINT: White.

SEASON: Spring through fall.

OTHER NAMES: Most members of this group have no common name.

COMPARE: *A. farinosa* has most of the features noted above for Grisettes, but it **lacks a volva** at the base of the stem. Caps are brownish, brownish-gray or whitish, and covered with **fine powder**. • Please also read about other Amanitas on pgs. 62–67.

NOTES: Grisettes are edible, but even most experts shy away from them due to possible confusion with **toxic** Amanitas. Definitely not for novices.

A.'vaginata'

A. populiphila

A. ceciliae

Funnel Caps

Infundibulicybe gibba, Infundibulicybe squamulosa

FROM THE SOIL NEAR TREES

SUMMER THROUGH LATE FALL

HABITAT: These saprobes grow from the ground near trees; they may grow singly but are more often found in groups or fairy rings (large circles).

DESCRIPTION: These light tan to pinkish mushrooms have distinctly funnel-shaped caps that are **smooth** and may be 3 to 4 inches across but are often smaller. They may be flat when young or have a wavy edge at maturity but always have a distinct **dimple** in the center. Caps may get paler with age but are always darker than the **crowded** gills, which are white or cream-colored and run down the stem. White mycelium (threadlike fungal filaments) are often attached to the bottom. Stems have no ring. • The **Common Funnel Cap** (*I. gibba*) is usually found near **oaks**. It has a smooth, light-colored stem that grows to 3 inches tall and may be slightly swollen at the base. • *I. squamulosa* is found under **conifers** and has a slightly darker cap and stem that are cinnamon to golden brown. The cap may be faintly scaly (called squamulose) and the cream-colored gills are **less crowded** than those of *I. gibba*.

SPORE PRINT: White.

SEASON: Summer through late fall.

OTHER NAMES: Funnel Clitocybe. The species listed above were originally included in the *Clitocybe* genus.

COMPARE: *C. eccentrica* grows on **wood and woody debris**, often in clusters; it first appears in **spring**, continuing into fall. The **whitish to pale yellowish-brown** caps are 2¼ inches wide or smaller, with rolled-under edges. Stems are up to 2 inches tall and often attached to the caps off-center; numerous white **rhizomorphs** (cord-like strands) are attached to the stem bases. • **Club-Footed Clitocybe** (pg. 165) generally has a more distinctively **swollen base**. Mature caps may become wavy and turned up on the edges; they often have a **knob** rather than a dimple in the center. • **The Sweater** (pg. 151; also known as Ivory Funnel Cap) has a pale, wavy cap less than 1⅝ inches wide; the top is often irregular and **mottled**. It grows in grassy areas and open woods. It is **toxic**. • *Arrhenia epichysium* (formerly *Omphalina epichysium*) grows on **rotted wood**; caps are less than 2 inches wide and **grayish-brown**, fading to tan.

NOTES: Common Funnel Cap is edible, but for experts only due to many inedible lookalikes. The Sweater is **toxic**; the others discussed above are inedible.

Common Funnel Cap

I. squamulosa

FROM DECAYING GROUND DEBRIS

LATE SUMMER THROUGH FALL

Aborting Entoloma

Entoloma abortivum

HABITAT: Growing in deciduous woodlands from decaying roots and other woody debris that may be underground; they are saprobes, getting nutrients from decaying matter. Entoloma often grow in clusters but may be found in small groups or singly, appearing in the same area for many years.

DESCRIPTION: Caps are **pale grayish-brown to dove-gray**; they are small and rounded when young, expanding and flattening out until they are up to 4 inches across, often with **wavy edges**. Stems are 2 to 4 inches tall and slightly paler than the cap; they are **moderately stout** and typically **wider at the base**, which is often covered with **whitish mycelium** (threadlike fungal filaments). The stem has no ring. Gills are closely spaced and are **gray** at first, turning **pinkish** with age; they are attached to the stem or run down it slightly. The mushroom has a cucumber-like odor.

SPORE PRINT: Salmon-pink.

SEASON: Late summer through fall.

OTHER NAMES: *Clitopilus abortivus*; the lumpy form (described below, shown at right) has a number of amusing names, including Earth Prune, Pig Snout, Stump Dumplings and Shrimp of the Woods.

COMPARE: Lead Poisoner (*E. sinuatum*; also called *E. lividum*) could be confused with Aborting Entoloma, but its cap may be up to **6 inches** across and is slippery when moist. • Twisted-Stalk Entoloma (*E. strictius*) has a brownish cap that is **slightly pointed** in the center; its stem is **slender and gray** with a subtle **twisting pattern**. Both of these Entoloma are **toxic**.

NOTES: The lumpy, stalkless mushrooms in the photo at right are often found in association with Aborting Entoloma and may be more common. For years, experts believed these were *E. abortivum* that had been parasitized during development by Honey Mushrooms (pg. 110). Recent studies reported by Dr. Tom Volk and others suggest that the reverse may be more accurate—the lumpy form may be Honey Mushrooms that have been parasitized by *E. abortivum*. The lumpy form is edible but has an odd texture and taste. The non-distorted form is edible but not recommended for beginners due to the possibility of confusing it with **toxic** lookalikes.

Caps of the lower mushrooms here are colored by spores dropped from the mushrooms above

Lumpy, aborted form

NEAR OR BENEATH LIVE OR DYING TREES

LATE SUMMER TO FALL

Honey Mushrooms (several)

Armillaria mellea and others

HABITAT: Growing in **clusters** at the base of living, dead or dying deciduous trees; also grows from hidden roots in open areas near trees. They are parasitic mushrooms, with black cord-like strands (rhizomorphs) that cause rot; the strands look like dark shoestrings and may be visible on tree trunks.

DESCRIPTION: Honey Mushrooms are a group of related species with variable characteristics. The classic example has **honey-colored** caps with **tiny dark scales or hairs** at the center, which is **darker**. The cap may be dry or tacky; the edge may be lighter in color. Young caps are small and rounded; they expand and flatten with age, growing to 4 inches wide or more. A **thin veil** covers the gills of young specimens. Stems are whitish at first, becoming darker and wooly near the base; they are 3 to 6 inches tall. Once the cap expands, a **prominent ring** is visible near the top of the stem; the ring may have a yellow edge. Stem bases may be fused together. Gills are white and fairly close, attached to the stem or running down it slightly; they may darken or turn spotty with age.

SPORE PRINT: White.

SEASON: Late summer to fall; found during moist periods.

OTHER NAMES: Honey Cap, Bootlace Fungus, *Armillariella mellea*.

COMPARE: Caps of *Armillaria gallica* are more **brownish** and its stems often have a wider base; it fruits alone or in small clusters. Its veil is **cobwebby** and the ring is filmy or nearly absent. • *Armillaria solidipes* (also called *Armillaria ostoyae*) is common in the fall on both conifer and hardwood stumps and logs. Its caps are **tan to brown** and usually **prominently scaly**. The stem has a persistent ring. • *Armillaria tabescens* (recently re-named *Desarmillaria tabescens*) is **cinnamon-colored**; its stem has **no ring** and its entire cap has a scattering of fine scales. • Several unrelated yellowish or brownish mushrooms may appear similar to Honey Mushrooms. **Deadly Galerina** (pgs. 58–59; **toxic**) has a **rust-brown** spore print; its ring is **thin** or absent. • **Big Laughing Gym** (pg. 161; **toxic**) has an **orangish-brown** spore print. • **Sulfur Tuft** (pg. 136; **toxic**) has a **purplish-brown** spore print; its ring is **filmy** or absent.

NOTES: Honey Mushroom caps are edible but mildly bitter; stems are too tough to eat but may be used in broth. Be sure to cook *very* thoroughly, to break down heat-sensitive toxins. Always check spore prints to eliminate **toxic** lookalikes.

Armillaria mellea

Hairs on cap
(*Armillaria mellea*)

Armillaria gallica

Armillaria solidipes

Thin veil
(*Armillaria gallica*)

SPRING THROUGH FALL

LBMs: Little Brown Mushrooms
Various species

HABITAT: Little Brown Mushrooms (LBMs for short) grow in all habitat types and may be found in woodlands and fields, on dead wood, or on debris.

DESCRIPTION: This catch-all term is used even by professional mycologists to refer to any of a number of common, **small to medium-sized brownish mushrooms** that are difficult to identify precisely—and are usually considered not worth the bother. *Alnicola, Naucoria, Panaeolus, Pluteus, Psathyrella* and *Psilocybe* are a few of the genera included in this group. Some *Agaricus, Agrocybe, Collybia, Entoloma, Galerina, Gymnopus, Inocybe, Mycena* and *Pholiota* also fall into this category, although some species in these genera can be more readily identified and appear elsewhere in this book. Some LBMs are **toxic**; none should be eaten due to the difficulty in identification.

SPORE PRINT: If you want to try to place your LBMs into a genus, the first step is making a spore print. Here are some generalizations to get you started; colors here apply to most species within the genera listed, although there may be exceptions. *Agrocybe, Alnicola, Galerina, Inocybe, Naucoria, Pholiota,* many *Agaricus* and some *Pluteus* have brownish spores (ranging from ochre to pinkish-tan to chocolate brown). *Collybia* have whitish, buff or pinkish spores. *Gymnopus* and *Mycena* have white spores. *Entoloma* and some *Pluteus* have pinkish spores. *Panaeolus*, many *Psathyrella* and some *Agaricus* have dark brown to blackish spores. *Psilocybe* and some *Agaricus* have purplish-brown spores.

SEASON: Early spring through late fall.

OTHER NAMES: Little Boring Mushrooms.

COMPARE: Some of the tiny fragile species discussed on pg. 74 are brownish. Also see "Fairy Ring Fungus" on pg. 160.

NOTES: It's frustrating to find a large crop of mushrooms that you can't identify—but it's also very common, since field guides can't cover everything you're likely to find. You may enjoy studying them to hone your observation skills and to see how far you get in attempting to identify them. Since you should never eat any mushroom that you can't identify with **absolute certainty**, you should never eat unidentified or poorly identified LBMs.

Agrocybe spp.

Entoloma spp.

Psathyrella spp.

Brown Alder Mushroom
(*Alnicola melinoides*)

FROM THE SOIL NEAR LIVE TREES

SUMMER THROUGH EARLY FALL

Black-Staining Russula
Russula dissimulans

HABITAT: Growing from the ground, scattered or in small groups, under deciduous trees or conifers; they are mycorrhizal, growing in a symbiotic relationship with living trees.

DESCRIPTION: The most distinctive feature of this somewhat generic-looking medium-sized mushroom is not immediately obvious: when it is cut or bruised the **flesh turns red**, then slowly becomes **black**. Young specimens have pillowy or convex caps that spread and flatten out with age, finally turning upward to form a shallow, wide-rimmed bowl up to 7 inches wide. Unlike some other *Russula* species, the skin on the cap **can't be peeled off easily**. Caps and stems are whitish at first, turning brownish or brownish-gray, often with a mottled appearance; both will eventually turn black. Stems are stocky, up to 3¼ inches tall and often almost half as wide; they are smooth and have no ring. Gills are **moderately widely spaced** and attached to the stem or running very slightly down it. They are white at first; like the rest of the mushroom, they turn red, then black, when damaged. The flesh is white and **brittle**, crumbling easily.

SPORE PRINT: White.

SEASON: Summer through early fall.

OTHER NAMES: Blackening Russula, Black-and-Red Russula.

COMPARE: *R. 'densifolia'* is another black-staining Russula that bruises red, then blackish, when cut. Its gills are more **closely spaced** than those of *R. dissimulans* and its cap is **sticky** when wet. • Some field guides list *R. nigricans* as a similar species that has **widely spaced** gills and microscopic differences; others say that *R. nigricans* is a European species that may not be found in North America. • *R. pectinatoides* has a buff-colored cap that is **slightly ribbed** around the edge; much of the **skin can be peeled off** the cap starting at the edge. It smells sweet and waxy, and it does not change color when cut. • Deceptive Milky (pg. 80) looks similar to young Black-Staining Russula, but it produces a **milky white latex** when cut.

NOTES: Black-Staining Russula is edible, but for experts only; there are too many inedible lookalikes. The other mushrooms listed above should be considered inedible.

Black-Staining Russula

Red staining

R. 'densifolia'

FROM THE SOIL NEAR LIVE TREES

SUMMER THROUGH FALL

Brownish Cortinarius (several)

Cortinarius spp.

HABITAT: *Cortinarius* species are mycorrhizal. Except as noted, the species discussed on this page are found near deciduous trees.

DESCRIPTION: Cortinarius have a **cobwebby veil** called a cortina (see pg. 13) covering the gills of young specimens. The veil disintegrates with age, sometimes leaving a ring remnant on the stem. The brownish spores typically darken the mature gills and may also coat the ring remnant, turning it brown. Caps are conical at first, becoming wider and fairly flat, often with a central hump. Stems are often swollen at the base. Gills are attached to the stem; with one exception, gills of all species listed here are closely spaced. Our area has numerous Cortinarius with brownish attributes; except as noted, those listed here are medium-sized, typically 3 to 4 inches wide and tall. • **Banded Cort** (*C. armillatus*) is up to **6 inches** wide and tall. Its cap is yellow-brown to brick-colored, with tan gills. The stem is paler than the cap and decorated with one or more **reddish-orange bands**. • Caps of *C. trivialis* are orangish-brown and **slimy**. Stems are whitish and moderately slimy at the top; the lower half is partially covered with **shaggy scales** in band-like patterns. It is sometimes considered a variation of *C. collinitus*, but the stem of *C. collinitus* is **violet** and lacks the scaly bands. • *C. corrugatus* has **wrinkled**, brownish-orange caps and whitish to yellowish stems. Gills of young specimens are **lilac-colored**. • *C. distans* are less than 3 inches wide and tall, with **widely spaced** gills. Caps are slightly **grainy**; fresh specimens are orangish-brown and moist, becoming paler and dry with age. They begin fruiting in **spring**, continuing into fall. • Young specimens of *C. croceus* have **silky**, **yellowish-brown** caps; gills and stems are **yellow**. With age, caps become dark reddish-brown with a paler margin; gills turn rust-colored. Found near conifers. • *C. infractus* has **olive-brown to grayish-brown** caps. Gills of young specimens are colored like the cap; stems are much paler. Found near both hardwoods and conifers.

SPORE PRINT: Rust-brown.

SEASON: Summer through fall; *C. distans* begins fruiting in spring.

OTHER NAMES: Some sources refer to *Cortinarius* species as Webcaps.

COMPARE: Also see Orange to Reddish Cortinarius on pg. 126.

NOTES: None of the species above should be eaten; some Cortinarius are **toxic**.

Banded Cort

C. trivialis

C. corrugatus

C. distans

FROM THE SOIL NEAR LIVE TREES

SUMMER THROUGH FALL

The Blusher

Amanita rubescens or *Amanita amerirubescens*

HABITAT: This mycorrhizal mushroom grows from the soil near living hardwoods or pines.

DESCRIPTION: At first blush, you might think the common name of this mushroom comes from reddish tones on the cap, which varies in main color from tan to yellowish, to bronze; however, it is the **pinkish to reddish discoloring or "blushing" of all parts** of this mushroom that characterize this species group. Blushing occurs from cutting, handling, insect holes or age and is darkest in the caps. Color change from handling happens slowly. Caps are up to 8 inches across, but typically smaller and covered with **yellowish warts**. As the cap expands, the warts fade to **gray** and diminish in prominence; they wash off easily with rain. Stems are white or tan, up to 6 inches tall and have a fragile ring or skirt. They are slender with a slightly swollen base, lacking a distinct volva (pg. 12). Gills are closely spaced and not attached to the stem; they are white, bruising pink or red.

SPORE PRINT: White.

SEASON: Summer through fall.

OTHER NAMES: Some mycologists believe that The Blusher is actually a group, with several related species; additional study is needed, and new names are likely in the future.

COMPARE: *A. flavorubens* is called the Yellow Blusher. The cap and patches are **bright yellow**. All parts **slowly bruise pink to red**, especially the stem, which is pale yellow to whitish; the ring is also yellow to whitish and often has a yellow edge. Compare with **Yellow Patches** (pgs. 65–66), which **does not bruise** when cut. • The **Eastern American White Blusher** (*A. rubescens* var. *alba*) has a **white to pinkish** cap with prominent warts and a **thicker** stem with a **more distinct bulb**.

NOTES: The Blusher is considered edible, but even experts often avoid this species, which can easily be mistaken for a deadly **toxic** Amanita (pgs. 62–67). The Blusher must be well cooked to destroy the hemolytic toxins that it contains; these toxins cause anemia, but they are destroyed by thorough cooking. You should never eat raw wild mushrooms, or specimens you haven't identified with 100% certainty.

The Blusher

A. flavorubens

Eastern American
White Blusher

FROM THE SOIL NEAR LIVE TREES

SUMMER THROUGH LATE FALL

Brownish Milk Caps (several)

Lactarius spp.

HABITAT: Milk Caps are mycorrhizal, growing from the soil near living trees.

DESCRIPTION: Milk Caps (*Lactarius* spp.) are brittle-fleshed, gilled mushrooms that produce **milky latex when cut**. Caps of the species discussed here are typically 1 to 4½ inches across, often with a small pointed knob at the center. Stems are typically as tall as the cap is wide; they have no rings. Gills are attached to the stem or running slightly down it; the species here have gills that are closely spaced to moderately close. • **Red-Hot Milky** (*L. rufus*) has a dry **reddish-brown** cap; the stem is paler than the cap, darkening with age. Gills are **tan**, turning darker or blotchy. Its latex is **white**, with a taste that is mild at first, becoming **very bitter or hot**. It grows near conifers and in mossy bogs. • The cap and stem of **Chocolate Milky** (*L. lignyotus*) are typically **dark brown** and **velvety**, although they range from smoky tan to nearly black and the stem may be paler than the cap, especially at the base. Gills are whitish, often with **brown edges**. Its latex is white; it turns pinkish as it dries and may stain the gills. This species is found near conifers; it also grows on well-decayed wood and in mossy areas. • The cap and stem of *L. fumosus* are **smoky brown** to dingy cream-colored; both are dry and smooth. Gills are white, becoming tan. Its latex is white and does not change color; the gills and flesh stain **pink to reddish** when damaged or exposed to the latex. Found with both hardwoods and conifers. • **Maple Syrup Candy Cap** (*L. helvus* or *L. aquifluus*) smells like **curry or burnt maple syrup**; the odor is more pronounced as the specimen dries. The cap is light brown and smooth when young, becoming scaly. Stems are **pale pink, orangish or orangish-brown**. Gills are whitish. The latex is watery and scant; it does not change color or stain the gills.

SPORE PRINT: Creamy white to pale yellow; *L. lignyotus* spores may also be orangish, while those of *L. rufus* may have a salmon-pink hue.

SEASON: Summer through late fall; Red-Hot Milky may also appear in late spring.

OTHER NAMES: Although usually referred to as Chocolate Milky, *L. lignyotus* is sometimes called Smoky Milky; however, most sources reserve that common name for *L. fumosus*.

COMPARE: Please see other Milk Caps on pgs. 80, 128 and 146.

NOTES: The Milk Caps discussed here are inedible; some are mildly toxic.

Red-Hot Milky

Chocolate Milky

L. fumosus

FROM DECAYING GROUND DEBRIS · SPRING THROUGH FALL

Yellow-Orange Waxy Caps (several)
Hygrocybe spp.

HABITAT: Waxy Caps fruit from the soil and humus in wooded areas that are generally a bit damp; they appear singly and in groups. Species listed below grow near deciduous trees; *H. flavescens* is also found in coniferous or mixed forests.

DESCRIPTION: The *Hygrocybe* listed here are small to medium-sized, with close to moderately close gills that feel **waxy**; stems have no ring. • *H. acutoconica* has **slimy** orangish-yellow caps with irregular edges; caps of young specimens come to a **conical point**. The sharp point flattens with age, becoming a softly pointed hump. Stems are often twisted and may be split vertically. Gills are yellow and free from the stem or barely attached. It **does not blacken** when bruised, which distinguishes it from *H. conica* (pg. 132). • Caps of *H. cantharellus* are scarlet at first, becoming orangish. They may be tacky in moist weather but are usually dry. The **long, thin** stems are colored like the cap, with a paler base. Gills are pale yellow to yellowish-orange and **run slightly down the stems**. • Caps of *H. flavescens* are **bright yellow**, becoming yellowish-orange; the center may be darker than the edges. The surface is slimy or sticky when fresh. Mature specimens are fairly flat, sometimes with a central dimple. Stems are bright yellow at first, fading a bit with age; they may be slightly flattened, and are often split vertically. The surface is slightly sticky or greasy. Gills are attached to the stem, often with a small notch; they are whitish at first, yellowing with age.

SPORE PRINT: White.

SEASON: Spring through fall.

OTHER NAMES: *H. acutoconica* is also listed as *H. persistens*.

COMPARE: Two small *Entoloma* species appear similar, but they have **conical caps** with a **sharp, pointed center** that looks like a small horn; spores are **salmon-pink**. **Yellow Unicorn Entoloma** (*E. murrayi*) is bright yellow to yellowish-orange overall; it grows in swampy areas and damp woods. **Salmon Unicorn Entoloma** (*E. salmoneum*) is **salmon-colored** overall; it grows from ground debris in deciduous forests and is also found in damp conifer forests. • Also see Orange Mycena (pg. 166) and Red Waxy Caps (pg. 132).

NOTES: Some *Hygrocybe* are edible, while others are toxic; none should be eaten due to difficulties with identification.

H. acutoconica

H. cantharellus

H. flavescens

E. murrayi

ON DECAYING WOOD

SPRING THROUGH LATE FALL

Fuzzy Foot

Xeromphalina campanella, Xeromphalina kauffmanii

HABITAT: Fuzzy Foot mushrooms are saprobes, getting their nutrients from decaying wood. They typically grow in dense clusters on dead wood but may be found scattered. *X. campanella* grows on dead coniferous wood, and *X. kauffmanii* grows on dead deciduous wood; other than the habitat differences they are impossible to tell apart with the naked eye.

DESCRIPTION: Although small, Fuzzy Foot are easy to spot. Caps are orange, yellowish or yellowish-brown and ¼ to 1 inch wide; they are **broadly convex** to nearly flat. The center is **darker and sunken**; edges have subtle ribbing and are thin enough to be somewhat translucent. Stems are slender and up to 2 inches long; they are yellow at the top, turning reddish-brown and **velvety** below. **Orange tufts** of stiff hairs called *hyphae* grow around the base. Stems have no ring. Gills are pale yellow to orangish and widely spaced; they run down the stem a fair amount. There are numerous **cross-veins** between the gills (visible with a hand lens).

SPORE PRINT: White to light buff.

SEASON: Spring through late fall; may appear into winter in warmer areas.

OTHER NAMES: Cross-Veined Troop Mushroom, Bell Omphalina and Golden Trumpet. Some sources list this as *Omphalina campanella*.

COMPARE: *X. tenuipes* has an **orangish-brown** cap up to **1¾ inches** wide; its stem is **brownish and velvety overall**. It grows from early spring through midsummer on dead deciduous wood. • **Orange Mycena** (pg. 166) is orangish overall and slightly larger. When handled, the mushrooms often **stain hands orange**. • Also see **Yellow-Orange Waxy Caps** on pg. 122.

NOTES: All mushrooms discussed above are regarded as inedible.

Cross-veins

Hyphae

Orange to Reddish Cortinarius (several)

Cortinarius spp.

HABITAT: *Cortinarius* species are mycorrhizal, associating with live trees.

DESCRIPTION: Cortinarius have a **cobwebby veil** called a cortina (see pg. 13) covering the gills of young specimens. The veil disintegrates with age, sometimes leaving a ring remnant on the stem. The brownish spores typically darken the mature gills and may also coat the ring remnant, turning it brown. Stems of the species in this paragraph **lack the bulbous base** found on many Cortinarius; gills are closely spaced and attached to the stems. • Red-Gilled Cort (*C. semisanguineus*) has a **reddish-brown to yellowish-brown cap** up to 2½ inches wide, a **yellowish stem** and **deep red gills**; found near conifers. • Dappled Cort (*C. bolaris*) has **yellowish-tan gills** and a cap up to 3 inches wide. Both cap and stem are pale and **mottled with numerous brick-red scales**; the cap may be so densely covered that it looks red overall. It is found primarily with hardwoods, especially oak. • Cinnabar Cort (*C. hesleri* or *C. cinnabarinus*) is **bright orange to reddish-orange overall** with a cap up to 3½ inches wide; often found with oak trees. • Orange Webcap (*C. mucosus*) has caps up to 4½ inches wide; they are **brownish-orange** and **very slimy** when fresh and young, fading with age. Stems are white and are also slimy on fresh specimens. • Blood-Red Cort (*C. sanguineus*) is **deep blood-red overall** with a cap less than 2 inches wide; it is a European species that is rarely reported in our area.

SPORE PRINT: Rust-brown.

SEASON: Summer through fall; Cinnabar Cort may appear in late spring.

OTHER NAMES: Cortinarius are sometimes called Webcaps.

COMPARE: *C. rubripes* has a lavender-brown cap that turns tawny or brownish-red; gills are **purplish** on young specimens. The stem is up to 3½ inches tall with a swollen, bulbous base that is **bright orangish-red**. • Also see **Brownish Cortinarius** on pg. 116.

NOTES: Many scientific names used for these Cortinarius refer to European species; some experts say these names should not be used for North American specimens, which have subtle differences. As experts attempt to categorize Cortinarius, new names are used, but not all experts agree on them. None of the species above should be eaten; some Cortinarius are **toxic**.

Red-Gilled Cort

Dappled Cort

C. hesleri

Orange Webcap

Orangish Milk Caps (several)

Lactarius and *Lactifluus* spp.

HABITAT: Milk Caps are mycorrhizal; except as noted, those discussed here grow near hardwoods, often favoring oaks.

DESCRIPTION: All Milk Caps produce **milky latex when cut**. Caps are rounded with a sunken center at first; most become vase-like with age. Stems have no rings. Gills are attached to the stem or run slightly down it; on most species here they bruise brownish. Except as noted, species on this page have close to moderately close whitish gills and produce white latex. • *Lactarius thyinos* is orange **overall**, and up to 3½ inches wide and tall. The cap has **concentric bands** that alternate from bright to pale orange. Its stem may be smooth or have shallow pockmarks; it is sticky on young specimens. Latex is **orange**. Caps, gills and stems **do not bruise or discolor greenish**. Found near **conifers**, often in swampy areas. • *Lactarius psammicola* also has a banded cap; its bands alternate between orange and buff. Caps are up to 5½ inches wide. The short, stocky stem is **whitish**, with **numerous pockmarks**. • *Lactifluus hygrophoroides* has a **velvety**, orangish-brown cap 2 to 4 inches wide. The dry to velvety stem is up to 2 inches tall; it is the same color as the cap or lighter. Gills are **widely spaced** and produce abundant latex. • **Tawny Milkcap** (*Lactifluus volemus*) has a **fishy odor**. Its smooth to velvety cap is orangish-brown and up to 5½ inches wide. The stem is 2 to 4 inches tall and colored like the cap or paler; it may have **faint vertical ribs**. It produces abundant latex that **stains all parts** of the mushroom **brown**. It grows near both deciduous and coniferous trees.

SPORE PRINT: Whitish, creamy or pale yellowish.

SEASON: Summer through fall.

OTHER NAMES: The species listed as *Lactifluus* above were formerly included in the *Lactarius* genus; some references still list them that way.

COMPARE: *Lactarius deliciosus* var. *deterrimus* appears similar to *Lactarius thyinos*, but all parts **bruise and discolor greenish**; its gills are more **closely spaced**. It grows near conifers. (*Lactarius deliciosus* is a European species that does not grow in our area.) • Some **Russulas** (pgs. 80, 114, 134, 156) appear similar but do not produce latex. • Also see **Brownish Milk Caps** (pg. 120).

NOTES: The *Lactarius* and *Lactifluus* species listed above are considered edible, although *Lactarius psammicola* has an acrid taste and may not be appealing.

Lactarius thyinos

Lactarius psammicola

Lactifluus hygrophoroides

Tawny Milkcap

Lactarius deliciosus var. *deterrimus* beginning to turn green

ON OR NEAR LIVE OR DEAD TREES

FALL THROUGH SPRING

Velvet Foot

Flammulina velutipes

HABITAT: On or near live or decaying deciduous trees and other woody debris that may be buried. They typically grow in clusters but may be found singly. They are saprobes, getting nutrients from decaying wood.

DESCRIPTION: These medium-sized mushrooms are a fairly common sight in late fall and again in early spring, when other edible mushrooms are scarce. The cap is typically orangish-brown to yellowish-brown but may be honey-colored or tan, particularly on older specimens; the edges are lighter in color. Caps are rounded on young specimens, becoming flatter and wider with age; mature caps are up to 2¾ inches across and may be wavy or distorted, particularly when crowded by neighboring specimens. The surface is **moist and slimy** during wet weather; when the caps dry, they are often glossy. Stems are up to 3 inches tall and have a **velvety texture**; they are pale on young specimens, darkening from the base up until they are **dark brown or blackish** overall except at the very top. The stem has **no ring**. Gills are white to creamy yellow, eventually developing subtle brownish bruises; they are fairly closely spaced and attached to the stem.

SPORE PRINT: White.

SEASON: Fall through spring; may occasionally appear during summer cold spells.

OTHER NAMES: Winter Mushroom, Velvet Shank, *Collybia velutipes*.

COMPARE: Deadly Galerina (pgs. 58–59) can appear very similar and may grow in the same locations, but it has **rust-brown** spores and a **thin ring** on the stem; as its name suggests, it is **deadly**. • Orange Mycena (pg. 166) appears somewhat similar to Velvet Foot and has white spores, but Orange Mycena is smaller; it is **orange overall** with **reddish gill edges**, and its stems are **sticky rather than velvety**.

NOTES: Velvet Foot caps are edible, although they are sticky and trap dirt; stems are tough and are generally not eaten. Make a spore print of every specimen assumed to be a Velvet Foot, and check the stem for a ring, to eliminate **toxic** Deadly Galerina. Velvet Foot is the same species as cultivated Enoki mushrooms; however, Enoki are grown in conditions that cause them to look completely different than wild Velvet Foot.

Dark stems

Red Waxy Caps

Hygrocybe spp.

FROM THE SOIL NEAR LIVE TREES

SUMMER THROUGH FALL

HABITAT: Waxy Caps fruit from the soil and humus in wooded areas that are generally a bit damp; they appear singly and in groups. All species listed below are found near hardwoods; *H. conica* and *H. punicea* also grow near conifers.

DESCRIPTION: *Hygrocybe* have **waxy** gills; stems have no ring and are often paler at the base. • Fresh, young specimens of *H. conica* have bright reddish to orange **conical** caps ½ to 1½ inches wide that are sticky to greasy. Stems are up to 3 inches tall and yellowish or orangish. Gills are closely spaced and attached to the stem; they are pale at first, darkening with age. **All parts turn black** when handled or with age. • *H. miniata* is less than 1½ inches wide and tall. Caps are bright reddish-orange to scarlet at first, fading to orange or yellowish. They are **rounded to flattened**, often with a central depression. The yellow to orangish gills are widely spaced and **run down the stem** slightly. • *H. punicea* has a shiny, sticky dark red cap up to **4 inches** wide; it is broadly conical to flattened. The stem is up to **4½ inches** tall and orangish to yellowish; it has a **fibrous texture**, often looking ribbed. Widely spaced gills are attached to the stem, sometimes slightly notched; they are yellow, orangish or dull reddish. • *H. cuspidata* is up to 1½ inches wide and 2½ inches tall. Young, fresh specimens have a sharply pointed cap that is slimy and scarlet; it fades to orangish with age. The stem is colored like the cap or lighter; it is often twisted. The orangish-yellow gills are fairly closely spaced and **free from the stem** or narrowly attached. • *H. coccinea* is less than 2¼ inches tall and wide and **scarlet-red overall**. The cap is broadly conical to flattened and shiny. The stem is dry or slightly sticky; it is **smooth**, not fibrous, which helps separate this species from *H. punicea*. Gills are fairly widely spaced and attached to the stem; the edges are paler than the sides.

SPORE PRINT: White.

SEASON: Summer through fall; *H. cuspidata* may start fruiting in late spring.

OTHER NAMES: *H. punicea* may be listed as Scarlet Waxy Cap; *H. conica* is often called Witches' Hat. Some sources list these species in the *Hygrophorus* genus.

COMPARE: Also see Orange Mycena (pg. 166) and Yellow-Orange Waxy Caps (pg. 122).

NOTES: Some *Hygrocybe* are edible, while others are toxic; none should be eaten due to difficulties with identification.

H. conica

H. miniata

H. punicea

H. cuspidata

FROM THE SOIL NEAR LIVE TREES

MIDSUMMER THROUGH MID-FALL

Reddish Russulas (several)

Russula spp.

HABITAT: Russulas are mycorrhizal, growing from the ground near living trees.

DESCRIPTION: Dozens of Russulas are reddish; many are impossible to accurately identify based on visual characteristics. Using DNA and microscopic evaluations, mycologists have determined that many North American species are different from those found overseas; names that had been applied to North American species are no longer valid. This paragraph presents information on several species found in our area that are visually distinct. Like all Russulas, they have **sturdy stems that lack rings**. Caps on young specimens are rounded, opening and turning upward to form a bowl-like shape; some or much of **the skin can be peeled off the cap**. Flesh is **white and brittle**. Gills of species listed here are closely spaced and attached to the stem or running slightly down it. • Caps of *R. mariae* are typically 2 to 3 inches wide and have a **dusty whitish coating** over a base that ranges from reddish, purplish-red to pinkish; mottling is not uncommon and some have olive or brownish tones. Stems are pale pinkish or purplish. Gills are white, becoming pale yellowish. Found near hardwoods. • **Rosy Russula** (*R. 'sanguinea'* or *R. rosacea*) is 2 to 4 inches wide and tall. Caps are **tacky** and **rosy-red** when young, fading with age. Stems are **pinkish**, or **whitish with a rosy blush**. Gills are white, becoming creamy to yellowish. It grows under pines. **The Sickener** (*R. 'emetica'*; **toxic**) appears similar to Rosy Russula, but caps are **slimy**; stems are **white to pale yellow**. It is found in bogs and mossy areas. • **Shrimp Russula** (*R. xerampelina* group) may be **6 inches** across (or more); they are often **wine-red or dull purple** but vary in color. Stems are 2 to 3 inches tall and white, sometimes with a reddish blush. Gills are yellowish to **orangish-yellow**; stem and gills **bruise brownish**. Shrimp Russula have a **fishy odor**; they grow in coniferous or mixed-wood forests.

SPORE PRINT: Pale yellow to creamy; Shrimp Russula's may be orangish-yellow.

SEASON: Midsummer through mid-fall.

OTHER NAMES: *R. mariae* is sometimes called Purple-Bloom Russula.

COMPARE: Wine Caps (pg. 167; delicious) grow on **wood chips or mulch**, stems have a **distinct ring**. Their spore print is **purplish-brown to blackish**.

NOTES: Rosy Russula is acrid and inedible; The Sickener is **toxic**. *R. mariae* and Shrimp Russula are considered good edibles when properly identified.

R. mariae

Rosy Russula

Shrimp Russula

ON DECAYING WOOD

FALL

Brick Tops

Hypholoma lateritium

HABITAT: These saprobes grow in clusters **on decaying deciduous logs and stumps**. They often appear on the same log or stump in successive years.

DESCRIPTION: These medium-sized mushrooms are fairly easy to spot in the fall because they are colorful and grow in tight clusters. Caps are chubby and rounded when young, with a rolled-under margin and a **thin, webby partial veil** over the gills. The caps flatten with age, becoming convex; they are up to 4 inches wide and **brick-red with pale edges**. The surface is smooth but may develop cracks with age. The veil often leaves a thin, filmy remnant near the top of the stem, but this remnant may not be present or noticeable; there is no other ring. The stem is up to 4 inches tall and up to ⅝ inch thick; it is often curved or bent as it twists its way out of the cluster. The top half of the stem is whitish or pale yellow, and there may be an irregular brownish stain near the cap where falling spores have been caught by the veil remnant. The base of the stem is **reddish-brown** and often mottled. Gills are dull **whitish** on young specimens, becoming **purplish-brown**; they are closely spaced and attached to the stem.

SPORE PRINT: Purplish-brown.

SEASON: Fall; may be found in late summer in some years and locations.

OTHER NAMES: Brick Caps, *H. sublateritium*, *Naematoloma sublateritium*.

COMPARE: Two related, slightly smaller species with similar growth habits are found in our area. **Sulfur Tuft** (*H. fasciculare*) has **yellowish** caps; its stem is tawny and up to 4¾ inches tall, and its gills are **yellowish**, becoming **greenish** to olive-brown. Sulfur Tuft is extremely bitter and considered **toxic**. The edible *H. capnoides* has an **orangish-brown** to tan cap and **gray** gills that turn **reddish-brown**; it grows on conifers. • **Wine Caps** (pg. 167; edible) have burgundy caps and a **cogwheel-edged ring**; they grow **from the ground** in wood chips and mulch.

NOTES: Young Brick Tops are edible and eagerly collected by some foragers, who note a nutty taste; others find them bitter. Be certain that the gills are whitish rather than yellow or greenish, to avoid the **toxic** Sulfur Tuft.

Brick Tops

Sulfur Tuft

H. capnoides

Bleeding Mycena

Mycena haematopus

ON DECAYING WOOD   SPRING THROUGH FALL

HABITAT: This saprobe grows **from dead hardwood**, typically in clusters that may be quite large.

DESCRIPTION: The cap is dry and up to 1½ inches across; it is conical to bell-shaped, with a ragged edge that is usually paler than the rest of the cap. Young specimens are pinkish to reddish-purple with a darker center, fading to pinkish-tan or brownish with age; thin ribs run from the center to the edges. The **thin**, hollow stems are brownish and up to 3 inches tall; there is no ring. Gills are closely spaced and attached to the stem; they are whitish, darkening with age. Caps and stems **ooze purplish-red liquid** when cut. This species is often attacked by *Spinellus fusiger*, a thread-like parasitic mold.

SPORE PRINT: White.

SEASON: Spring through fall.

OTHER NAMES: Bleeding Fairy Helmet.

COMPARE: Lilac Mycena (*M. pura*; also called Lilac Bonnet) grows singly to scattered **from the ground** under hardwoods and conifers. The cap is bell-shaped, often with a low bump in the center and ribbed edges; with age the cap flattens out and may be up to 2¼ inches across. This species is hygrophanous (pg. 11), changing color in response to moisture levels; it also changes color as it ages. Young, fresh caps are generally lilac or purplish, but caps may also be pinkish, yellowish, whitish or tan. Stems are colored like the cap or paler. They are up to **4 inches** tall and moderately thick; there is no ring. The whitish gills are moderately closely spaced and attached to the stem; a small notch or tooth may be observed next to the stem. Spores are white. Lilac Mycena typically **smells like radish**. • Lilac Fiberhead (*Inocybe lilacina*; also listed as *I. geophylla* var. *lilacina*) resembles young, fresh specimens of Lilac Mycena; it is lilac to purplish with a bump in the center of the cap. Gills of young specimens are covered by a **cobwebby white veil**. The spore print is **brown**. • Tan to Grayish Mycenas (several) appear similar to older specimens of the Mycena listed above; see pg. 96. • Blewits (pg. 142) have caps up to 6 inches across, with stocky stems and a **sweet, floral fragrance**. Spores are **pale pink to pinkish-buff**.

NOTES: Some sources list Bleeding Mycena as edible but of poor flavor. Lilac Mycena and Lilac Fiberhead are both **toxic**.

"Bleeding"

Bleeding Mycena
(top 3 photos)

Attacked by
Spinellus fusiger

Lilac Mycena

Purple-Gilled Laccaria

Laccaria ochropurpurea

FROM THE SOIL NEAR LIVE TREES

MIDSUMMER THROUGH FALL

HABITAT: Growing from the ground, scattered or in groups, in mixed forests, particularly under oak, beech and white pine. They are mycorrhizal, growing in a symbiotic relationship with living trees.

DESCRIPTION: When fresh, young and moist, this mushroom has a lilac to light brownish-purple cap; as it matures, its color fades to gray or white. Caps may be smooth or finely scaly. On very young specimens, caps are small and rounded, often perched atop a grossly **swollen, bulbous** stem. The cap enlarges and flattens out with age; it may be up to **6 inches** wide at maturity, often with wavy edges and a depressed center. Gills are **purple, thick and widely spaced**, with a waxy texture. They are attached to the stem and may run down the stem for a short distance. Stems are **stocky**, up to **7 inches** tall and often somewhat twisted or curved. They are colored like the cap or slightly darker; they typically have a dry, fibrous texture and coarse hairs or scales on the surface. There is no ring. The base is often slightly swollen and covered with soft lilac-colored mycelium (it may be necessary to dig around the base to see the swelling and mycelium).

SPORE PRINT: White or pale lilac.

SEASON: Midsummer through fall.

OTHER NAMES: None.

COMPARE: Amethyst Laccaria (*L. amethystina*; also called Purple Laccaria and Amethyst Deceiver) is much smaller than Purple-Gilled Laccaria and is **violet overall** when young; with age the cap and stem fade to buff, gray or brownish. Caps are less than **1½ inches** wide; stems are **slender** and 1 to 4 inches tall. **Common Laccaria** (pg. 90) is tan to orangish, and resembles faded specimens of Amethyst Laccaria. • **Sandy Laccaria** (*L. trullisata*; also spelled *trullissata*) has purple gills, but its cap is less than 3 inches wide; it grows in **sandy areas**. • **Blewits** (pg. 142) are purplish when young but have **closely spaced gills** and a **pinkish** spore print. • **Purplish Cortinarius** (pg. 144; **toxic**) have a **cobwebby veil** over the gills of young specimens and **rust-brown** spores.

NOTES: Caps of Purple-Gilled Laccaria and Amethyst Laccaria are edible, with a mild flavor; the stems are tough and fibrous and are generally not eaten.

Purple-Gilled Laccaria

Amethyst Laccaria

Blewit

Clitocybe nuda

HABITAT: Blewits are saprobes, mushrooms that get nutrients from decaying organic matter, including leaf litter, compost, grass clippings and wood mulch. Found under brambles and hedgerows and in deciduous and coniferous forests. They grow singly or in small groups and may grow in a ring.

DESCRIPTION: Young Blewits are **lavender, violet-blue or purplish** overall; stems are paler. Mature specimens are **tan to brownish**, often with slight mottling; gills may retain some purplish coloration, particularly around the cap edge. Gills are closely spaced and attached to the stem; they may be slightly notched at the stem, appearing to curve upwards. Caps are 1½ to 6 inches wide with a smooth surface. Caps of young Blewits are softly rounded with slightly rolled-under edges, but as the mushrooms age the caps flare out and may develop wavy edges and irregular tops; some have a rounded point in the center. Stems are generally 1 to 3 inches tall and **stocky** with a rough texture; there is no ring. The base is often swollen or bulbous and may have a network of **fine purplish mycelium** (threadlike fungal filaments). Blewits have a **sweet**, floral fragrance.

SPORE PRINT: Pale pink to pinkish-buff.

SEASON: Late summer through late fall.

OTHER NAMES: Wood Blewit, *Lepista nuda*, *Tricholoma nudum*.

COMPARE: Other purplish mushrooms may be encountered; some, such as *Cortinarius* spp. (pg. 144), are **toxic**. Young Cortinarius have a **cobwebby veil** over the gills, and mature Cortinarius have **rust-brown spores**. • Some *Laccaria* (pg. 140; edible) are purplish but the gills are **widely spaced** and spores are **white**. • Lilac Mycena (pg. 138; toxic) is smaller, with a cap less than 2 inches wide and a **thin, hollow stem**; it has a **radish-like** odor and **white** spore print. It may turn tan with age.

NOTES: Blewits are edible but not recommended for amateurs due to similarities to **toxic** Cortinarius species. Always look for any trace of a cobwebby veil (present on Cortinarius but not Blewits) and make a spore print of every mushroom assumed to be a Blewit before eating it. Blewits should never be eaten raw.

Maturing Blewits

Young Blewits

Lilac Mycena

FROM THE SOIL
NEAR LIVE TREES

LATE SUMMER
THROUGH LATE FALL

Purplish Cortinarius (several)
Cortinarius spp.

HABITAT: *Cortinarius* species are mycorrhizal, growing from the soil in a symbiotic relationship with living trees.

DESCRIPTION: Cortinarius have a **cobwebby veil** (called a cortina; see photo on facing page) covering the gills of young specimens. The veil disintegrates with age, sometimes leaving a ring remnant on the stem. Gills of the species listed here are closely spaced except for Violet Cort, whose gills are somewhat widely spaced. Spores are brownish; they typically darken the mature gills and may also coat the ring remnant, turning it brown. Caps are conical at first, becoming wider and fairly flat. Stems of some species have a swollen base. Our area has at least five *Cortinarius* species with purplish attributes. • Silvery-Violet Cort (*C. alboviolaceus*) is **pale violet to silvery lilac** overall with a **dry, silky cap** up to 4 inches wide; its stem is **club-like**. It favors birch or beech trees. • Violet Cort (*C. violaceus*) is **dark violet overall** when young, turning brownish with age; the cap is dry, covered with **fine white tufts** and is up to 5 inches across. The stem is slightly club-like but not as broad as that of Silvery-Violet Cort. It is found near conifers. • *C. iodes* (also called *C. heliotropicus*) has a purplish cap less than 2 inches wide that often has **yellowish spots**; the stem is pale and both cap and stem are **slimy**. It grows near deciduous trees, favoring oaks. *C. iodeoides* is nearly identical to *C. iodes*, but its slime is bitter, while that of *C. iodes* is not; other differences are microscopic. • Found around conifers, *C. traganus* has a lavender to violet cap up to 5 inches wide that may be **cracked or patchy in the center**. The stem exterior is the color of the cap, but the interior is rusty brown. • *C. azureus* is **pale purple overall** with a cap less than 3 inches wide; in our region it grows only in the eastern part in association with **beech trees**.

SPORE PRINT: Rust-brown or cinnamon-colored.

SEASON: Most common from late summer through late fall.

OTHER NAMES: Some sources refer to *Cortinarius* species as Webcaps.

COMPARE: Blewits (pg. 142; edible) are also purplish but lack the cobwebby veil; their spore print is **pale pink to pinkish-buff**. • Some *Laccaria* (pg. 140; edible) are purplish but the gills are **widely spaced** and spores are **white**.

NOTES: None of the species above should be eaten; some Cortinarius, including Silvery-Violet Cort, are **toxic**.

Silvery-Violet Cort

Cortina

Violet Cort

Bluish to Greenish Milk Caps (several)

Lactarius spp.

HABITAT: Milk Caps are mycorrhizal, growing from the soil in a symbiotic relationship with living trees. *L. chelidonium* prefers pine trees; the others discussed here associate with both coniferous and deciduous trees.

DESCRIPTION: Milk Caps (*Lactarius* spp.) are a large family of brittle-fleshed, gilled mushrooms that produce **milky latex when cut**. Caps of young and middle-age specimens are rounded with a sunken center and rolled-under edges; many become vase-like with age. The species on this page have **stocky** stems up to 3 inches tall; their gills are closely spaced and attached to the stem or running down it slightly. Stems have no rings. • **Indigo Milky** (*L. indigo*) is the most stunning. Its cap and stem are **deep blue to grayish-blue**, sometimes with greenish bruises; caps are up to 5 inches wide or larger, often with darker rings or scattered dots. Gills are **deep, rich blue**, turning yellowish as spores develop. When cut, all parts **immediately turn dark blue**, then greenish; the **gills ooze** a bit of **dark blue** latex. • Caps of *L. chelidonium* are up to 4 inches wide; they are generally **buff-colored and mottled with pale blue or green** when young, turning yellowish-brown and finally **mottled greenish-bronze**. Gills are **tan** to brownish-orange, sometimes with greenish areas. When cut, caps and stems turn bluish, then greenish; gills bruise greenish. Fresh specimens ooze a small amount of **yellowish-brown** latex when cut. • *L. atroviridis* have **rough or pockmarked** caps up to 6 inches wide and stems that are **mottled with dark green, moss-green, olive or tan**. Gills are **pinkish**, bruising greenish or brownish. When cut, all parts ooze a fair amount of **white** latex.

SPORE PRINT: Cream, buff, white or yellowish.

SEASON: Summer through fall.

OTHER NAMES: Milky Caps, Milkcaps, Milky.

COMPARE: Some Russula in our area have greenish attributes (pg. 171), but their gills are **whitish** and **do not produce the milky latex** when cut.

NOTES: Indigo Milky and *L. chelidonium* are edible; *L. atroviridis* is not considered edible.

Indigo Milky

L. chelidonium

Fairy Inkcap

Coprinellus disseminatus (also listed as *Coprinus disseminatus*)

This miniscule mushroom is fun to find because it grows in eye-catching numbers. It is a saprobe, growing from well-rotted stumps and logs of deciduous trees in spring, summer and fall. A member of the Inky Cap family (pgs. 28–29), its caps are **off-white** and egg-shaped when young, but darken with age, becoming gray and bell-shaped at maturity. The caps develop **prominent striations** as they grow, making them look almost **pleated**, and they retain a **tan or brownish spot at the top**. Gills are white, darkening to gray and finally black, due to the black spores. It is also called the Non-Inky Coprinus because the gills do not turn to liquid like other ink caps. The tiny fragile stems grow up to 2 inches tall with caps less than one inch at maturity.

COMPARE: Fuzzy Foot (pg. 124) is another small mushroom that grows in large numbers on rotting wood, but has an **orange to bright yellow** color; its gills are **pale yellow to orangish**. • *Mycena* species (pgs. 96, 138, 166) are slightly larger and grow in groups that are not quite as numerous as Fuzzy Foot or Fairy inkcaps. *Mycena* species are sometimes called Fairy Bonnets, or Fairy Helmets. • There are many other tiny, fragile mushrooms (pg. 74); making a spore print is helpful in narrowing down their genus.

NOTES: Fairy Inkcap is edible, but has a delicate texture giving it the alternate name of Trooping Crumble Cap. That and the small size make it poor table fare.

Silky Volvariella   Smooth Volvariella

Silky Volvariella
Volvariella bombycina

Also known as Tree Volvariella, this saprobe grows **directly from wood**, including living deciduous trees, dead trees or fallen wood. Young specimens are encased in an egg-shaped **universal veil** that breaks open to reveal the bright white caps, which are covered with **silky hairs** and up to 8 inches across. Slender stems grow up to 7 inches tall and have no ring, but are **sheathed at the base** by a mottled, tan sack. Gills are closely spaced, not attached to the stem and are white at first, turning pale **salmon-pink**, the color of the spores. Summer through fall.

COMPARE: Smooth Volvariella (*Volvopluteus gloiocephalus*, formerly *Volvariella speciosa*) grows from late spring through fall in grassy areas, on disturbed ground and on mulch or dung. Caps are white to pale gray and sticky when fresh and young, appearing **shiny** when dried. The cup at the base may be visible, or hidden underground. Spores are **pinkish-brown**. • Several white *Amanita* species (pgs. 62–67), including **deadly toxic** Destroying Angel, appear similar, but have prominent **rings** on the stems; spore prints are **white**. • *Leucoagaricus naucinus* (also listed as *Lepiota naucina* and *Leucoagaricus leucothites*) has a distinct ring on the stem when young, but the ring may deteriorate or disappear with age. There is **no cup** at the stem base, which is frequently swollen and bulbous.

NOTES: Both Tree and Smooth Volvariella are edible but should be avoided by all but well-experienced foragers due to the possibility of confusing them with the **deadly** Destroying Angel (pg. 64).

Snowy Waxy Cap

Cuphophyllus virgineus (also known as *Hygrocybe virginea*)

This small saprobe is found in grassy areas, pastures, parks and mossy patches, sometimes near forest edges; it grows from decaying matter which is often buried. It is white overall and may appear slightly translucent. The cap is up to 2 inches wide and feels **waxy or slippery** but not slimy; it may be slightly humped or wavy, and older specimens may appear to be turned inside-out. Stems are smooth and up to 3¼ inches tall; there is no ring. The **widely spaced gills run down the stem** for a short distance; they are **thick and waxy or greasy-feeling**. Snowy Waxy Cap has a white spore print and is found from summer through fall.

COMPARE: Ivory Waxy Cap (*Hygrophorus eburneus*) is slightly larger and its cap and stem are **very slimy**, especially when wet; it may turn slightly yellowish with age. • Golden-Spotted Waxy Cap (*Hygrophorus chrysodon*) has a white cap with a slightly sticky surface and fine **yellowish-gold flakes** that may wash away or fade with age; it is often found near conifers. • Species in the *Limacella* **genus** (particularly *L. illinita*) may resemble Snowy Waxy Cap, but their gills are **slimy** and **free from the stem**; caps are **slimy**. • The **Sweater** (pg. 151; **toxic**) is similar in size to Snowy Waxy Cap, but its caps are **mottled** and its gills are **closely spaced**.

NOTES: Snowy Waxy Caps are edible but not tasty; not recommended for amateurs due to the possibility of confusing them with toxic species. This may also be listed as *Camarophyllus virgineus* or *Hygrophorus virgineus*.

The Sweater

Clitocybe rivulosa (also known as Ivory Funnel Cap and *C. dealbata*)

This small, **toxic** mushroom appears in pastures, grassy areas and open woods; it often grows in a ring. It is white, pale grayish-white or buff-colored overall; the cap may appear pinkish when it is moist and often becomes **mottled with darker, wet-looking splotches**. Mature caps are generally ½ to 1⅝ inches wide; the edge is turned under. The cap surface is irregular but smooth; it may be slippery on young specimens but becomes dry with maturity. Stems are 1 to 1½ inches tall and may be a slightly darker shade than the cap; the cap is often attached to the stem slightly **off-center**. The stem has no ring. Several specimens may grow together from a common base. Gills are **closely spaced** and **run down the stem for a short distance**; they are creamy white at first, turning **tan to pinkish-tan** with age. Its spore print is **white**; it is found from mid to late summer.

COMPARE: The Sweetbread Mushroom (pg. 76) is similar in overall appearance but is generally larger and its spore print is **pinkish**. · Funnel Caps (pg. 106) are up to 4 inches across and pinkish-tan with a **deep funnel shape**. · Snowy Waxy Cap (pg. 150) and other pale waxy caps appear similar, but their caps are **waxy or covered with sticky slime**.

NOTES: The Sweater contains the **toxic** compound muscarine, which causes intense sweating, salivation, tear formation and intestinal distress.

Onion-Stalked Lepiota
Leucocoprinus cepistipes (also listed as *Lepiota cepistipes*)

These common saprobes grow on debris, such as wood chips, mulch or compost piles and sawdust heaps; also found in lawns, parks and gardens. The cap is 1 to 3 inches wide and covered with small, **powdery white granules** that become scale-like with age. The cap is **white** or very pale pink and round to egg-shaped when young, expanding and becoming softly conical to almost flat; as it ages, the cap becomes cream-colored to yellowish-tan with a darker center that is smooth and knob-like. The **slender** stem is up to 5 inches tall; its base **widens slightly**, resembling a green onion in shape, accounting for its common name. There is **no cup** around the stem base. Young specimens have a thin veil over the gills; the veil disintegrates as the cap expands, leaving a **thin ring** on the upper stem. Gills are closely spaced and not attached to the stem; they are white when young, turning tan with age. The cap and stem bruise yellowish-brown to brownish when handled. They grow in clusters from midsummer to early fall. Spores are white.

COMPARE: Yellow Parasol (*Leucocoprinus birnbaumii* or *Leucocoprinus luteus*; **toxic**) is similar but is pale to bright **lemon-yellow** overall; it commonly appears in **flower pots** and in sheltered areas growing on leaf litter, compost and other debris. • *Lepiota cristata* has a **red-scaled** cap less than 2 inches wide and a **very thin stem**; it has a foul odor. • Many *Amanita* species (pgs. 62–67; **toxic**) have patchy caps and swollen bases; some have a **cup** at the stem base.

NOTES: All species above should be considered inedible; several are **toxic**.

Elm Cap   Train Wrecker

Elm Cap
Hypsizygus ulmarius (also listed as *Pleurotus ulmarius*)

From late summer through fall, look for these saprobes growing from **a wound, scar or knothole** on live deciduous trees, primarily boxelder and, less frequently, elms. Elm Caps are often mistaken for Oyster Mushrooms (pgs. 34–37), but the Elm Cap has a **stem that is distinct from the cap**, whereas Oyster Mushrooms have only a very short, flowing stem or none at all. Elm Caps are **white, creamy or tan** overall. Young specimens have smooth, rounded caps that expand and flatten with age and may be **up to 6 inches across**; the surface may develop cracks. Stems are 2 to 4 inches long and may be attached to the caps off-center; they are often curved. The moderately spaced gills are **attached to the stem but do not run down it**; the stem has no ring. The spore print is white to buff.

COMPARE: Beech Mushrooms (*H. tessellatus*; edible) are related to Elm Caps, but its caps are **pinkish-buff** and **subtly marbled** with darker areas that resemble water spots. It grows in clusters on a larger variety of deciduous trees, including aspen and maples. • The **Train Wrecker** (*Neolentinus lepideus*; young caps edible) grows in clusters on decaying wood, including logs, stumps and railroad ties; its cap has numerous **fine brown scales**. Gills of mature specimens have **jagged edges** and run down the stem, which has **curved whitish to brownish scales**.

NOTES: Elm Cap is a good edible, although not as favored as Oyster Mushrooms; stems are tough and are generally not eaten. Elm Caps and Beech Mushrooms are available in grow-it-yourself kits; the cultivated mushrooms are sold as Shimeji.

Yellow Fieldcap

Bolbitius titubans (also known as Egg Yolk and *B. vitellinus*)

This small, brightly colored mushroom grows in loose groups on hay piles, in grassy areas, on compost heaps and on dung. Caps of young, fresh specimens are **bright yellow, egg-shaped and slimy**. They are ¾ to 1 inch wide and are fairly smooth, with a fragile, thin texture. The caps change very quickly to grayish or tan, flattening and expanding to nearly 2 inches wide; they develop fine ribbing from the edges nearly to the center of the cap, which typically still retains some yellow. Stems are **whitish to pale yellow** and are typically **shaggy looking**; they are 1½ to 3 inches tall and hollow, and there is **no ring**. Gills are closely spaced and barely attached to the stem, pulling away with age; they have a soft texture. Young specimens have yellow gills, which are soon colored reddish-brown by the **rust-brown** spores; the **gills may liquefy** in wet weather. They prefer cool weather and are found in spring through early summer, then again in fall.

COMPARE: Mica Caps (pg. 100) and other members of the *Coprinus* genus grow in straw and have gills that liquefy, but the cap colors are more muted and the spores are **black**. • Tan to Grayish Mycena (pg. 96) appear quite similar to faded Yellow Fieldcaps, but their spores are **white**; gills are typically whitish. • Spring Fieldcap and other *Agrocybe* (pg. 88) are generally larger and more sturdy; they usually have **remnants of a universal veil**, including white fragments on the cap edges and **rings** on the stems.

NOTES: Yellow Fieldcap are edible when young but are fairly bland and soft.

Plums and Custard

Tricholomopsis rutilans (also known as *Tricholoma rutilans*)

This attractive mushroom, also known as Variegated Mop, grows scattered or in small clusters from **decaying conifer stumps and logs** that may be underground. Both cap and stem are **yellow** and have a coating of **reddish to purplish-red fibers and scales** that are sometimes so dense on the cap that it may appear entirely red. Caps of mature specimens are up to **4¾ inches** wide, often with a wavy or scalloped edge. Stems are stocky and up to 4 inches tall; the base may be somewhat flattened. The stem has no ring. Gills are **deep yellow** and closely spaced; they are attached to the stem or slightly notched. The flesh is yellow. The spores are **white**. It grows from late spring through fall, particularly during cool periods.

COMPARE: Decorated Mop (pg. 84) is smaller, with a cap that is generally less than 3 inches across and a stem that is less than 3 inches tall. It is typically **golden yellow overall** and **lacks the reddish fibers**; it has **tiny brown scales** that are concentrated on the center of the cap. • Some *Russula* species (pg. 134) have reddish or purplish-red caps; stems may be pale or colored like the cap and the spores are **creamy yellowish to pale orangish-yellow**. Russulas grow directly **from the soil**. • Brick Tops (pg. 136) grow in **tight clusters** from decaying decid-uous logs and stumps. They have caps that are brick-red with pale edges; gills are **white** and the spore print is **purplish-brown**.

NOTES: In spite of its delicious-sounding name, Plums and Custard is a poor edible.

Yellow Russulas (several)

Russula spp.

Several yellow-capped Russula species grow in our area; they are identified by habitat, slight variations in appearance and microscopic analysis. The listed species have a yellowish cap that is 3 to 4 inches wide at maturity; the center is depressed and the surface is often tacky when moist. Stems are sturdy and smooth; there is no ring. Gills are white, cream-colored or yellowish. They are attached to the stem and fairly closely spaced. Spore prints are white, cream-colored or yellowish. Species listed here are found in summer and fall. • *R. claroflava* (also listed as *R. flava* and *R. ochroleuca* var. *flava*) is called Yellow Swamp Russula because it grows in **boggy conifer-birch** forests. Stems are white, turning **gray** when bruised. • *R. flavida* has a **yellow stem**; its cap may be slightly orangish. The stem does not change color when bruised. *R. flavida* grows near oaks and other deciduous trees. • Mature gills of *R. lutea* are **ochre**; the cap may be apricot-colored. Stems are white. Its spore print is **bright yellow to ochre**. It grows in deciduous forests. • *R. ochroleucoides* is less common. It has a **velvety**, yellow to orangish cap that has reddish hues when young. The white gills become yellow near outer cap edge.

COMPARE: Almond-Scented Russula (*R. grata*; formerly *R. laurocerasi*) is larger, with a dull yellow cap up to 5 inches wide; it **smells like almonds**.

NOTES: The Russulas listed above are edible. Most have a mild taste; *R. flavida* is generally mild-tasting, and *R. lutea* is said to have a fruity flavor.

Golden Pholiota (several)

Pholiota aurivella, P. limonella, P. squarrosoadiposa

Golden Pholiota is a name used for several Pholiota species that can't be positively separated from one another without a microscope; the three listed above are often grouped together. The **yellow** to yellowish-orange caps are up to 6 inches wide and **very slimy**, with **irregularly placed reddish-brown to purplish scales** that may eventually fall off. Young caps have a webby partial veil over the gills that often leaves a thin band-like remnant near the top of the stem; there is no other ring. The stem is up to 4 inches tall; it is cottony and white at the top, becoming **scaly** and yellowish to brownish yellow below the veil remnant. Gills are cream-colored, turning tan to **reddish-brown** with age; they are closely spaced and attached to the stem. Spores are **rusty brown**, and may darken the veil remnant. Golden Pholiota appear from midsummer through late fall in clusters or singly on living or dead deciduous and coniferous trees, logs and stumps.

COMPARE: Decorated Pholiota (pg. 86) have tan caps that are covered with **pointed tan to rusty brown scales**. The spore print is **white**. • Scaly Pholiota (pg. 86; **toxic**) has a **dry, pale yellow to tan** cap with prominent, **spiky brown** scales. Its gills turn **greenish** before turning brownish from the spores.

NOTES: Golden Pholiota is often listed as an acceptable edible once the cap is peeled; other sources state that it is bitter and may cause intestinal problems.

The Gypsy
Cortinarius caperatus (also known as *Rozites caperata*)

The Gypsy is mycorrhizal, growing **from the soil** in a symbiotic relationship with deciduous trees and conifers. It seems to prefer acidic soil near **conifers** and blueberry bushes and can be found singly or in large groups. The cap is up to 5 inches wide and **yellowish** to light brown; it is covered with fine, **silky white fibers**, mainly in the center, making it appear slightly **frosted**. Caps are conical to slightly knobbed and are often wrinkled (*caperata* means "wrinkled" in Latin). The **attached gills** are closely spaced and putty-colored when young. They are initially covered by a partial veil that breaks to form a **white ring** on the stem, which is white to light tan and may be swollen at the base. Gills darken with age to a **rusty brown** color that matches the spore print. It fruits from late summer through fall.

COMPARE: Other *Cortinarius* species (pgs. 116, 126, 144) may look similar in some regards, but buttons typically have a **cobwebby cortina** (partial veil) and mature specimens lack the ring on the stem. • *Agaricus* species (pg. 82) may be tan with a prominent ring, but the gills are **not attached** to the stem and spores are **dark brown**. • Big Laughing Gym (pg. 161) grows in clusters on **wood** and has a **dark-capped** ring.

NOTES: The Gypsy is being studied for antiviral properties. It is a good edible when properly identified; some of the other species listed above are **toxic**.

Pale Brittlestem
Psathyrella candolleana

This mushroom is very common but hard to identify. It is a saprobe, growing singly or in small groups from stumps and wood chips, often in lawns and gardens in spring and summer. A key feature to distinguish it from numerous other LBMs (pg. 112) is the **flimsy white veil tissue** found on the edge of young caps. Dome-shaped or slightly conical caps are 1 to 3 inches across, flattening with age; color is highly variable and changes based on moisture (called *hygrophanous*; pg. 11). Young caps are yellowish-brown, fading to a **parchment white with gray areas** when wet. Thin, fragile white stems are 1½ to 3 inches tall. A veil remnant is visible as a ring at first; it quickly disappears, leaving only wisps as a partial ring or remnant. The **crowded** gills are white when young; with age they change to pinkish-gray, finally turning dark purplish-brown, the color of the spores.

COMPARE: Common Fieldcap (pg. 88) is similar in size, color and habitat, but has **widely spaced** gills. • Mica Caps (pg. 100) grow in dense clusters in the same habitats and seasons, but caps are dotted with **small granules**; edges **lack the veil remnants**. • Caps of Tippler's Bane (pg. 29) are **pewter-gray to grayish-brown**. The gills turn to a black liquid when mature.

NOTES: Pale Brittlestem, Mica Caps and Common Fieldcaps are edible, but they are small, fragile and unremarkable. Tippler's Bane is edible but should not be consumed with alcohol. Accurate identification of all of these species is difficult. You should never eat anything you can't identify with absolute certainty.

"Fairy Ring Fungus"

Marasmius oreades (also known as Scotch Bonnet)

Although this mushroom is referred to as the Fairy Ring, that name is also used for other species that have circular growth habits, so it is best to use the scientific name, *Marasmius oreades*. It is found in grassy areas and is common in urban settings; it grows in small clusters, often in a ring where a tree has been removed. The cap is **buff or tan** and is often slightly darker in the center. Caps are rounded at first but flatten out quickly; they are typically somewhat **wavy with a central hump**. Mature specimens are up to 2 inches wide. The stem is up to 3 inches tall and fairly slender; it is generally colored like the cap. It feels somewhat felt-like and has a rubbery, tough consistency. There is no ring. Gills are cream-colored and **fairly widely spaced**. They are typically attached to the stem but **never run down it**; sometimes the gills appear slightly notched where they are attached to the stem. Spores are white. These mushrooms fruit from spring through fall.

COMPARE: Numerous small to medium-sized mushrooms can be confused with *M. oreades*. **The Sweater** (pg. 151; **toxic**) grows in similar habitat and is about the same size and shape. Its gills are **closely spaced** and **run down the stem** slightly, and its cap is often mottled with wet-looking splotches. • Also see **Spring Fieldcap** (pg. 88), **Common Laccaria** (pg. 90), **Pale Brittlestem** (pg. 159) and **LBMs** (pg. 112) for other mushrooms that may appear somewhat similar to Fairy Ring Fungus.

NOTES: Although its flesh is somewhat tough, *M. oreades* is edible, but beginners must seek expert help to avoid **toxic** lookalikes.

Big Laughing Gym

Gymnopilus junonius (formerly *G. spectabilis* and sometimes called Waraitake)

With its large stature and frequently clustered growth habit, this mushroom is hard to miss; it grows in mixed woods from summer through fall on rotting trees and woody debris that may be buried. Caps of mature specimens are up to **8 inches across**; the thick stem is up to **8 inches tall**. Caps and stems are yellowish-brown, golden or brownish-orange; gills are yellowish to rusty. The cap is dry and may be finely scaly. Stems, which are often curved or twisted, have a **ring** near the top that typically becomes darkened by spores; below the ring, stems are **streaked with coarse fibers**. Gills are closely spaced and attached to the stem or running down it slightly. Its spores are bright orangish-brown to rust-brown.

COMPARE: *G. luteus* is less than 4 inches wide and 3 inches tall, with a **slender** stem; its ring is often **very faint**. • *G. luteofolius* has a **scaly, reddish-brown** cap up to 3 inches wide; its stem is up to 4 inches tall and brownish with pale streaks, and it generally has a ring. • *G. sapineus* and *G. penetrans* (sometimes considered variations of a single species) are less than 3 inches wide and tall. Caps are orangish-yellow and often scaly; stems have **no ring**. They are sometimes called Rustgills because the gills develop **brown splotches** before turning completely rust-brown. Found with conifers.

NOTES: Big Laughing Gym has a pleasant odor but a bitter taste. It is hallucinogenic, causing fits of laughter, mood swings and other bizarre behavior. Other *Gymnopilus* may have similar effects; none should be eaten or used as a drug.

False Matsutake

Matsutake

Tricholoma 'caligatum,' Tricholoma magnivelare

Two Matsutakes are found in our area in fall; both are mycorrhizal. False Matsutake (*T. 'caligatum'*) grows near **hardwoods**; American Matsutake, *T. magnivelare*, associates with **conifers** and is rare in our area. Caps of both are whitish with brownish fibers. Gills are crowded and attached to the stem, sometimes notched; they are white when young and covered with a veil. When the cap expands, veil remnants sheathe the lower part of the stem, terminating in a **prominent, flaring ring** toward the top of the stem. Below the ring, the stem is adorned with **brownish scales or fibers**. Spores of both are white. False Matsutake caps are generally 2 to 4 inches wide and have a denser fibrous coating, appearing **brownish**; stems are up to 3 inches tall, and gills darken with age. American Matsutake are **larger**, with paler caps up to **7 inches** wide and stems up to **6 inches** tall; gills develop orange spots with age. American Matsutake have a **unique, strong aroma** that is a blend of spicy, fruity and musty. False Matsutake generally have a mild fungal aroma.

COMPARE: Caps of *Catathelasma ventricosum* may be up to **12 inches** across and are white, streaked with **grayish** fibers. Stems are up to 6 inches tall, with a **double ring**; the stem often appears to bulge above the tapered base. Found near conifers. • *T. murrillianum* is the West Coast version of American Matsutake.

NOTES: American Matsutake are a highly prized edible. False Matsutake are edible but not as choice; some people find them bitter, while others report a mild flavor with a hint of spiciness. Palatability may vary with individual collections.

Platterful Mushroom

Megacollybia rodmanii (also known as *M. platyphylla*, *Tricholomopsis platyphylla*)

From spring through summer, this mushroom can be found **singly** or in **small groups**, growing from **dead and decaying wood**, stumps and buried woody debris. Its cap is up to 7 inches wide and is grayish, brown or grayish-brown, streaked with **fine, dark fibers** running from the center to the edges; it may look **silky**. On mature specimens, the top of the cap may be uneven; edges are often wavy and/or cracked. Stems are up to 5 inches tall; they are white and have **fine, white vertical fibers**. There is no ring on the stem. White mycelium (threadlike fungal filaments) are often visible at the base. Gills are white to cream-colored and moderately widely spaced; they are attached to the stem, and the edges near the cap may appear **ruffled or wavy**. Its spore print is **white**.

COMPARE: Deer Mushroom and Black-Edged Pluteus (pg. 92) may appear somewhat similar, but both have **salmon-pink** spores. • Fried Chicken Mushroom (*Lyophyllum decastes*; edible) is the same stature as Platterful. Its cap may be grayish, brownish or yellowish-brown, but it lacks the dark fibers. It has a white stem, white gills and white spores. It grows in **dense clusters** in **grassy areas** and along roads from summer through fall.

NOTES: Platterful Mushrooms are edible when young; some people may experience gastrointestinal problems, so try only a small portion at first. *M. platyphylla*, a name that has been used for this species in the past, has been determined to be a European species that does not appear in North America.

green = key identification feature   163

Velvet-Footed Pax

Tapinella atrotomentosa (also called *Paxillus atrotomentosa* and Velvet Rollrim)

This saprobe is found from summer through fall in woodlands and urban parks, growing on **decaying conifer stumps and debris**; it also appears on the ground, emerging from decaying roots or stumps that may be buried. It can be common at times in older conifer woodlands. Caps are dry, dull to velvety, and yellow-brown to brown. This medium to large mushroom is 2 to 6 inches across. The cap margin is **rolled under** at first; the cap becomes flat in age, often with a depressed center. The cap edge is often paler that the rest of the cap. Flesh inside the cap is thick and pale buff colored. When young, the stems are proportionally large in relation to the caps. The 2 to 5 inch stem is robust and covered with a **brown to blackish wooly coating**. It may be centrally attached, but is usually off-center. The stem has no ring. At times, several stems may be fused at the base, forming pairs or small clusters with overlapping caps. The cream to yellowish gills are closely spaced and run down the stem. Near the stem, the gills are forked or may have cross veins. The gills are easily separated from the cap. Velvet-Footed Pax has a mild to slightly sour odor. Its spores are yellowish to tan.

COMPARE: Velvet Footed Pax is a distinctive species. It slightly resembles the Brown Roll-Rim (pg. 71), which **lacks the fuzzy hairs** on the stem.

NOTES: Velvet-Footed Pax is considered inedible due to its poor taste; many sources list it as toxic. It is used to make dye to color wool and silk.

Club-Footed Clitocybe

Ampulloclitocybe clavipes (also known as *Clitocybe clavipes*)

Growing in woodlands, primarily coniferous, from decaying roots and other woody debris which may be underground; may also be found in mixed-wood forests. They grow singly, scattered or in loose groups and may grow in a ring. This mushroom's distinguishing feature is its **broad, club-like base**, although it may not be notable in every specimen. Young specimens often have a disproportionately tiny cap, ½ to 1 inch wide, sitting atop a stem with a narrow neck and a bulbous base. The cap expands with age, becoming flat with a rolled-under edge and, often, a knob in the center. On mature specimens the cap flares up to form a **shallow, wavy-edged bowl** up to 3¼ inches wide. Caps are smooth or felty and tan, reddish-brown or dark brown, typically with a light margin and darker center. The stem is cream-colored to brownish, **stout** and up to 2½ inches tall; the base is typically **swollen** and may be up to 1¼ inches wide. The stem has no ring. Gills are white or cream-colored and moderately close; they **run down the stem** for some distance. It has a white spore print and grows from late summer through fall.

COMPARE: Numerous *Clitocybe* species (pgs. 76, 106, 151) may appear similar, and many of them can't be easily separated from one another without the use of a microscope. Some, such as The Sweater (pg. 151), are **toxic**.

NOTES: Club-Footed Clitocybe should be considered inedible.

Marginate gills

Orange Mycena
Mycena leaiana

This little showstopper is a saprobe, growing in tight clusters **on dead wood** of deciduous trees from summer through fall. When young, the **bright orange** color makes it easy to identify; it **glistens with slime** when wet and is tacky to the touch. With age, it fades to yellowish or cream, sometimes appearing like other *Mycena* species (pg. 96). Young caps are bell-shaped and ½ across or less; as they grow, they become more convex and can be up to 2 inches wide, with ribbed edges. Another distinct feature is the **darker, reddish-orange** color on the **edges** of the lighter orangish to salmon-colored gills (called *marginate*). Gills are closely spaced and attached to the stem, which is yellow to orange. Stems are thin, hollow, fibrous, and 1 inch to 3 inches long. Many stems grow out of a central spot; coarse white hairs are often visible at the base. It has a white spore print.

COMPARE: *Hygrocybe cantharellus* (pg. 122) have long, thin stems and tacky orange caps, but grow **from the ground** rather than wood. • Fuzzy Foot (pg. 124) is yellowish-orange and grows on decaying wood, but the caps are much smaller and it often grows in **great numbers.** • Velvet Foot (pg. 130) has orange to brown caps that are slimy when wet, but the caps are larger. It has white to cream colored gills and a **velvety** stem that turns **brown** with age.

NOTES: When cut, the stem and gills produce orange fluid that can stain your skin. Edibility is not known, and consumption is not recommended. Orange Mycena is so photogenic you might not want to pick it!

Wine Caps

Stropharia rugosoannulata (also called Wine-Cap Stropharia, Garden Giant)

Young specimens have pillowy caps with a **thick white partial veil** underneath; the bottom of the veil has **irregular edges**, resembling a gear or cogwheel. The cap expands and flattens with age and is generally 2 to 5½ inches wide, sometimes larger. It is **burgundy to reddish-brown**, with a dry, smooth surface; older specimens fade to tan and can develop cracks, especially in dry weather. There is a persistent ring on the upper stem; the ring retains the **gear-shaped edges**. Stems are typically 4 to 6 inches tall and white or cream-colored; they are moderately stout and typically wider at the base, which often is surrounded by whitish mycelium (threadlike fungal filaments) that may be visible in the growing substrate. Gills are closely spaced and attached to the stem; they are white at first, turning **grayish-lilac to purplish-black**. Wine Caps grow from spring through fall on wood chips, mulch and straw, and in cultivated areas. They are present but less common during summer. Spores are **purplish-brown to blackish**.

COMPARE: Some *Russula* species (pg. 134; inedible or **toxic**) have reddish caps; stems have **no ring** and spores are **creamy yellowish to pale orangish-yellow**. • Brick Tops (pg. 136; edible) have brick-red caps; stems have a **filmy ring remnant or no ring**. • Some *Amanita* species (pgs. 62–67; **toxic**) have reddish caps and rings on the stem, but they have **white spores** and a **cup** around the stem base.

NOTES: Wine Caps are delicious; make a spore print to avoid **toxic** lookalikes. Wine Caps are available in grow-it-yourself kits, for outdoor gardens.

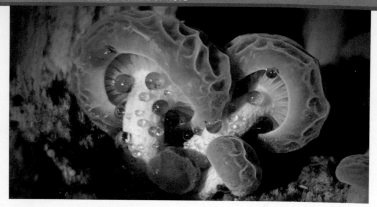

Wrinkled Peach

Rhodotus palmatus

This mushroom is small and uncommon, but striking in appearance. It is a saprobe and can be found growing in the summer, singly or in small groups, from well-rotted logs of deciduous trees, especially maple, basswood and elm. Young caps are **salmon-pink** with a distinctive **netted or veined texture**, so it is also called the Netted Rhodotus or Rosy Veincap. Immature caps may be less than an inch across and dome-shaped with rolled under edges, but can grow up to 4 inches across. As the cap expands it flattens, fading to peach or pale orange coloring. The textured surface also diminishes on the **rubbery**, sometimes slimy cap. Stems are 1 to 3 inches long; they are typically off-center and curved. There is no ring. Stem color is pale pink to nearly white; young stems often have **fluid droplets** ranging in color from peach to pink to red. The attached gills and spore print are also pinkish.

COMPARE: Because these grow from logs and the stem is often off-center, old clusters can be mistaken for **Orange Mock Oyster** (pg. 229), which have **fuzzy caps** and **no stem**. • **Velvet Foot** (pg. 130) is an orangish mushroom that grows from rotted elm; it has a **dark** stem and **white** gills. It grows in spring and fall.

NOTES: Wrinkled Peach is not considered edible, and reportedly has a bitter taste. More frequent sightings might be related to the growing interest in mushrooms, not the occurrence of this species. It has been called rare and even threatened (redlisted) in Europe.

Red-Tinged Lepiota

Leucoagaricus rubrotinctus (also listed as *Lepiota rubrotincta*)

This small yet distinctive saprobe can be found from summer to fall, decomposing organic matter in woodland or landscaped settings. Brown to burnt-orange buttons are less than one inch and nearly flat on top, appearing **squarish**. Caps expand up to 3 inches across, fading to tan, orange or pinkish and developing a **scaly, cracked surface** over a whitish background. Cap edges are slightly shaggy and often cracked. Like other Parasol Mushrooms (pg. 78) it retains a **smooth central disc** which is colored like the scales, giving it the alternate name of Red-Eyed Lepiota. The slender white stems are up to 4 inches tall; with age they become hollow and may discolor. Like many Amanita species (pgs. 62–67), it has a swollen base that may be hidden in the humus. It has a **fragile but persistent white ring** that can develop pink or orange edges with age. The closely spaced gills are white and not attached to the stem. The spore print is white.

COMPARE: Nearly identical *Leucoagaricus rubrotinctoides* is slightly larger; **cap scales are absent** but it has an even darker central disc. • Onion-Stalked Lepiota (pg. 152) grows from leaf litter but it has a **pale cap** with **scaly, white granules**. The gills turn tan with age and both the cap and gills bruise with handling. • Tawny Grisettes (pg. 104) are larger overall and **lack the ring** on the stem; caps do not crack and have **distinct ribbing** on the cap margin.

NOTES: Edibility is unknown; consumption is not recommended as they can be confused with other **toxic** *Lepiota* and *Amanita* species.

Pinkmottle Woodwax

Hygrophorus russula

This mycorrhizal mushroom associates with oaks, often growing in large groupings in mixed woods, summer through late fall. It is also called False Russula; its overall appearance and **firm** white to pink flesh mimic members of that genus, but other characteristics place this species in the *Hygrophorus* genus (also called waxy caps). Young caps are reddish to pinkish and rounded, with a rolled-under edge; they are **slimy**, often collecting dirt. With age, they dry out and flatten, growing up to 5 inches across. Stocky stems are **fibrous, not brittle** and up to 3 inches tall. They are white, turning pink with age. Crowded white gills run down the stem and may be **speckled pink or red or turn completely pink** when old. Spores are white.

COMPARE: Several pink to purple *Lactarius* species look similar, but typical to that genus, gills **produce milk when cut**. *L. argillaceifolius* has up to 7 inch, **dull lilac** colored caps. The cream-colored gills produce off-white milk that **stains brown**. *L. vinaceorufescens*, the Yellow Latex Milky, has caps with **pink to red bands of color**. Its cream to pinkish gills ooze white milk that quickly turns **yellow**; it grows with pines and is **toxic**. *L. subpurpureus* grows near hemlock and is known for the **red** milk it produces. Caps are **pink to red**; gills are pink, turning **green** with age. It has a peppery taste. • Numerous **Russulas** are reddish to pinkish; see pg. 134.

NOTES: Pinkmottle Woodwax is edible and rarely attacked by bugs, but some say they have a bland taste and leave a waxy feel in your mouth. Do not confuse them with **toxic** Russulas (pg. 134). *Lactarius* species listed above should not be eaten.

R. 'virescens'

Green-Capped Russulas (several)
Russula spp.

Russulas are mycorrhizal, growing from the soil in a symbiotic relationship with living trees; they may be found singly or in small groups from summer through fall. Caps on young specimens are pillowy, spreading and flattening out with age, then turning upward to form a shallow, wide-rimmed bowl; some or much of **the skin can be peeled off the cap**. Stems are **sturdy** and **lack rings**. Gills are white to cream-colored and attached to the stem; gills of the species discussed here are closely spaced. The flesh is white and **brittle**. • Two species are referred to as Quilted Green Russula. *R. 'virescens'* is a name in common usage, although this is a European species that does not grow in North America. The species found here has a greenish-yellow cap up to **6 inches across** that is dotted with **small patches**; the stem is up to 3½ inches tall. The cap of *R. parvovirescens* (formerly *R. crustosa*) is less than 3½ inches across; it is **bluish-green** and the patches are up to ¼ **inch** wide. • **Tacky Russula** (*R. aeruginea*) has a yellowish-green cap that is less than 3½ inches across; it is **smooth and uniformly** colored, lacking the patches.

COMPARE: *R. cyanoxantha* and *R. variata* have caps that are typically **purplish or brownish mottled with green** and gills that feel somewhat **greasy** and **soft**, while gills of the species discussed above are firm. *R. cyanoxantha* has gills that are mostly unforked, while gills of *R. variata* have **numerous, conspicuous forks**.

NOTES: Quilted Green Russulas are considered a delicious edible. The other Russulas discussed here are not as favored; *R. variata* is often somewhat acrid.

green = key identification feature   171

Fringed Polypore
Lentinus arcularius

ON DECAYING OR DOWNED WOOD

SPRING (GROWING SEASON)

HABITAT: Fringed Polypores are saprobes, mushrooms that get their nutrients from decaying organic matter. They grow from fallen trees, branches and sticks of hardwoods, especially birch and poplar. They also grow on buried wood, giving them the appearance of growing from the ground.

DESCRIPTION: This small funnel-shaped mushroom, which is generally less than 2 inches across and tall, has a beautiful pore surface under the cap. The **large, angular pores** are arranged around and run slightly down the stem, creating a **honeycomb-like pattern** that is white to pale yellow, turning tan with age. The cap is brown, with fine, lighter-colored cracks that expand as it grows. It is covered with **fine hairs** that extend to the edges. This **hairy cap edge** is the easiest way to separate this from other similar mushrooms. It grows early in the spring and can be found singly or in large groups. The tough, thin stems are also tan to brown like the cap. There is no ring on the stem.

SPORE PRINT: White.

SEASON: Grows in spring; present year-round.

OTHER NAMES: Spring Polypore, Early Brown Funnel Polypore, *Polyporus arcularius*.

COMPARE: Winter Polypore (*L. brumalis*; formerly *P. brumalis*) is a similar size and is found in the same habitat, but its cap is **darker**. The pore surface is **finer**, and angular to rounded. When young, the cap is hairy like Fringed Polypore, but it becomes **smooth and velvety** as it grows; the **cap edge is hairless**. It grows later in the summer through fall. • Big Black Foot and Little Black Foot (pg. 174) could be mistaken for Fringed Polypore and are found in the same habitat, but as the common names suggest, both have stems that are **partially black**. Both have a fine **white pore surface** under the caps. Big Black Foot is much larger than any of the other species listed above, with caps up to **8 inches** across.

NOTES: All of the mushrooms listed above cause white rot of dead trees, and old specimens can be found year-round. They are not edible due to their tough texture and lack of flavor, though Fringed Polypore is being studied for medicinal properties.

Pores

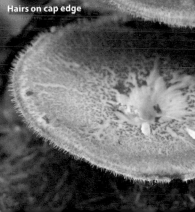

Hairs on cap edge

Black Foot Mushrooms

Cerioporus varius, Picipes badius

HABITAT: These saprobes get their nutrients from decaying organic matter, and cause white rot of dead wood. They grow singly or in groups from fallen trees, branches and sticks of deciduous trees.

DESCRIPTION: Two Black Foot species are common in our area. Both have thin, smooth, funnel-shaped caps that grow flatter as they expand, often developing a **wavy edge**. Under the cap they have a **fine white pore surface** that runs partway down the stem. The stem may be whitish, tan or brown at the top but is always **black at the bottom**; there is no ring. The stem location varies from centered to completely off to one side and everywhere in between. It may be so short that these mushrooms often look like a shelf fungus at first glance. • Little Black Foot (*C. varius*) has a uniformly colored cap that is light cream, tan or brown (*varius* means "variable" in Latin); it is up to 4 inches across. • Big Black Foot (*Picipes badius*; also listed as *Polyporus badius, Polyporus picipes* and *Royoporus badius*) is much larger, with caps up to **8 inches** across. It is typically much **darker or reddish brown**. The center is often nearly black, becoming lighter towards the wavy outer edge.

SPORE PRINT: White.

SEASON: Grows from early summer through fall; present year-round.

OTHER NAMES: *C. varius* is also called the Elegant Polypore, and listed as *Polyporus varius* or *Polyporus elegans*. Some describe *Polyporus elegans* as a distinct species that is larger than *C. varius* and has faint ridges radiating outward on the cap; it may also be called Light Cap Black Foot (*C. leptocephalus* or *Polyporus leptocephalus*), although some references describe that as a separate species.

COMPARE: Rooting Polypore (*Polyporus radicatus*) has a **long, rooting stem**, most of which is often broken off when the specimen is picked. The above-ground portion of the stem is **dull yellowish to orangish** and up to 2¼ inches long; the buried part is blackish. • Winter Polypore (pg. 172) has the same habitat and growth pattern and is small, like Little Black Foot, but it has a **darker, more velvety** cap surface and a light tan to brown stem that is **not black** at the bottom.

NOTES: These tough, leathery mushrooms can be found year-round. They are not edible but are often used in dried floral arrangements.

Little Black Foot

Big Black Foot

Rooting Polypore

Scaber Stalks (several)

Leccinum spp.

HABITAT: These mycorrhizal mushrooms typically grow from the ground near birch, aspen and poplar. They are also found with mixed hardwoods and in open, grassy areas near stands of trees; some may also associate with conifers.

DESCRIPTION: The hallmark of *Leccinum* species are **scabers**, minute raised scales covering the stems. The scabers of the species discussed here are generally darker than the stems and often darken further with age, becoming more prominent. Caps of the species listed here are dull and smooth when dry but slippery when wet; stems are **whitish** with no rings. The pore surface is white to yellowish and deeply sunken next to the stem; pores darken with age. • Members of the *L. insigne* group are sometimes called Orange-Capped Leccinum because of their cap color, which may be **apricot, orange or reddish-orange**; they often become brownish with age. Caps are typically 2 to 4 inches across at maturity; stems are sturdy and 3 to 5 inches tall. They are also called Aspen Boletes, due to their frequent association with that species. *L. vulpinum* is similar but its cap is reddish-brown; it is associates with conifers. • Caps of **Brown Birch Bolete** or Common Scaber Stalk (*L. scabrum*; also called *Boletus scaber*) are **yellowish-brown to grayish-brown** and less than 4 inches across; stems may be bluish-green at the base and are usually slender. The flesh **remains white or turns pale pinkish** when cut. It is found near birch trees. • White Birch Bolete (*L. holopus*) is very similar to Brown Birch Bolete but its cap is **dingy white**, often developing a greenish to bluish tinge; the stem base often stains bluish. Its scabers are pale and coarse on young specimens, darkening with age. It is found in **damp areas** such as bogs and soggy birch woods.

SPORE PRINT: Yellowish-brown to olive-brown.

SEASON: Summer through fall.

OTHER NAMES: Orange-Capped Leccinums were previously referred to as *L. aurantiacum*, which is a European species.

COMPARE: Dotted-Stalk Suillus (pg. 188) has minute dots on the stem that are **more subtle** than the raised scales on Scaber Stalks.

NOTES: The *Leccinum* species listed here were considered good edibles, but reports of gastrointestinal sickness from across the country have created a call for further study. They are currently not recommended.

Orange-Capped Leccinum

Brown Birch Bolete

White Birch Bolete

Yellow-Pored Boletes (several)
Various species

HABITAT: These species are mycorrhizal, and found near living hardwood trees.

DESCRIPTION: The mushrooms described here have medium to deep yellow pore surfaces; except as noted, pores do not bruise when damaged. Stems have no rings. • Although it doesn't appear in many guidebooks, *Hemileccinum subglabripes* is not uncommon in our area. Caps are generally 3 to 4 inches wide and brownish-orange to tan with a smooth surface that may be tacky in damp weather. Slender stems are up to 4 inches tall and yellow with **subtle scabers** (minute raised scales; see Scaber Stalks, pg. 176) that are colored like the stem, making them inconspicuous. Stems may be smooth and bright yellow at the top; the lower part is often streaked with dusky red, although it may be faint, and stems may turn faint blue or reddish when cut. Pores are fairly fine; the pore surface is deeply sunken next to the stem. **Corrugated Bolete** (*Xerocomus hortonii*) is similar, but its caps are reddish-brown to brownish and look **very wrinkled**. • **Butter Foot Bolete** (*Boletus auripes*) has tan to brownish caps that are up to **8 inches** across, with a finely **velvety** surface. Stems are stocky and bright yellow with a **fine, net-like pattern** on the top half or overall. Pores are fine. • *Aureoboletus auriporus* has reddish-brown caps up to 3 inches across; they are sticky when fresh, becoming velvety. Stems are up to 4¾ inches tall and are **sticky** when fresh. They are yellowish near the cap and **streaky red** below; **white mycelium** (threadlike fungal filaments) are often seen at the base. The pores are fairly fine, **bruising pink to reddish**. • *A. innixus* often grows in **clusters**, and is often called Clustered Brown Bolete. Stem bases may be slimy and are often bulbous, tapering to a root-like projection; **yellowish mycelium** is often seen at the base. Pores are fairly fine when young, coarsening with age.

SPORE PRINT: Olive-brown; Butter-Foot Bolete's spores are yellowish-brown.

SEASON: Summer through fall.

OTHER NAMES: *H. subglabripes* is also listed as *Leccinum subglabripes*; it, and the *Xerocomus* and *Aureoboletus* above, were originally part of the *Boletus* genus.

COMPARE: Larch Bolete (pg. 180) has a yellow pore surface that bruises rust-colored. It has a partial veil that leaves a **visible ring zone** on the stem.

NOTES: All species listed above are edible; *Hemileccinum subglabripes* may cause digestive upset if eaten fresh, but is reportedly safe to eat after drying.

Stem detail

Hemileccinum subglabripes

Butter Foot Bolete

Aureoboletus auriporus

FROM THE SOIL NEAR TREES

FALL

Slippery Jack, Slippery Jill

Suillus luteus, Suillus salmonicolor

HABITAT: These mycorrhizal mushrooms grow in scattered clusters near living conifers. In our area, Slippery Jack prefers red pine and white pine; Slippery Jill is typically found with jack pine.

DESCRIPTION: *Suillus* species are called Slippery Boletes because the cap surface is **slimy** when moist; dried caps may appear shiny and often have debris stuck to them. Another feature is the partial veil over the pore surface that produces a ring on the stem; above the ring, the stem has **fine, glandular dots**. What makes Slippery Jack and Slippery Jill distinctive is the **prominent, folded-over ring** created when the veil breaks and collapses onto the stem; the rings are **slimy** when moist. Pores **do not change color** when bruised. • **Slippery Jack** (*S. luteus*) has **brown to reddish-brown** caps with a whitish to yellow pore surface that darkens with age. Caps are up to 5 inches across and may become tan or yellowish with age. Stems are up to 3 inches tall and one-third as wide; they are white below the ring and typically yellowish above it. The ring is white, gradually becoming **purplish**. • Caps of **Slippery Jill** (*S. salmonicolor*) are **pale orangish-brown to salmon-colored** with radial streaks; they are typically 2 to 3 inches wide. Stems are up to 4 inches long and one-quarter as wide; they are covered with **fine, dark dots overall**. The pore surface of young specimens is salmon-colored, becoming brownish. The ring on the stem is band-like and often thickened on the bottom and lacks the purplish tones.

SPORE PRINT: Cinnamon-brown.

SEASON: Fall.

OTHER NAMES: Slippery Jill is also listed as *S. subluteus* and *S. pinorigidus*.

COMPARE: Larch Bolete (*S. grevillei*; also listed as *S. clintonianus*) grows near **larch (tamarack) trees**. Its yellow cap is up to 5 inches across and turns **orange or rust-colored** with age; the bright yellow pore surface **bruises brownish**. Its veil becomes a cottony **ring zone**; the stem below the ring has brownish to reddish-brown streaks.

NOTES: The mushrooms above are edible, and are best when young and fresh. Unpeeled caps remain slimy after cooking; the skin may be sour or bitter, and may cause digestive problems. Most cooks peel the caps before cooking; however, some people get a rash from handling the sticky, uncooked caps.

Slippery Jack

Slippery Jill before veil breaks

Slippery Jill with ring

Bitter Boletes

Tylopilus spp.

HABITAT: The species below are mycorrhizal, growing from the soil singly or in groups. They associate with hardwoods, particularly oak; *T. felleus* is also found with conifers.

DESCRIPTION: The *Tylopilus* species described here have pore surfaces that are whitish at first, becoming **pinkish** and darkening with age. Stems have no rings; white mycelium (threadlike fungal filaments) is often seen at the base. • *T. felleus*, the species that is generally referred to as Bitter Bolete, is a large, meaty mushroom with caps up to **12 inches** across; it is often mistaken for the King Bolete (pgs. 44–47). The spongy pore surface often bulges out from under the cap; it **bruises brown** with handling. Tan stems are 3 to 6 inches tall, typically bulbous at the bottom and thinner at the top with pronounced, **brown** reticulation (a net-like pattern). Flesh may discolor pink or brown when cut. • *T. plumbeoviolaceus* is also called the Violet Gray Bolete. Velvety caps are less than 6 inches across and are dark purple to purplish-brown, fading to gray or brown. Stems are a striking **violet** color with **white streaks**. They are 3 to 5 inches tall and often bulbous or enlarged at the bottom. Flesh is white and **does not stain** when cut; the pore surface may bruise brown when very old. • Caps of *T. rubrobrunneus* are up to 7 inches across and reddish-purple to purplish-brown, fading to tan with age. The pore surface bruises dark pink to brown. The flesh is white and does not discolor when cut. Stems are tan to brown and **smooth**, typically lacking reticulation; they discolor **grayish-green** when handled.

SPORE PRINT: Pink to brown.

SEASON: Summer through fall.

OTHER NAMES: Bitter Tylopilus.

COMPARE: *Porphyrellus indecisus* (pg. 47; also listed as *T. indecisus*) is nearly identical to *T. felleus*, but has a mild taste. Stems are less bulbous, **faintly patterned** and lighter in color; they stain brown easily. • *T. badiceps* is another mild-tasting Tylopilus; caps are reddish-brown and mistaken for *T. rubrobrunneus*, but the cap edge may have a **slight angle**, giving it a flatter look.

NOTES: The bitter boletes listed here are not toxic, but are generally not eaten due to the intensely bitter flavor. However, not everyone's taste buds are sensitive to bitter, so a few people report eating and enjoying them.

T. felleus

T. plumbeoviolaceus

T. rubrobrunneus

Ash Bolete
Boletinellus merulioides

HABITAT: Ash Boletes always grow from the soil. They fruit singly but often prolifically under **ash trees** or in areas with ash trees nearby; the mushrooms have a symbiotic relationship with an aphid that is associated with ash trees.

DESCRIPTION: This mushroom has a mottled brown cap that is **tacky** but not slimy when wet and looks almost polished or iridescent when dry and mature, much like the King Bolete (pgs. 44–47). Like many other boletes, it has a spongy yellow pore surface underneath the cap. Compared to other bolete varieties, however, it is easily recognized by its irregularities. The pore surface has a network of **ridge-like veins** running from the stem to the cap edges. The pores, which are large and somewhat angular, are arranged between the veins to form a **mesh-like surface**. The veins and pores run down the stem, which is **short, brown and not centered under the cap**; in many cases the stem grows completely off to one side. The caps, which are up to 8 inches wide, are **lobed and irregular**, growing very close to the ground on a stem that is generally 2 inches tall or shorter; the stem has no ring. If you come across a large group of these, it looks like a bag of russet potatoes has been dumped in the grass. The pore surface **bruises brown to bluish** after much handling.

SPORE PRINT: Olive-brown.

SEASON: Summer through fall.

OTHER NAMES: *Gyrodon merulioides*.

COMPARE: The pore surface of Leathery Veiled Bolete (*Paragyrodon sphaerosporus*; found near **oaks**) is similar to that of the Ash Bolete, but it lacks the ridge-like veins. Pores are hidden under a **tough veil** (pg. 62) that breaks only when the caps get large; even mature species have flaps of the leathery veil attached to the stem and cap edges. It should not be eaten because it may have toxins that accumulate in the body over time, like the related *Paxillus* species (pg. 71).

NOTES: Ash Boletes are edible but not desirable, which is unfortunate because you are apt to find many at a time and they can be decent sized.

Ash Bolete

Veins on Ash Bolete pore surface

Leathery Veiled Bolete

Graceful Bolete

Wrinkled Bolete

Graceful Bolete

Austroboletus gracilis (also listed as *Tylopilus gracilis, Porphyrellus gracilis*)

This elegant mycorrhizal mushroom grows singly or in groups from the ground near trees, primarily conifers. It has a **fairly small cap** and a **long, slender stem** that is typically thinner at the top than at the bottom and often curves gracefully. Caps are 1 to 3 inches across, often with a velvety texture; the surface may crack with age. They are brownish, ranging from reddish-brown to brownish-gray to yellowish-brown; some may be yellowish, and this may represent a different variety in the same group. Stems are 3 to 7 inches tall and similar in color to the cap or paler, often with faint vertical ridges or, sometimes, a net-like pattern. White mycelium (threadlike fungal filaments) is often seen at the base. There is no ring on the stem. The pore surface is white, turning pinkish with age and **bruising brown**; the pores are fairly large, and the pore surface is often sunken around the top of the stem. The flesh does not stain when cut. The spore print is pinkish-brown to cinnamon-brown. Graceful Bolete is found from summer through fall.

COMPARE: Several mushrooms resemble Graceful Bolete, particularly when their cap surfaces **crack with age**. The two here associate with **oaks**. • Caps of Wrinkled Bolete (*Leccinum rugosiceps*) are up to **5 inches** across and **wrinkled** when young. Stems are decorated with **scabers** (minute raised scales; see Scaber Stalks, pg. 176). The pore surface is **yellowish**. • *T. sordidus* has **grayish to dark brown** caps that are velvety when young and a whitish to grayish pore surface.

NOTES: Graceful Bolete is edible but not choice; the others should not be eaten.

Russell's Bolete

Boletellus russellii (also listed as *Aureoboletus russellii* and *Boletus russellii*)

If all mushrooms were as easy to identify as this somewhat uncommon species, life would be easier! Its stem is the major point of identification; it is **heavily textured** and often quite **shaggy-looking**, covered with **vertical ridges** that are created by highly raised, elongated reticulation, the net-like pattern that helps identify Boletes. Stems are typically thin and long—they may be nearly 8 inches tall—and often curvy, but they may also be shorter and even appear stubby at times. They are **pinkish-tan to reddish-brown**, and the base is often sticky in damp weather. Caps, which have rolled-under edges, vary in color; they are often yellowish-brown but may be pinkish-brown, cinnamon-colored or even grayish. They are rounded and usually velvety when young, flattening in age and developing **surface cracks or patches**; mature caps may be up to 5 inches across. There is no ring. Pores are angular and yellowish to greenish-yellow; they may become brighter yellow when rubbed. Its spore print is olive-brown. It is mycorrhizal and prefers deciduous trees, especially oak, but may be found near conifers; it fruits from summer through fall.

COMPARE: Frost's Bolete (pg. 70) has a similarly ornate stem, but it is **deep red overall**. Its pore surface **bruises blue**, as does its stem. • Graceful Bolete (pg. 186) has a long, graceful stem with **faint vertical ridges** or a net-like pattern; its stems look nearly smooth compared to the shaggy stems of Russell's Bolete.

NOTES: Russell's Bolete is listed as edible, as are the other species noted above.

Dotted-Stalk Suillus

Suillus granulatus (also listed as *Suillus weaverae*)

Dotted-Stalk Suillus is mycorrhizal, growing from the soil near pines. Caps are **pinkish-buff, brown or tan**, often spotted or streaked with cinnamon-brown. They are typically 2 to 4 inches wide and shiny when dry but sticky when damp. The pore surface is spongy and cream-colored, becoming coarse and yellow with age. When young and fresh, the spore-producing tubes may weep a milky fluid, giving this the alternate name of Weeping Bolete. Stems are up to 3 inches tall and **white** with **minute tan dots** that are **more concentrated at the top**; stems become yellow with age, particularly at the top. There is **no ring**. Flesh is white to yellow and **does not change color** when cut. Spores are cinnamon-brown. Found from spring through fall.

COMPARE: Spicy Suillus (*S. punctipes*) have a strong fragrance that is often described as **spicy or almond-like**. The slimy, yellowish-brown caps are covered with a **pale, dull coating** when young. Pores of young specimens are **brownish**, becoming dingy yellowish with age. Stems are **heavily covered overall** with brownish glandular dots. • Chicken Fat Mushroom (pg. 192) is usually smaller than Dotted-Stalk Suillus, with **reddish streaks** on the **flat yellow caps**. It has a **thin, yellow stem**. • Slippery Jack and Slippery Jill (pg. 180) have a partial veil that breaks to form a **prominent ring** on the thick white stem.

NOTES: Dotted-Stalk Suillus and the compares listed here are good edibles; as with other *Suillus*, caps should be peeled to prevent stomach upset (see pg. 192).

Red-Cracked Bolete

Xerocomellus chrysenteron (also listed as *Boletus chrysenteron*)

This mycorrhizal species grows from the ground, scattered or in groups, near deciduous and coniferous trees. Caps are **olive-brown to brownish**, often with a reddish edge; the surface develops **pinkish to reddish-tinged cracks**. Smooth and velvety at first, caps grow to 3 inches wide, cracking as they expand. Pores are angular and moderately sized. The pore surface is **yellow** on young specimens, aging to brownish; when damaged, it slowly **bruises bluish**. The flesh inside is white to yellow and **slowly stains blue** when cut. The stem is up to 2½ inches tall and may appear subtly ridged; it is yellow at the top, turning reddish to purplish-red toward the bottom. The stem **bruises bluish-green**. There is no ring. Its spore print is olive-brown, and it grows from early summer through fall. This species is frequently infected with, and consumed by, white mold.

COMPARE: *X. truncatus* is identical except for microscopic features. • *Boletellus pseudochrysenteroides* has **brick-red** caps that crack to reveal pinkish to whitish flesh. When this mushroom is sliced vertically, the yellow flesh of the cap **quickly discolors blue**; flesh inside the stem is **dark red**. It is uncommon in our area.

NOTES: Red-Cracked Bolete is edible, although the flesh is bland and mushy. Caution must be taken to avoid **toxic** Brick-Cap Bolete (pg. 69) and other look-alikes, which also may crack when old; these mushrooms **stain blue immediately** when cut. Expert Dr. Michael Beug warns that Red-Cracked Bolete can cause gastrointestinal distress when consumed with alcohol.

Painted Suillus

Suillus spraguei (also known as *Suillus pictus*)

Young, fresh specimens of this lovely mushroom have yellowish caps decorated with a **dense layer of scales and fibers** that are brownish-rose, pinkish, reddish or brick-red. The scales may disintegrate with age, leaving the caps smooth and yellowish-brown to buff. Caps are dry and up to 4¾ inches wide, often with whitish veil remnants hanging from the edge. Stems of mature specimens are typically about 3 to 4 inches tall and fairly sturdy. A grayish to whitish ring is present towards the top of the stem at first, but it soon disappears; below the ring area, the stem is **shaggy** and **streaked with brownish or reddish fibers**. The angular pores are yellowish and may be arranged in rows that radiate from the stem; they may bruise brownish to reddish. Flesh is yellow, remaining unchanged or turning slightly pinkish when bruised. Spores are cinnamon-brown. Painted Suillus are mycorrhizal; in our area they associate with **white pine** and are found from late summer through fall, primarily in the northern half.

COMPARE: Hollow Bolete (*S. cavipes*) fruit only under **larch** (tamarack) trees. At a quick glance, it resembles Painted Suillus, but a closer look reveals that its caps are densely covered with **whitish hairs over a brownish base**. The bottom half of the stem is **brown** and **hairy**, with a **hollow** interior. Some sources say *S. cavipes* is the name of a European species that does not appear in North America.

NOTES: Although they are not regarded as choice, both of the species listed above are edible; they lack the slimy skin found on the caps of other *Suillus* species.

Ornate-Stalked Bolete

Retiboletus ornatipes (also known as *Boletus ornatipes*)

Ornate-Stalked Bolete is found in groups, scattered or singly under deciduous trees, particularly beech and oak; it also grows on mossy banks. This mushroom gets its name from the **coarse mesh-like texture** (reticulation) covering the entire stem. The texture is created by ridges that are yellow at first, turning **orangish-brown** when handled or with age. The stem is stocky and up to 6 inches tall; it is **bright yellow** and somewhat **powdery**, and turns brownish with age. Yellow mycelium (threadlike fungal filaments) may be present at the base of the stem, which may be tapered; there is no ring. The cap is up to 8 inches wide; it is yellowish, brownish or olive-colored with a **dry or felt-like** surface. The pore surface is bright yellow, turning darker with age or handling. The flesh is bright yellow. Its spore print is olive-brown, and it grows from midsummer through early fall.

COMPARE: Gray Bolete (*R. griseus* or *B. griseus*) has **white to grayish** stems with **white** reticulation that becomes brown with age. Caps are **gray to grayish-brown**; pores are **whitish, gray or dull tan**. • King Bolete (pgs. 44–47) is up to **10 inches** wide and **7 inches** tall. Its stem is **whitish** with **pale** reticulation that is **much finer** than that of the Ornate-Stalked Bolete. It prefers conifers but also grows near oak and other deciduous trees. • Butter Foot Bolete (pg. 178) has yellow stems and brownish caps, but the reticulation is **much finer** and often only on the upper half of the stem, which is frequently wider at the base.

NOTES: Ornate-Stalked Bolete is edible but some specimens may be very bitter.

green = key identification feature   191

Chicken Fat Mushroom

Suillus americanus

This mushroom is also called the White Pine Bolete because it grows singly, scattered or prolifically from the soil near **white pine** (exclusively). Of the many *Suillus* species, Chicken Fat is distinct because of its **small size**; it is typically less than 4 inches wide and tall. It has **yellow** caps that are **slimy** or slippery in moist weather; both the color and greasy feel account for its common name. Caps are fairly flat when mature, with only a slight peak in the center; they are often marked with reddish streaks. There may be veil remnants hanging on the cap edge; the stem may have a faint ring but it is usually absent. The stem is **slender** and often bent; it has small, raised **brown dots** and **stains brown** when handled. The flesh is yellow and **stains pinkish-brown** when cut or bruised. Pores are fairly large and angular; like the cap, the pore surface is yellow. Chicken Fat Mushroom has a cinnamon-brown spore print and is found from late summer through fall.

COMPARE: *S. intermedius* (also listed as *S. acidus*) is less common and is generally found under red pines. The stem has **brown to black dots** and it bruises blackish; it has a **thin, sticky ring** that flattens with age.

NOTES: Both of the mushrooms listed here are edible. The caps remain slimy when cooked and are often peeled before cooking; however, some people get a skin rash from handling the sticky, uncooked caps.

Chestnut Bolete

Gyroporus castaneus

There's something about the appearance of this **smallish** Bolete that makes you want to gather it for the table. Perhaps it's the way that the **chestnut-brown to yellowish-brown cap and stem** contrast with the pure white pore surface. Or it may be the fact that you're likely to find good quantities of this mushroom, which typically grows scattered or in groups near oak and other hardwood trees, in grassy areas and along edges and trails of forested areas; some reports place it in the vicinity of conifers. Caps are 1 to 4 inches wide, often with a velvety surface; edges may split with age. The **smooth** stems are moderately **thin**, up to 4 inches tall and fairly **equal in width** from top to bottom; the inside is **cottony** on young specimens, becoming **hollow** or chambered with age. The pore surface is white on young specimens, aging to light yellow; pores do not change color when bruised. The spore print is **light yellow**. Look for it from summer through fall.

COMPARE: Red Gyroporus (*G. purpurinus*) is about **half the size** of the Chestnut Bolete; the cap and stem are **burgundy-colored** rather than chestnut-colored. It is much less common in our area than Chestnut Bolete. • King Bolete (pgs. 44–47) is much larger, up to **10 inches** wide and 7 inches tall. Its stems are **whitish** to pale brown and covered with a **mesh-like texture** (reticulation) of the same color; they have a **bulbous** base. Its spore print is **olive-brown**.

NOTES: Both of the Gyroporus above are considered good edibles. Unfortunately, bugs seem to enjoy them as well; stems are often compromised by insects.

Shiny Cinnamon Polypore

Coltricia cinnamomea (also known as *Boletus cinnamomeus*)

This small, attractive mushroom grows singly or in small groups **from the ground** in mixed wooded areas; it is common in mossy areas and is often found along paths, even in hard soil. Its brown cap is **thin** and wavy, featuring **concentric brown rings** of varied color and texture, depending on age and weather conditions. Young ones are **shiny**, becoming velvety with age. Caps are mostly round and less than 2 inches wide. The short brown stem is up to 2 inches tall and has no ring. Sometimes funnel shaped, caps flatten out as they grow. Two or more individuals may fuse together, creating irregular shapes. Underneath the cap is a thin, **brown** pore surface. Its spore print is **cinnamon-brown**; it grows from late summer through fall but may be found year-round.

COMPARE: Tiger's Eye (*C. perennis*) is larger, with caps up to **4 inches wide**. It shows a wider range of colors, from yellow to brown to gray, in **strong ring patterns**. It is found in areas with **pines**. • Little Black Foot (pg. 174) is large like Tiger's Eye but lacks the distinct rings. The pore surface is **white**, and the bottom part of the stem is **black**. It grows **on wood**. • Winter Polypore (pg. 172) is small like Shiny Cinnamon Polypore but lacks the rings. It has a **white to pale yellow** pore surface. Like Little Black Foot, it grows **on wood**.

NOTES: Even when fresh, this fungus is tough and leathery. It dries well and is used in decorative arrangements. It is being studied for medicinal uses.

Chrome-Footed Bolete

Harrya chromapes (also known as *Leccinum chromapes, Tylopilus chromapes*)

With its pinkish cap, this beautiful bolete is easy to spot in the woods. They are mycorrhizal, growing in a symbiotic relationship with living conifers and deciduous trees; they grow singly or scattered. Caps are **pinkish** and up to 6 inches across at maturity, although they are generally smaller; they turn tan with age. They are dry and often have a suede-like surface. Most of the stem is cream-colored to pale pink and **covered with fine scabers** (minute raised scales) that are generally **pinkish** but may be brownish; the bottom part of the stem is **bright yellow**. The stem is up to 6 inches tall on large specimens; the base may be pinched or narrowed. There is no ring. The pore surface is finely textured and somewhat sunken around the stem; it is white on young specimens, becoming yellowish, then pinkish and, finally, brownish with age. The flesh is white to pinkish; the flesh and the pore surface do not bruise. Its spore print is pinkish-brown; it is found from spring through fall.

COMPARE: Both the cap and stem of **Lilac Bolete** (pg. 46) are **lilac-colored** when young; stems lack the scabers and the yellow base of Chrome-Footed Bolete. • **Violet-Gray Bolete** (pg. 182) has a **dark purple** cap that becomes brownish or purplish-gray with age. Its stem is **violet with white streaks**; it has no scabers.

NOTES: Violet-Gray Bolete is too bitter to eat; the others listed are edible.

Bicolor Bolete or Two-Color Bolete

Baorangia bicolor (formerly *Boletus bicolor*)

It is clear how this lovely mushroom gets its name. Fresh examples have a **red cap, red stem and bright yellow pore surface**. It can grow quite large, with caps up to 6 inches across. As it matures, the smooth cap surface becomes paler, more pinkish and sometimes cracked; the pore surface becomes orangish, then olive-yellow, with age. Stems grow up to 4 inches tall and may be yellow towards the top; there is no ring. The pore surface **stains a dramatic blue**. Bicolor Bolete can be distinguished from **toxic** blue-staining boletes (pgs. 68–70) by the way its yellow interior flesh stains blue **slowly and faintly**, if at all. This mushroom grows from the ground near oaks and other hardwoods. It may be scattered, in tight little clusters or alone. Its spore print is olive-brown, and it is found from summer through fall. It is said to smell like chicken bouillon.

COMPARE: Brick-Cap Bolete (pg. 69; **toxic**) looks very similar, but **all parts stain blue instantly**; it is said to smell like curry but that trait may not be noticeable. Its stem is **yellowish to brownish-yellow**, becoming streaky reddish at the base. • *Boletus bicoloroides* is similar to Bicolor but its cap and stem are darker red; its stem is **red overall**. In our area, it is found in the northeast in mixed coniferous woods.

NOTES: Many consider Bicolor Bolete almost as choice as the King Bolete (pgs. 44–47). However, some report gastric distress after eating Bicolors, while others are not affected. It is advised to consume them only after expert identification and always well cooked; try just a small amount at first.

Old Man of the Woods

Strobilomyces 'floccopus' (also listed as *Strobilomyces 'strobilaceus'*)

This distinctive mushroom grows from the ground near oaks and other deciduous trees; the mycelium (threadlike fungal filaments) has a symbiotic relationship with tree roots. It grows alone or scattered, not in large groups. The cap is 1 to 6 inches wide; when young, it is white and covered with **shaggy black patches**. The stem is 2 to 6 inches tall and proportionally thinner than stems of other Boletes; it is **grayish to black** with a **shaggy** texture. The pore surface is white and sunken, darkening and bulging from under the cap with age. At the button stage, a partial veil covers the pore surface; as the cap expands, the veil leaves obvious flaps around the cap edges and may leave a faint ring on the stem. Both pore surface and flesh **bruise red** at first, then black. All parts of the mushroom become black with age. Its spore print is dark brown to black. Found from summer through fall.

COMPARE: *S. confusus* looks identical but is usually **slightly smaller**; the black patches are **more pointy and firmer** to the touch. A microscope is used for positive identification. • **Black Velvet Bolete** (*Tylopilus alboater*) is similar to mature Old Man in coloring and size. It has a **black** cap and stem that are both **smooth**, not shaggy like Old Man. The stem is **slightly thicker** and may bulge at the base. Like Old Man, it has a white pore surface that bruises red at first, then black.

NOTES: The mushrooms listed here are edible but not considered desirable. *S. floccopus/S. strobilaceus* is a European species; it is not an exact match for the species found in North America.

Stinkhorns (several)

Phallus and *Mutinus* spp.

HABITAT: Stinkhorns are saprobes, getting their nutrients from decaying organic matter. They are found in woods and fields and also appear in gardens, lawns and other cultivated areas; they often grow from wood chips.

DESCRIPTION: Stinkhorns start their lives encased in a universal veil, appearing like an egg (see pg. 62 for more details). Stinkhorns grow rapidly, rupturing the egg and attaining full stature of 6 to 9 inches in a day or less. A volva (a cup-like remnant of the universal veil) remains at the base of the stem, although it may be buried. Stems are hollow and slightly rough. Heads are covered with **dark, foul-smelling slime** that carries the spores; the tip is often free of slime. Flies strip away the slime, exposing the paler surface below. • **Common Stinkhorn** (*Phallus impudicus* and *P. hadriani*) have **ridged, pitted** heads and **whitish** stems. The volva of *P. impudicus* is whitish; that of *P. hadriani* is purplish. • **Ravenel's Stinkhorn** (*P. ravenelii*) is similar to Common Stinkhorn, but its head is **smooth to slightly granular**; the volva is **pinkish-tan**. • **Netted Stinkhorn** (*P. duplicatus*; also listed as *Dictyophora duplicata*) is similar to Common Stinkhorn but has a **white net-like skirt** hanging off the bottom edge of the head; the net encircles the stem loosely, hanging down to the ground. • **Devil's Stinkhorn** (*P. rubicundus*) has an **orangish to pinkish** stem with a **netlike** texture, a smooth, **cap-like head** and a tan volva. • **Dog Stinkhorn** (*Mutinus caninus, elegans* and *ravenelii*) closely resemble Devil's Stinkhorn, but there is **no distinct head**; it is merely a curved stem with brownish slime at the top that is eventually carried away by flies, leaving the bare stem.

SPORE PRINT: Impossible to make; likely brownish to olive-brown.

SEASON: Summer through fall.

OTHER NAMES: Common Stinkhorns are also called Morel Stinkhorns.

COMPARE: Common Stinkhorns may be mistaken for Morels (pgs. 24–27), but the caps of Morels are **not slimy** and there is **no volva** at the base of the stem. Morels grow in **spring**, while Stinkhorns grow in summer to fall.

NOTES: Mature Stinkhorns are inedible; cooked eggs are edible but revolting.

Common Stinkhorn

Ravenel's Stinkhorn with split egg

Netted Stinkhorn

Devil's Stinkhorn

Dog Stinkhorn

NEAR LIVE TREES   SUMMER THROUGH FALL

Elfin Saddles (several)

Helvella spp.

HABITAT: These unusual-looking mushrooms grow from the ground near living deciduous trees and conifers; they may also grow in grassy locations, along paths and in disturbed areas. Found singly or in small groups.

DESCRIPTION: Several Elfin Saddles are found in our area; they have thin-fleshed caps that appear **folded, lobed or saddle-like**. Stems of species discussed here are **chambered or hollow** and typically up to 4 inches tall; the flesh is brittle. • Fluted White Helvella (*H. crispa*) is the most common in our area. It has a **wide, heavily ribbed stem** that is whitish and may have a faint pink tinge. The cap is whitish to pale tan. It is saddle-shaped or irregularly folded and up to 2 inches across; the underside is **finely hairy**. • Smooth-Stalked Helvella (*H. elastica*) has a whitish to cream-colored stem that is **smooth** and **fairly slender**; it is **round** in cross-section. The cap is yellowish-brown, light brown or gray and usually less than 2 inches across. It typically has two lobes that appear to be folded together; edges are rolled slightly inward, giving a pillowy appearance. *H. latispora* is similar, but its caps are paler and have **irregular edges** that give it a **ruffled** appearance. • Fluted Black Helvella (*H. lacunosa*) has a whitish to grayish stem that is wide and heavily ridged, with numerous pockets or cavities among the ridges; the stem may be up to **6 inches** tall. The cap is **dark gray, dark brown or black**; it is irregularly lobed and may seem **convoluted or brain-like**. It is usually about 2 inches across but some of the lobes may extend to nearly 4 inches across.

SPORE PRINT: White.

SEASON: Summer through fall.

OTHER NAMES: Elfin Saddle is a common, catch-all name for the species listed above. Some mycologists currently consider *H. sulcata* as a synonym for *H. lacunosa*, while others believe it is a variant.

COMPARE: Saddle-Shaped False Morel (*Gyromitra infula*; **toxic**) is similar; some sources list it as *H. infula*. Its tan to brownish caps are up to 5 inches tall and have two or three lobes. Stems are colored like the cap and up to 4¾ inches tall. They grow on **rotted wood** and woody debris that may be underground.

NOTES: Elfin Saddles are sometimes listed as edible but are poor table fare; they may cause stomach upset and should be considered inedible.

Fluted White Helvella

Smooth-Stalked Helvella

Fluted Black Helvella

Saddle-Shaped False Morel

Birch Polypore
Fomitopsis betulina

HABITAT: Found growing exclusively on birch trees, stumps and logs; more common on dead wood than on living trees. They grow as individual specimens, although there are typically multiple polypores on each tree. They cause brown rot, acting as both parasites and decomposers.

DESCRIPTION: Although this polypore takes several forms and appears in various colors, it is easy to recognize. It looks like a **pillowy growth** that may be shaped like a half-dome, a hoof, a projecting disk, a kidney or a half-bell that may be distorted. The top surface is dull white, gray or tan; it is **smooth** at first, often developing wide **cracks that expose the pale inner flesh**. The edge of the cap is rolled inward, creating a **thick, rounded overhang** that surrounds the pore surface. The cap may grow to 10 inches across but is usually smaller. There is no stem, although some specimens may have a thick neck at the point of attachment. The underside is whitish to buff, with small pores that may become tooth-like with age.

SPORE PRINT: White.

SEASON: Birch Polypore grows from spring through summer; they often persist over winter, appearing as darkened specimens the next year.

OTHER NAMES: Birch Bracket, Birch Conk, *Piptoporus betulinus, Polyporus betulinus*.

COMPARE: Tinder Polypore (pg. 212) grows in a similar fashion, but the surface is **banded** and it grows on a **wide variety of trees**. • Several other mushrooms that grow on trees may resemble Birch Polypore at a quick glance, but they have **gills** rather than pores. These include **Oyster Mushrooms** (pgs. 34–37), **Elm Caps** (pg. 153) and **Bear Paw Lentinus** (pg. 227).

NOTES: Birch Polypore has long been used for medicinal purposes; indeed, it is one of the mushrooms found with the "Tyrolean Iceman," a mummified body from the mid-Neolithic era (the body was carbon-dated to between 3350 and 3100 BC) that was discovered in the Italian Alps in 1991, and is on display at the South Tyrol Museum of Archaeology in Bolzano, Italy. Birch Polypore are bitter and generally regarded as inedible.

ON DEAD AND DECAYING WOOD

PRESENT YEAR-ROUND

Turkey Tail
Trametes versicolor

HABITAT: Grows on dead wood such as fallen logs, stumps and standing dead trees; typically found on wood from deciduous trees but may occasionally grow on conifer wood. They are decomposers, causing white rot.

DESCRIPTION: These common shelf mushrooms grow as **thin, overlapping fan-shaped caps**. They may grow in a rosette, or may cover the wood like a scaly carpet. Individual caps have **concentric bands** of color. The outer band is **cream-colored or tan**, and the rest of the bands are shades of gray, blue, brown or reddish-brown; caps may develop greenish tones with age due to algae growth. The surface is silky or velvety (a hand lens may be needed to see the hairs, but they can be felt with the fingers); the bands often alternate from smooth to hairy. Caps are **thin, leathery and flexible**; they range from 1 to 4 inches wide. Edges are **ruffled, scalloped or wavy**. The undersides are whitish, pale gray or yellowish and covered with **very fine, round pores**. The caps have no stem, although they may narrow to a neck at the point of attachment.

SPORE PRINT: White to pale yellow.

SEASON: These grow from spring through fall; the caps are persistent and may be found for several years, continuing growth in successive seasons.

OTHER NAMES: *Coriolus versicolor, Polyporus versicolor.*

COMPARE: Several other shelf mushrooms that grow on wood appear similar to Turkey Tail but are distinguished by various features. • Caps of **Hairy Turkey Tail** (*T. hirsuta*) are **densely hairy** and **typically gray to whitish** overall; the outer band is typically **brownish** and the pores are larger than those of Turkey Tail. • Caps of **False Turkey Tail** (*Stereum ostrea*) are **smooth underneath, with no pores**; its caps often appear elongated. • Caps of **Hairy Curtain Crust** (*S. hirsutum*) are **densely velvety**; they are often **fused together**, forming a shelf-like or crust-like layer with wavy edges. They are often orangish. • The upper side of **Gilled Polypore** (pg. 233) is similar to Turkey Tail, but the underside is covered with white **gill-like structures** rather than pores. • **Purple Tooth** (pg. 232) has **purplish teeth** underneath rather than pores.

NOTES: Turkey Tail and the lookalikes listed above are tough and inedible. Some are used medicinally and are being studied for anti-cancer properties.

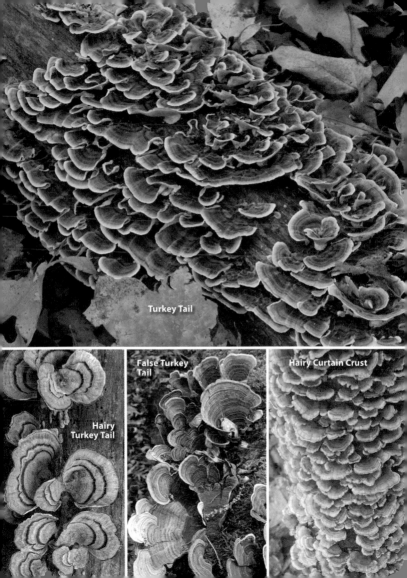

Turkey Tail

Hairy Turkey Tail

False Turkey Tail

Hairy Curtain Crust

Artist's Conk

Ganoderma applanatum

ON DEAD OR DECAYING WOOD (TYP.)

PRESENT YEAR-ROUND

HABITAT: Found growing on living or dead trees, stumps and logs, primarily deciduous but also coniferous; more common on dead wood than on living trees. They grow as individual specimens, although there may be multiple polypores on each tree. Artist's Conk causes white rot, acting as both a parasite and decomposer.

DESCRIPTION: A tough, woody perennial that grows as a stemless, semicircular shelf, often with irregular, wavy or slightly scalloped edges; it may also appear hoof-like. Caps range from 2 to **25 inches** across; the body is thick on the side that attaches to the growing substrate, becoming thinner towards the edge. The top surface is **dull, dry and very hard**; it is tan, gray or brownish, often with concentric bands of color. It often develops ridge-like bands as it continues to grow each year; it may also become warty or bumpy and often develops furrows that run from the center toward the edge. The underside is covered with **fine white pores** that instantly turn **dark brown when scratched or bruised**; with age, the pore surface becomes buff-colored and less sensitive to scratches. If the mushroom is cut from top to bottom, **layers** of pores representing each year's growth will be visible. The mushrooms produce copious amounts of brown spores that are often seen on the growing substrate, or on plants and other nearby objects.

SPORE PRINT: Brown.

SEASON: Perennial; present year-round.

OTHER NAMES: Artist's Bracket, *G. megaloma*.

COMPARE: Tinder Polypore (pg. 212) is a tough, dull polypore that is less than 8 inches across; its pore surface is **tan or gray** and does not bruise.

NOTES: Because it turns dark brown when scratched, Artist's Conk is often used as the medium for scratch art. The cap must be fresh, and the drawings should be done a few days after removing the cap from the tree. Once the cap dries out, it turns buff-colored; the brown engraved lines remain, creating an unusual piece of art. Tea made from the dried mushrooms is sometimes used medicinally.

Spores caught by spiderweb

Scratch art on Artist's Conk

NEAR LIVE, DEAD OR DYING TREES

PRESENT YEAR-ROUND

Dyer's Polypore
Phaeolus schweinitzii

HABITAT: A wood-rotting parasite, this mushroom is usually found at the base of conifers (rarely deciduous trees) growing from buried roots. It can sometimes be found growing directly from dead or dying wood.

DESCRIPTION: The color and shape of this fungus is quite variable, depending on the age and growing conditions. Single specimens can grow into large rosettes, up to a foot across, with overlapping shelves. Like the Tooth Mushrooms (pg. 262), this mushroom tends to envelop surrounding material as it expands and may simply look like a formless blob. When young, it is typically spongy and brown with a **yellow margin** and a velvety surface. With age, it becomes woody and dark brown to black, with intense yellow, orange or rust-brown bands of color. Underneath is a **greenish-yellow pore surface** that **bruises brown**. The pores are **large and rough**, becoming angular and almost tooth-like or maze-like with age. The entire mess grows from a stubby, brown stem.

SPORE PRINT: White to creamy yellow.

SEASON: Summer through late fall; grows annually but found year-round.

OTHER NAMES: Velvet Top Fungus, *Polyporus schweinitzii*.

COMPARE: Yellow-Red Gill Polypore (pg. 235) is smaller, with rosettes less than 5 inches across. Underneath are distinct, **deep gill ridges** that are **golden brown**; they may be fused and maze-like. • Orange Hydnellum (pg. 262) has fused or clustered caps up to 6 inches across. Caps are very bumpy and orange to brownish with a paler edge. Underneath are white **teeth** that turn brown with age except for the tips, which remain white. Textile dyers use it to get green to blue colors. • Examples of *Ganoderma* species (pgs. 206, 218) growing from buried roots may look like the Dyer's Polypore, but they have a **fine, white** pore surface underneath.

NOTES: Though not edible, the Dyer's Polypore is a favorite of textile dyers because it contains an intense yellow pigment. This same mushroom, used with a dye bath or wool treated with iron sulfate, produces a beautiful green color. Yellow-Red Gill Polypore is regarded as inedible.

Bruised pore surface

Young specimen

Dyed wool yarn

ON DEAD TREES, STUMPS AND LOGS   FALL

Resinous Polypore
Ischnoderma resinosum

HABITAT: Resinous Polypore are saprobes, mushrooms that get nutrients from decaying organic matter. They grow on dead trees, both standing and fallen, as well as on stumps; they may occasionally appear on dying trees in areas where the wood has already succumbed to injury or disease. Generally found on wood of deciduous trees, occasionally conifers. They may grow singly but are often seen in overlapping clusters.

DESCRIPTION: This mushroom's appearance changes considerably over time. Very young specimens are rounded or lumpy; they are thick, soft and **velvety**, with reddish-brown centers and a white margin. **Amber resin droplets** sometimes appear on cap edges. As the specimens age, they become wider and flatter; they are semicircular, often with wavy or scalloped edges. Mature specimens are up to 7½ inches across and roughly ¾ inch thick. They are brownish to reddish-brown, often retaining the white margin; the color may be fairly consistent or it may be zoned into concentric rings. Old specimens become wrinkled and develop black, crusty-looking bands interspersed with brownish bands; the surface becomes dry and tough and may develop cracks that radiate from the center to the edges. The underside of young specimens is covered with white pores that **bruise brownish**; with age, the pore surface becomes tan.

SPORE PRINT: White.

SEASON: Fall.

OTHER NAMES: Late Fall Polypore.

COMPARE: Young specimens of **Oak Bracket** (*Pseudoinonotus dryadeus*; formerly *Inonotus dryadeus*) produce amber droplets, but cap surfaces are **buff-colored to tan**; with age, both cap surfaces turn brownish, and the surface appears **pockmarked**. They often grow in overlapping clusters; large specimens may be **over a foot across**. In our area, they are found only **on oaks** (live or recently cut stumps), typically near the base. • Yellow-Red Gill Polypore (pg. 235) looks similar to mature specimens of Resinous Polypore but is under 5 inches across and has **slot-like pores and gills** underneath. It has a **corky** texture.

NOTES: Young, tender specimens of Resinous Polypore are edible when gently stewed; they have a moderately soft texture. Oak Bracket and Yellow-Red Gill Polypore are regarded as inedible.

Young Resinous Polypore
with resin drops

Middle-aged Resinous Polypore

Mature Resinous Polypore

Young Oak Bracket

Cluster of Oak Bracket

Pore surface

Tinder Polypore

Fomes fomentarius (also known as *Polyporus fomentarius*)

Found on living or dead deciduous trees, stumps and logs, particularly birch and beech trees, this hard, tough-crusted gray to grayish-brown mushroom looks like a half-dome. It grows directly on the woody substrate and has no stem. The top side is **banded or ridged** both in texture and color; it is dull, dry and hard to the touch. The underside is **brownish, tan or gray** and covered with fine, rounded pores. Caps are generally 2 to 8 inches across. Young specimens may be as tall as they are wide. With age they become thicker and expand in width, particularly near the bottom; old specimens often appear **hoof-like**. The surface may develop **slight cracks**. They grow as individual specimens, although there may be multiple polypores on each tree. The spore print is white. Growth takes place in spring and summer; specimens persist on the trees year-round. They cause white rot, acting as both parasite and decomposer.

COMPARE: Birch Polypore (pg. 202) is similar, but it **lacks the banding** and grows only on birch trees. • **Artist's Conk** (pg. 206) has white pores that instantly bruise brown.

NOTES: This mushroom is also called Firestarter Mushroom, Tinder Conk and Hoof Fungus, and is known as Amadou in Europe. It has long been used as a fire-starter and antibiotic, and was carried by Neolithic peoples who probably knew of its multiple uses (see pg. 202 for more information on the Tyrolean Iceman).

Berkeley's Polypore

Bondarzewia berkeleyi (also known as *Polyporus berkeleyi*)

This polypore can grow to impressive sizes; clusters may be several feet across, with individual caps that are up to **10 inches** wide. They cause white rot, acting as both parasites and decomposers and are found near living, dying and dead deciduous trees, particularly oak; they typically grow at the base of a tree or from the ground over buried roots. Very young specimens look like a grouping of **knobby fingers**; these develop into caps that are fleshy and somewhat tough. Mature specimens grow as a **rosette** of overlapping caps that are roughly fan-shaped; the caps narrow down into a neck-like stalk. A tough, yellowish-brown stem may be found at the base of the rosette. Top surfaces are **cream-colored, tan or yellowish**, often with concentric bands of color that may be obvious or subtle; caps become dull orangish-brown with age. The surface is dry and may be smooth or lightly hairy. The **whitish** lower surface is covered with medium-fine pores that descend the stalk. Flesh of young specimens produces a milky sap when squeezed. Its spore print is white; it grows from midsummer through fall.

COMPARE: Hen of the Woods (pgs. 54–55) appears similar, but its caps are less than 3 inches across and are more delicate. • Chicken of the Woods (pgs. 32–33) is **brightly colored**; pores of the most common variety (*Laetiporus sulphureus*) are **yellow**.

NOTES: The finger-like stage is edible but developed caps are very bitter.

Smoky Polypore

Bjerkandera adusta (also known as *Polyporus adustus*)

From above, this polypore often looks like a cluster of generic-looking tan or grayish caps blanketing a dead deciduous tree; they are semicircular or irregularly shaped and have no stem. They are saprobes, getting their nutrients from decaying wood; they prefer the wood of deciduous trees but may be found on conifer wood. The caps are typically overlapping or fused together. They are 1 to 3 inches wide and **thin**, with a **velvety** surface and leathery texture; they are whitish, grayish or tan, frequently with concentric bands of color but sometimes fairly monotone. The surface underneath is covered with tiny pores that are **smoky gray**; they become darker when handled or with age. The edge is frequently whitish on both sides of younger specimens, turning black with age. The spore print is white. They are found year-round.

COMPARE: Big Smoky Bracket (*B. fumosa*) is a related shelf mushroom that has a **buff to pale gray** pore surface. It may grow to nearly **6 inches** wide, and the caps are **thicker** and more fleshy than those of Smoky Polypore. Young specimens of Big Smoky Bracket smell like anise.

NOTES: When young, both of the *Bjerkandera* species discussed here may grow with only rudimentary caps or may appear nearly capless; they look like spreading patches of white or tan foam with blobs of velvety color. Both species are considered inedible.

Dryad's Saddle

Cerioporus squamosus (also known as Pheasant Back, *Polyporus squamosus*)

Both common names for this mushroom seem appropriate. The cap is elaborately patterned with flattened, dark brown scales that create a **feather-like pattern** on top of a tan to creamy yellowish background. It is semicircular or kidney-shaped, appearing like a **small saddle** suited to a woodland fairy. Some specimens have a short, thick stem that is attached off-center; it is cream-colored at first, turning black with age. Other specimens are attached directly to the wood. Dryad's Saddles act as parasites on living deciduous trees (particularly elms) and as decomposers of dead wood such as stumps and fallen logs. Caps may grow to over 12 inches across but are usually smaller; they often grow in small clusters but may also appear singly. The underside is covered with whitish to creamy yellow pores that are fairly large and angular; they do not bruise when handled. Flesh is soft when young, with a scent like **watermelon rind**. The spore print is white. Dryad's Saddle are most common in spring, but are also found in summer and fall.

COMPARE: With a round, scaly cap that is **2 to 5 inches** across, *P. craterellus* resembles a small Dryad's Saddle. However, the scale pattern is more subtle and may be absent. The cap has a central **funnel-like** indentation; **soft wrinkles** run from the center to the edge. The stem is always present and **does not blacken**.

NOTES: Young Dryad's Saddle are edible when cooked, as are *P. craterellus*. Caps of Dryad's Saddle develop a tough, corky texture with age, becoming inedible.

Hexagonal-Pored Polypore
Neofavolus alveolaris

The small, bright caps of this mushroom can be a beautiful sight in the early spring woods. This polypore grows singly or in groups on branches and sticks of deciduous trees; it is usually seen on branches that have fallen to the ground. Caps are semicircular or kidney-shaped and may be up to 4 inches across but are typically much smaller. Young caps are tan to **bright orange** with a **feathered** surface (described as scaly in many field guides). Underneath the caps are white, **hexagonal-shaped** pores radiating from and running down the short to non-existent stem. Older caps may be white after exposure to the elements. Its spore print is white, and it is found from early spring through fall.

COMPARE: The Fringed Polypore (pg. 172) has a round cap that has a **hairy edge** and a **centrally attached brown stem**. • Dryad's Saddle (pg. 215) has large angular pores, but its cap is much **larger**, growing up to a foot and a half across on trunks and stumps of dead or dying trees. Its surface is white with a **feathery-looking pattern** created by **dark brown scales**.

NOTES: This small mushroom has many names; it is also called Hickory-Stick Polypore, *Polyporus alveolaris*, *P. mori*, *Favolus alveolaris* and *F. canadensis*. Though tough, this mushroom is edible; young caps are a little more tender. It causes white rot of the wood it grows on.

Cinnabar-Red Polypore

Pycnoporus cinnabarinus (also known as *Trametes coccinea, Polyporus cinnabarinus*)

It's hard to miss this stunning mushroom in the woods; its bright **orangish-red** coloration draws the eye. It grows as a stemless semicircular or kidney-shaped cap that is attached to fallen or dead deciduous trees, particularly oak; it is occasionally reported on conifers. It typically is not found on very old, rotten wood. Caps are up to 5 inches across; they are up to ½ inch thick with a thinner edge and are **tough and leathery**. They grow singly or in overlapping clusters. The surface is finely hairy on young specimens, becoming hairless but rough-textured, wrinkled or pockmarked with age; the color may fade to yellowish-orange. The underside is covered with **fine, bright reddish-orange pores** that are rounded or somewhat angular. Its spore print is white, and it grows from spring through fall in our area.

COMPARE: Tender Nesting Polypore (*Hapalopilus nidulans*) is a smaller polypore whose cap is **brownish-orange to cinnamon-colored**. Its pores are angular and **dirty orange to yellowish-brown**. • Beefsteak Fungus (pg. 220) is **deep red** and has a **very soft** texture. • Reishi (pg. 218) may have a deep red cap, but it has concentric bands of different hues and a **varnished surface**; the outer edge is generally **cream-colored or yellow**.

NOTES: Cinnabar-Red Polypore and Tender Nesting Polypore are inedible. Beefsteak Fungus is edible when young. Reishi is used medicinally.

Stemless form (*G. sessile*)　　Stemmed form (*G. lucidum*)

Reishi

Ganoderma sessile, G. tsugae (also called Ling Chih, Varnished Polypore)

These two species appear very similar, and are distinguished largely by habitat. Both are saprobes that fruit on living or dead trees, as well as from buried roots; **G. sessile** is found on **hardwoods**, particularly maple, while **G. tsugae** appears on **conifers**, primarily hemlock. Both have fan-shaped caps with lumpy, **glossy** surfaces; they often develop wrinkles from the center to the edge. Caps are **firm** and 3 to 6 inches across, sometimes larger; they typically have concentric zones of color, primarily **brownish-red to reddish** with a lighter edge, but they may also be mostly one color. There may be a thick, lumpy neck-like stem; *G. tsugae* is more likely to have this stem, while *G. sessile* is more commonly stemless. The undersides of both are covered with fine whitish pores that turn brownish with age and handling. They fruit singly or in overlapping clusters from spring through late fall, and may persist into winter; the spore print is brown. *G. sessile* is also listed as *G. lucidum*, which is an Asian species that does not occur in most of the U.S.

COMPARE: *G. sessile* also grows in urban areas on buried roots. Mowing and foot traffic cause this terrestrial mushroom to develop **multiple, overlapping, misshapen lobes.** • Artist's Conk (pg. 206) is a large, firm fan-shaped bracket, but its top side is **dull tan, gray or brownish.** • Beefsteak Fungus (pg. 220) is **solid, bright red** on top, with no banding or glossiness; it has a **very soft** texture.

NOTES: Reishi has been used for over 2,000 years in China to enhance longevity, boost the immune system, lower blood pressure and treat cancer.

Red-Belted Polypore

Fomitopsis pinicola (also known as *Fomitopsis mounceae, Fomes pinicola*)

This mushroom grows on both living and dead trees and is frequently found on stumps and downed wood; it seems to prefer conifers but also grows on deciduous wood. Specimens may grow alone or there may be many on a single tree. It is perennial, persisting for several years. Each year it grows a new band of flesh on the outer edge of the older flesh, which is **hard and woody**. The new band is white to yellowish; there may be beads of moisture on its surface. As the mushroom grows, older portions darken, becoming reddish, then reddish-brown, gray and finally blackish; there is typically a **bright or deep red band** near the outer white edge. Younger bands typically have a glossy surface that looks lacquered; on some specimens the entire surface is glossy. The mushroom is typically hoof-shaped but may also be fairly flat, looking like a thick fan. Pores are **cream-colored**, bruising yellow on young growth. The spore print is whitish.

COMPARE: Reishi (pg. 218) is glossy and reddish to reddish-brown, but it does not have the distinct, multiple layered bands of woody flesh. • *Phellinus everhartii* (pg. 223) appears similar to Red-Belted Polypore, but it lacks the reddish band on the edge and the pore surface is **brownish**; it grows only on living oak.

NOTES: Red-Belted Polypore has an important role in breaking down woody waste in forests, helping to create material for new soil. It also acts as a parasite on living trees, causing brown rot.

Beefsteak Fungus

Fistulina hepatica

This colorful mushroom is very noticeable. It grows singly or in small clusters on stumps and dead or dying trees; it is also found at the base of living trees. It prefers oak but also grows on chestnuts and other deciduous trees. Caps are **deep to bright red or purplish-red** and generally fan-shaped or tongue-like, often with irregular or wavy edges; they are up to 10 inches across and typically **½ to 1½ inches thick**. The texture is **soft and fleshy**; it may be somewhat gelatinous, slimy or sticky. Caps may appear streaked or mottled; edges may be darker than the center. The pore surface underneath is whitish to pinkish-yellow on fresh specimens, turning reddish-brown when bruised. Unlike most other mushrooms with pores, the tubes are **separate** rather than fused together (a hand lens is needed to see this). Fresh specimens produce a **reddish liquid** when squeezed; the cut surface is red and really does resemble beefsteak. The spore print is pinkish or salmon-colored. Beefsteak Fungus grows from midsummer through fall.

COMPARE: Reishi (pg. 218) may have a deep red cap, but its texture is **very firm** and it often has concentric bands of different hues. • Cinnabar-Red Polypore (pg. 217) is bright orangish-red and thin with a **tough** texture.

NOTES: Beefsteak Fungus is edible but has a bitter or tart taste; young specimens are preferred. Oak that has been parasitized by this fungus is prized by woodworkers because it develops dark, rich tones.

Blue Cheese Polypore

Postia caesia group (also known as *Tyromyces caesius* and *Oligoporus caesius*)

This soft, watery polypore is a saprobe that is found on decaying wood, both deciduous and coniferous. It grows singly or in groups that are often overlapping. Caps are roughly semicircular with wavy edges but may also be irregularly lumpy; they are up to 3 inches across and have no stems. The surface is **dirty white to grayish** and is covered with fine hairs that may be grayish-blue; it develops **bluish-gray or bluish tones** with age or handling. The bottom surface is whitish to gray, becoming grayish-blue or grayish-purple with age or handling; pores are small, but coarse and angular when closely inspected. The flesh is spongy and whitish, bruising grayish-blue; it has a pleasant fragrance. Its spore print is **pale blue**; it grows from midsummer through fall.

COMPARE: White Cheese Polypore (p. 230) looks identical to very young blue cheese polypore, but has a **white** spore print. • Green Cheese Polypore (*Fomitopsis spraguei* or *Niveoporofomes spraguei*) is typically larger, up to **6 inches across**. It is grayish to whitish overall except for the edges, which are **reddish-brown** on young, growing specimens; the edges become **greenish** when bruised. **Watery droplets** may be present on the top and edges of young specimens.

NOTES: The true *Postia caesia* does not occur in North America, but a handful of related species are found here; these are often listed simply as the *Postia caesia* group. Neither of the polypores discussed here are edible; some say they have a soapy taste.

Cup stage Bracket stage

Little Nest Polypore

Poronidulus conchifer (also known as *Trametes conchifer, Boletus conchifer*)

This fascinating saprobe starts its life as a tiny **cup-shaped** fungus that is typically about ½ inch across and grows on dead hardwood, favoring elm. The upper surface usually features concentric zones of color, ranging from white to grayish to brownish. A **small stem** is present at the point of attachment to the substrate, giving this stage a goblet-like appearance. As the fungus grows, the edge of the cup expands outward so the specimen looks like a **shell-shaped bracket** that can be nearly 2 inches across and up to 1 inch deep; a remnant of the cup depression is sometimes obvious at the base. The bracket stage has subtle zones of color that are whitish, pale gray or pale brown; **soft wrinkles** radiate from the center to the edge. The pore surface of the bracket stage is **whitish, becoming yellowish** with age. The flesh is tough and dry. The spore print is white. This species is present from spring through fall; it typically grows in groups.

COMPARE: Bird's Nest Fungus (pg. 275) resembles the cup stage of Little Nest, but Bird's Nest specimens **contain flattened spheres** (the "eggs"). • Smoky Polypore (pg. 214) has caps that are similarly zoned and colored, but the pore surface underneath is **gray**. • Shiny Cinnamon Polypore (pg. 194) has a flat, velvety cap that features **concentric brown rings**; it has a brown stem up to 2 inches long. It grows **from the ground**. • Mature, bracket-shaped Little Nest specimens resemble faded *Trametes* species (pgs. 204, 234)

NOTES: Both stages of this fungus are inedible.

Willow Bracket

Phellinus igniarius (also known as *Fomes igniarius* and False Tinder Conk)

This tough, woody bracket looks like a half-dome or hoof. The top is dark gray to black; it develops **multiple, plate-like cracks**, often looking **charred**. The underside is brownish to gray and covered with fine, rounded pores. Caps are 2 to 6 inches across. This species causes heartwood rot, and is found on birch, willow, cottonwood, alder and other hardwoods. Growth takes place in spring and summer, but the polypore is present year-round. Its spore print is white.

COMPARE: Several other *Phellinus* species are found in our area. They are difficult to identify based on appearance, which varies greatly even within a species; the host tree provides the best clue. • Aspen Bracket (*Phellinus tremulae*) is found only on **aspen** species, growing from **branch scars and wounds**. It is flatter, projecting from the tree in a **sloped** fashion. • Pine Bracket (*Porodaedalea pini*; also called *Phellinus pini*) infests primarily **conifers**. Its surface has bands of colors ranging from tan to dark reddish-brown; the underside is brownish-yellow, with irregular pores. • *Phellinus everhartii* appears primarily on **oak** trees; the edge of the cap is paler than the top. • *Phellinus robiniae* is found on **black locust** and related trees. It may be up to **15 inches** across; mature specimens often have green algae on top.

NOTES: *Phellinus* are inedible. Willow Bracket is used by some native groups in Alaska to prepare Iqmik, an addictive chewing mixture. Ashes from the burned polypore are mixed with tobacco, which amplifies the effect of the nicotine.

ON DECAYING WOOD

EARLY SPRING THROUGH LATE FALL

Hairy Panus
Panus neostrigosus

HABITAT: Hairy Panus is a saprobe, getting its nutrients from decaying wood. It grows singly, in loose groups, or more often in tight clusters on dead deciduous wood, especially on cut or fallen logs and stumps.

DESCRIPTION: This mushroom, which is less than 4 inches across, presents itself in many different forms, from an almost stemless shelf to a short-stemmed funnel; it may be pink, purplish, tan or orangish. However, caps are **always furry**, a feature accentuated by the rolled-under cap edges. Gills are fine and closely spaced; they are colored like the cap when young, turning white with age. When a stem is present, it may be off-center with the **gills running down it** to meet the short, furry base.

SPORE PRINT: White.

SEASON: Early spring through late fall.

OTHER NAMES: Ruddy Panus, *Lentinus strigosus*, *Panus lecomtei*, *Panus rudis*.

COMPARE: The **Smooth Panus** or **Conch Panus** (*Panus conchatus*; also listed as *L. conchatus* and *L. torulosus*) is slightly larger than Hairy Panus, with a more obvious stem. It has a **smooth cap** and is more purplish, especially when young. • **Styptic Panus** (*Panellus stipticus*) is generally 1 inch across or less and grows in overlapping shelves. The semicircular cap fans outward from a short stem near the inside edge. Caps are tan, buff-colored or whitish; the top is velvety and edges are rounded or lobed. Gills are **abruptly attached** to the stem and do not run down it. They are light brown and forked, with numerous **cross-veins** (visible with a hand lens). Gills of young, fresh specimens glow in the dark (called bioluminescent), giving this species the alternate name of Luminescent Panus. • Orangish specimens of Hairy Panus may be mistaken for a pale **Orange Mock Oyster** (pg. 229), but Mock Oyster is **stemless** and more **brightly colored**; it has a **pink to tan** spore print.

NOTES: These mushrooms can be found in many seasons, shriveling up in dry weather and re-hydrating when wet; they are inedible. Styptic Panus is used in traditional Chinese medicine as a blood thickener and purgative.

Hairy Panus

Smooth Panus

Styptic Panus

Split Gill
Schizophyllum commune

These small mushrooms act as both parasites and decomposers, getting their nutrients from the wood of decaying or dead deciduous trees; they may also grow on processed lumber. Although small and easily overlooked, they have intriguing features when viewed closely; a hand lens is helpful. Caps are **fuzzy** and white to grayish above. They are up to 2 inches wide and are fan-shaped or irregularly lobed; edges are minutely scalloped. They grow scattered, layered or in rosettes. Undersides are pinkish-gray, with **doubled or split** gill-like structures that fan out from the center to the edge. These "gills" are really a folded pore surface; they pull together in dry weather to protect the spores within but open to release them when moisture is present. In fact, the entire mushroom will curl up and appear even smaller when dry but rehydrate and regain its shape when wet. This tough little shelf can last for many seasons. Its spore print is white; it is found year-round.

COMPARE: Caps of *Trametes pubescens* (pg. 234) are **velvety** but not fuzzy; they have a **white pore surface** below that yellows with age. They are inedible.

NOTES: Many experts call Split Gill the most common and widespread mushroom in the world! Though small and tough, it is edible and considered a survival food or even a traditional food in some cultures, particularly in southeast Asia. It is being studied for its medicinal properties.

Bear Paw Lentinus
Lentinellus ursinus

This mushroom is a saprobe, getting its nutrients from decaying wood. It may grow singly but is usually found in overlapping clusters on dead deciduous trees, occasionally conifers. Bear Paw Lentinus gets its name from *ursa*, the Latin word for bear, due to its brown color and **hairy surface**. Lacking a stem, fan-shaped caps grow to about 4 inches across with a lobed or wavy edge. They are usually lighter colored on the outer edges; some specimens may be tan all over and resemble an Oyster Mushroom (pgs. 34–37). However, unlike Oysters, the cap surface is **fuzzy**, especially near the base. Underneath, the **closely spaced**, white to pinkish gills have a distinct, **serrated** edge. Its spore print is white, and it is found from summer through late fall.

COMPARE: Fox Lentinus (*L. vulpinus*) is a similar size but caps grow from a **short stem** that may fuse with neighboring stems to form a thicker base. • The **Brown Leaflike Oyster** (*Hohenbuehelia grisea*) is much smaller, with caps that are less than 2 inches wide. They are faintly furry and are **bluish-black to dark brown** when young, fading to tan with age. • *H. petaloides* has a wide neck, appearing like a rounded spatula; its cap is **smooth**.

NOTES: *l entinellus* species are said to have an extremely bitter or hot taste and are not collected for the table. This mushroom is also called Bear Lentinus, Bear Paw and Saw Tooth.

Creps (several)
Crepidotus spp.

These small, **flimsy** caps grow in loose groups on well-rotted deciduous wood, especially fallen logs and branches; when you first see them, you may think you've found a batch of baby Oyster Mushrooms (pgs. 34–37). Creps have white to tan caps with **crowded gills** underneath that fan out from where they are attached to the wood; there is no stem. When growing from the bottom of a log, they may be nearly circular. The gills are white at first, darkening to light brown; the spore print is brown. Creps are found from summer through late fall; they are common even in dry weather. • The **Flat Crep** (*C. applanatus*) is the most common, growing up to only 2 inches across; it is also called Little White Crep and Flat Oysterling. • The caps of the **Peeling Oysterling** (*C. mollis*) may grow slightly larger and have **minute brown scales** on top when dry. The flesh is **gelatinous**, giving it the alternate name of Jelly Crep.

COMPARE: The Orange Crep or Yellow Gilled Crep (*C. crocophyllus*) has buff to yellowish caps **overlaid with brownish fibers** that may be sparse or heavy. Gills of young specimens are **yellowish to orange**, turning brown with age.

NOTES: These fragile Oysterlings are not edible. Since Oysters have thicker flesh and often a short stem with gills running down it, you will know after inspecting only a couple whether you have an edible treat, or just Crep.

Orange Mock Oyster
Phyllotopsis nidulans

Orange Mock Oysters grow singly or in loose groups but mostly in dense overlapping clusters on dead and fallen wood of deciduous trees and conifers. They are saprobes, getting their nutrients from dead and decaying organic matter. Though somewhat small, these **fuzzy** little shelves are easy to spot because of their **bright yellow to orange** color. Caps are up to 3 inches across. Underneath the cap are closely spaced gills that are the same bright orange color and radiate out from the **stemless** connection point to the wood. Often the edge of the cap is rolled under, especially when young. The brightly colored cap surface fades to tan with age, but remains intensely furry at every stage. They typically have a strong, unpleasant odor, but this may be absent. Their spore print is pink to tan; they grow from late summer through late fall.

COMPARE: Most **Oyster Mushrooms** (pgs. 34 -37) are **cream-colored, tan or grayish-brown**, although caps of the Golden Oyster are bright yellow; however, true Oysters have **smooth** caps and **whitish** gills. • *Panus* **species** (pg. 224) grow on wood and have densely **furry** caps, but they are not bright orange like the Orange Mock Oyster. • **Chicken of the Woods** (pgs. 32–33) is a prime edible shelf mushroom that is bright orange, but the underside is covered with **tiny pores** rather than gills and the top sides are **smooth** rather than fuzzy or hairy.

NOTES: Orange Mock Oysters are generally regarded as inedible.

Marshmallow Polypore
Spongipellis pachyodon

Acting as both a saprobe and parasite, this polypore is found on hardwoods, favoring oak. Individual caps are less than 2 inches across and whitish to faded yellow overall; the surface may be finely hairy, and there is no stem. The underside is initially covered with small, angular pores. As the specimen ages, the pores become distended, forming **long, irregular tooth-like projections** that are up to ⅜ inch long. Caps frequently overlap, and may not be perceptible; sometimes the growth is simply a spreading, sheet-like pore surface that may be nearly 8 inches across. Its spore print is white. Growth occurs from midsummer into fall, but the specimens are present into winter.

COMPARE: *S. unicolor*, also called Marshmallow Polypore, is a soft **dome-shaped** cap, 4 to 8 inches across, that grows singly or in small groups. Both surfaces are buff to cream-colored. The underside is covered with large, angular pores that become slot-like or tooth-like with age. • **White Cheese Polypore** (*Tyromyces chioneus* or *T. albellus*) is semicircular and 1 to 4 inches across; it often grows in overlapping clusters. Its texture is soft and **watery**; it is white on both surfaces when young, yellowing with age. The pores of young specimens are so **fine** that the underside looks smooth. It has a noticeably **pleasant odor**. • **Milk-White Toothed Polypore** (pg. 272) is a white to tan **crust fungus** with short, hard teeth.

NOTES: All species listed here grow on deciduous trees. None are edible.

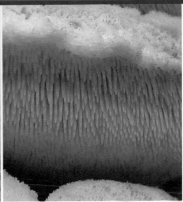

Northern Tooth

Climacodon septentrionale (also known as *Climacodon septentrionalis*)

This large, creamy white shelf mushroom is a parasite, causing heart rot of deciduous trees, especially beech and maple; it fruits prolifically on the trees it has infected. The thick, tough caps can grow up to a foot across in densely overlapping clumps up the side or base of a tree. From a distance, it might look like a nice batch of Oyster Mushrooms (pgs. 34–37) or a pale version of the Chicken of the Woods (pgs. 32–33), but close viewing reveals quite different features. Growing from a thick, solid base, Northern Tooth caps are **fuzzy and bumpy** on top with clear zones of growth. Under the cap is a crowded surface of spore-bearing **teeth**. The entire fungus turns yellowish-brown when old and develops a rancid scent that some compare to rotting ham. Its spore print is white, and it grows from summer through late fall.

COMPARE: Hen of the Woods (pgs. 54–55) grows from the ground at the base of **oaks** and has a **fine white pore surface** under its caps, which are **smaller and thinner** than those of Northern Tooth. • All surfaces of *Hericium* species (pgs. 48–49) are **draped with white teeth**; several *Hericium* have branching forms.

NOTES: This large fungus is not edible, and worse than that, it likes to attack sugar maples! The name implies that it is a northern species (*Septentrionale* means "northern" in Latin), but it is just as common in the southern parts of our area. It is also called Shelving Tooth.

green = key identification feature   231

Purple Tooth
Trichaptum biforme (also known as *Trichaptum biformis*)

These fan-shaped saprobes grow in overlapping layers on dead and dying decid-uous trees, often in a rosette. The fans are **very thin** and up to 3 inches across. The species name *biforme* ("two forms") was chosen because when young this mushroom has a **purple** pore surface that develops into **teeth** with age, fading to mauve or tan; new growth on the outer edge is brighter. The top is hairy and whitish to grayish when young, with **bands** of **pink, purple, tan or brown**. It becomes smooth and faded with age, often turning green from algae. The spore print is white. It grows from spring through early winter but is found all year.

COMPARE: *T. abietinum* is usually **smaller** and grows on **conifers.** • Mossy Maze Polypore (*Cerrena unicolor*; previously *Daedalea unicolor*) are typically fan-shaped caps up to 4 inches across with irregular, wavy edges. Tops are velvety to hairy and have bands of color, from whitish to grayish to green from algae. Undersides are **whitish to gray** and appear **maze-like**, becoming tooth-like with age. • Turkey Tail and its many lookalikes (pg. 204) grow in the same manner and have bands of colors but undersides are covered with **smooth whitish, pale gray or yellowish pores**. • From above, caps of Gilled Polypore (pg. 233) look very similar to Purple Tooth, but they have **white gill-like structures** underneath.

NOTES: The mushrooms listed above are decomposers, multiplying and persist-ing for years until the wood is totally broken down.

Oak Maze Gill
Daedalea quercina

This white, grayish to light brown mushroom grows on dead hardwood, particularly oak. It looks unremarkable until you turn it over to see the **deeply ridged** pore surface that looks like an intricate **maze**. This spore-producing surface is white at first, turning tan with age. The cap has a velvety surface and can grow to 8 inches wide, 3 inches out from the tree and **3 inches thick**. The spore print is white. It grows from summer into fall; individual specimens last for many years. It may surround sticks or other debris as it grows rather than pushing them away

COMPARE: Caps of Gilled Polypore (*Lenzites betulina*) grow only to about 4 inches wide and less than an inch thick. Underneath is a firm pore surface composed of **thick, white gill-like structures**. *Betula* is the Latin genus name for birch and this is also called the Birch Mazegill, though it can be found on other deciduous trees and conifers. The cap surface has **distinct bands of color**, often including green from algae growth. • Thin-Maze Flat Polypore (*Daedaleopsis confragosa*) grows mainly on birch and willow. Its bumpy to wavy cap surface varies in color from all-white, to gray or dark brown with **strong concentric zones**. It is also called Blushing Bracket, due to the tendency of its finer white to tan maze-like pore surface to **bruise pink to reddish** when young. Nearly identical *D. septentrionalis* grows only on birch.

NOTES: All of the mushrooms listed above are inedible but quite decorative.

Lumpy Bracket

Trametes elegans (also listed as *Lenzites elegans* and *Daedalea elegans*)

This **firm-textured** saprobe grows on decaying deciduous wood. It is semi-circular to kidney-shaped with somewhat irregular edges and usually 1 to 5 inches wide, although it may be larger. The top surface is **hairless** and whitish, buffy or gray; it often has concentric bands of varying texture. The point of attachment to the wood is often lumpy, resembling a thick, stubby stem. Underneath, the whitish pore surface has a **variety of pore shapes**; they may be round, elongated, angular or maze-like, even on the same cap. The spore print is white. It grows from spring through fall and is found singly or in small groups that may be overlapping.

COMPARE: Several other mushrooms appear similar and grow on the same substrate. • *T. pubescens* (also called *T. velutina*) has cream-colored to yellowish caps that have a **finely hairy** surface when young and fresh. **Soft wrinkles** often run from the center to the edges. Several caps may fuse together. The underside is dull white to yellowish and covered with small angular pores. • False Turkey Tail (pg. 204) has **elongated** caps that are **smooth underneath**, with no pores. • Mossy Maze Polypore (pg. 232) are typically fan-shaped caps with irregular, wavy edges. Tops are velvety to hairy and have bands of color, from whitish to grayish to green from algae. Undersides are **whitish to gray** and appear **maze-like**, becoming tooth-like with age.

NOTES: The mushrooms above are all tough and inedible.

Yellow-Red Gill Polypore
Gloeophyllum sepiarium (also known as Conifer Mazegill)

This woody, fan-shaped to irregularly shaped saprobe grows on dead conifers, as well as construction lumber and, occasionally, on hardwoods; it may appear singly but often fruits in overlapping shelves or rosettes. From the top it looks like many other shelf mushrooms, but the underside is covered with a series of **irregularly shaped gill-like structures and elongated pores** that looks like an intricate **maze**. The maze is tan to brownish with pale edges. Individual caps are subtly zoned and yellowish-brown when young, becoming reddish-brown or dark brown; new growth on the edge is yellow, orangish or white. The top surface is **hairy to velvety**; caps may be up to 4½ inches across and 3 inches from front to back. There is no stem; the cap fans out from the point of attachment to the wood. Spores are white. This species is present year-round; individual specimens get darker over time. It causes brown rot of the wood.

COMPARE: From above, **Mustard Yellow Polypore** (*Phellinus gilvus*) often looks quite similar to Yellow-Red Gill Polypore, but the surface underneath is covered with **very fine dark pores** that range from purplish-brown to reddish-brown to grayish-brown. The top surface is dark reddish-brown or yellowish-brown, becoming blackish with age; new growth on the edge is mustard-yellow. Caps may be almost **6 inches** across and have a rough texture that is often velvety.

NOTES: These mushrooms are inedible but very handsome.

FROM THE SOIL

EARLY SUMMER THROUGH FALL

Common Puffball

Lycoperdon perlatum

HABITAT: Grows **from the ground**, usually in large groups or clusters. They are common in the woods but are also found in grassy urban areas.

DESCRIPTION: Common Puffballs have generally **spherical tops** that may be up to 3 inches in diameter but are usually smaller. Rather than true stems, they have **elongated bases** that vary from 1 to 3 inches tall, making the mushrooms look like upside-down pears; however, they often grow in tight clusters so only the spherical tops are visible. The outer skin is white, cream-colored or tan and is covered in **minute spines** that may disappear with age, leaving a slightly rough surface. As with other Puffballs (pgs. 41–43), the outer skin encases the interior spore-producing flesh. Initially smooth, white and edible, the flesh becomes yellowish-green and inedible, finally turning into a brown powder. Each sphere develops an opening at the top to release, or puff out, the spores.

SPORE PRINT: Brown.

SEASON: Early summer through fall; dried specimens can be found year-round.

OTHER NAMES: Gem-Studded Puffball, Devil's Snuff-Box, *L. gemmatum*.

COMPARE: The slightly smaller **Pear-Shaped Puffball** (*Apioperdon pyriforme*; also listed as *L. pyriforme* and *Morganella pyriformis*) is similar to the Common Puffball but it grows from **decaying wood**, typically in dense clusters; the surface is less spiny, appearing nearly smooth by maturity. • The edible **Peeling Puffball** (*L. marginatum*) is up to 2 inches across; its skin is covered with **spines that have pyramidal bases**. It may be confused with species of **Spiny Puffball** (*Vascellum curtisii*, *L. pulcherrimum*, *L. echinatum*), which are marble-sized and inedible. Peeling Puffball can be recognized at maturity when the skin **falls off in large sheaths**, revealing a smooth, brown surface.

NOTES: Most puffballs are edible when young but can be mistaken for various cap-and-stem species in the button stage, including **deadly** Amanitas (pgs. 62–67), **toxic** Agaricus (pg. 82) or the egg stage of Stinkhorns (pg. 198). Small puffballs growing from the ground should always be cut in half to make sure they are not overripe or young examples of another species such as an Amanita button (pg. 62); also see Earthballs, pg. 240. The ripe spores should not be inhaled, as they can cause respiratory distress.

Common Puffball

Pear-Shaped Puffball

After releasing spores

Spiny Puffball

FROM THE SOIL NEAR TREES

SUMMER THROUGH LATE FALL

Earthstars (several)

Geastrum spp.

HABITAT: Grows from the ground singly or in groups near hardwoods and conifers. They are saprobes, getting their nutrients from leaf litter and dead wood; often found in large numbers near the stumps of dead trees.

DESCRIPTION: Earthstars begin their lives as small, smooth, tan egg-shaped balls that have a pointed beak at the top. The skin splits and unfolds into a **star-shaped base** surrounding the central sphere, which is a tough skin encasing the spore mass, much like a Puffball (pgs. 41–43, 236). The star may be hidden by the dirt and debris it collects. With age, the sphere turns darker brown and the beak at the top opens to release the ripened spores. There are numerous species, each distinguished by slight variations. • Rounded Earthstar (*G. saccatum*) is the most common; it is less than 2 inches across, including the opened rays of the star. It is attached to the ground at a **central point;** the sphere nestles in the bowl-shaped base of the star, which is buff-colored on the side facing up. The spore beak sits in a **depressed ring** that is slightly fuzzy and colored differently than the rest of the sphere. Sessile Earthstar (*G. fimbriatum*) is very similar, but has a **wider connection** to the ground and **lacks the ring** around the spore beak. • Collared Earthstar (*G. triplex*) is up to **4 inches** across. The star's rays are pale pinkish or tan on the side facing up. The rays often fold under and crack into layers; the top layer forms a **collar-like rim** around the base of the sphere. The area around the spore beak is pale and slightly fuzzy; it may be slightly depressed but not as much as Rounded Earthstar.

SPORE PRINT: Brown.

SEASON: Fruiting summer through late fall, present year-round.

OTHER NAMES: Some Native American tribes traditionally called them Fallen Stars and thought their appearance foretold of celestial events.

COMPARE: The Hygroscopic Earthstar (*Astraeus hygrometricus*) is also called the Barometer Earthstar because the rays **react to moisture**. In dry weather, they curl up to protect the interior but open when it rains to let the drops hit and disperse the spores. The rays can open wide enough to push the brown spore mass off the ground to give the spores a chance to be carried farther by wind. It is usually found in dry, sandy areas.

NOTES: The Earthstars listed here are inedible but are fascinating and beautiful.

Rounded Earthstar

Collared Earthstar

FROM THE SOIL NEAR TREES · SUMMER THROUGH FALL

Common Earthball
Scleroderma citrinum

HABITAT: Growing from the ground, singly or in groups, near living conifers and hardwoods; they are mycorrhizal and have a symbiotic relationship with the trees. They are fond of wet wooded areas and grassy lawns but are always near trees; they occasionally grow directly on rotted wood.

DESCRIPTION: This small sphere could almost be mistaken for a puffball, but it has a **yellowish to tan** exterior that is covered with a **dark brown, crackled texture**. This surface is actually a thick, tough skin surrounding the mass of spores. The sphere is 1 to 4 inches across; as it grows, it often flattens out slightly and may become oblong or slightly lobed. The interior is initially white like a puffball, but much **firmer**. As it matures, the interior darkens, turning **purplish-black** and, finally, **warmer brown**. Like a puffball, it develops a hole or expanding crack at the top through which the ripe, powdery spores are eventually released. Earthballs have **no stem** but are well-attached to the ground or wood by a cluster of roots.

SPORE PRINT: Black to dark brown.

SEASON: Summer through fall.

OTHER NAMES: Pigskin Poison Puffball, Hard Puffball, *S. aurantium*, *S. vulgare*.

COMPARE: The **Potato Earthball** (*S. bovista*) is less than 2 inches across and has a **smooth** brownish surface, like a potato. It may narrow at the bottom where it is attached to the ground. With age it develops **fine cracks** on the surface; the spore mass inside becomes black to purplish-black. • The **Leopard Earthball** (*S. areolatum*) has thinner skin that is **cream to light brown** with fine, dark brown scales on the surface. • The **Earthstar Puffball** (*S. polyrhizum* or *S. geaster*) prefers **sandy soils**. It forms mostly underground so is typically **dirty brown**; it leaves quite a mark as it bursts through the soil. Its skin is **thick**; when it splits open to release its **purplish-brown** spores, it resembles a blackened Earthstar (pg. 238). • Small edible **Puffballs** (pg. 236) appear similar to some Earthballs, but their interiors are **soft and white**, becoming **yellowish**. When fully mature, Puffballs are filled with **brown powder**; they never have the firm, dark centers found in maturing Earthballs. • Also see the **Skull-Shaped Puffball** and the **Purple-Spored Puffball** on pgs. 42–43.

NOTES: Earthballs are **toxic**; take care not to confuse them with Puffballs.

Common Earthball

Interior

Potato Earthball

Earthstar Puffball

Wolf's Milk Slime

Lycogala epidendrum (also known as *Lycoperdon epidendrum*)

This slime mold is common and widespread; when it is in the fruiting stage it is very noticeable because of its color and quantity. Individual specimens are **spherical** or cushion-shaped and **⅛ to ½ inch** in size; the surface is **soft** and **slightly roughened**. Young specimens are pale pink, turning pinkish-orange before becoming deep **pinkish-red to reddish-orange**; they are filled with a pinkish to reddish paste-like mass that oozes out when a sphere is punctured (visible on one specimen in the photo above). When the spores mature, the outer surface becomes dark brown, tan or olive-colored; the mass inside becomes pale and powdery. Wolf's Milk Slime grows scattered or in clusters on well-rotted wood; it is very common on downed logs that have been decaying for some time. It is found from late spring through late fall.

COMPARE: Several other **slime molds** appear similar in color to Wolf's Milk Slime; please see Slime Molds on pg. 268. • **Red Tree Brain** (*Sterellum rufum*; also listed as *Peniophora rufa*) looks like **flat, coarsely wrinkled cushions** about ¼ inch across. The cushions are **dull reddish** to reddish-orange with a **tough** texture; they feel **waxy** to the touch. They grow in colonies on the bark of dead deciduous trees, primarily aspens, from spring through fall.

NOTES: Like all slime molds, Wolf's Milk Slime starts out as a slimy mass of proto-plasm that develops fruiting bodies in order to spread spores.

Carbon Balls

Daldinia childiae (also listed as *Daldinia concentrica*)

These round to irregularly blob-shaped fungi are typically less than an inch across but can be up to 4 inches; they grow in **dense clusters** on fallen logs of deciduous trees, especially beech and ash. Light gray to pinkish-brown at first, they become black and shiny like coal when mature. Cutting them in half reveals the **concentric growth rings** that give them the Latin species name *concentrica*. The surface may appear **finely dotted** with spore-releasing openings before the ripe, **black** spores cover the surface of the balls and often become a sooty halo around them. They are found year-round.

COMPARE: Gorse Cramp Balls (*D. vernicosa*) is a similar species that has a **narrow base** that does not produce spores but still grows new layers, getting taller each year. • Dead Man's Fingers (pg. 254) grow in a similar, clustered fashion but are grayish to greenish when young and are typically more **elongated** like fingers. They have a black exterior, but the interior is firm and **white**. • Wolf's Milk Slime (pg. 242) is much smaller and **bright pink** when young, with a wet, slimy texture; it turns brown and hard with age.

NOTES: Though not edible, this common mushroom is also called King Alfred's Cakes or Cramp Balls in reference to old folklore. They are also called Coal Fungus and can be used in the woods for starting fires, like charcoal.

ON DECAYING WOOD   SPRING

Devil's Urn
Urnula craterium

HABITAT: Devil's Urns are saprobes, getting their nutrients from decaying deciduous wood. They are found on downed branches and logs and also on buried wood, appearing to grow from the ground; they frequently grow in moss. Found singly or in clusters that are often linear.

DESCRIPTION: These mushrooms look like something from the underworld. Young specimens are an **inverted teardrop with a narrow opening** at the top; the base narrows down into slender, seamlessly connected **solid** stems that may be buried in ground litter and hard to spot. As specimens age, the opening becomes wider, revealing a **hollow** interior; when stems are visible, the mushrooms look like **black goblets**. Cups are generally 1½ to 2½ inches across and up to 4 inches tall; they are tough and leathery. Their insides are blackish-brown to jet black and smooth; the outside is scruffy and grayish to brownish, turning black with age. The edge of the cup appears **torn** or toothy.

SPORE PRINT: Whitish to pale yellowish.

SEASON: Spring, typically early; often appears before Morels (pgs. 24–27).

OTHER NAMES: Black Tulip Fungus, Crater Cup.

COMPARE: Hairy Rubber Cup or Peanut Butter Cup (*Galiella rufa*; also listed as *Bulgaria rufa*) also resemble goblets with torn edges, but they contain a **tan to yellowish-brown gelatinous substance**. The outside is blackish to brownish and **downy**. Cups are less than 1½ inches across and feel **rubbery** when squeezed. **Summer through fall.** • **Black Trumpet** (pgs. 50–51) is **trumpet-shaped**, with **rolled-over edges** turning outward; its stem is **completely hollow. Summer through fall.** • **Common Brown Cup** (pg. 246) are **brownish, irregularly shaped** cups with **brittle** flesh; they have **no stems**, and fruit **into early summer.** • Young specimens of **Black Bulgar** (*B. inquinans*) are typically ½ to 1½ inches wide and tall. They resemble a **partly filled bowl** that often has distorted edges. The **black** center is smooth and shiny while the exterior is brown to blackish with a rough surface. There may be a stubby stem-like attachment to the wood, or the bowl may be attached directly. Specimens **flatten** out with age, becoming dull black overall. **Late summer into fall.**

NOTES: Black Bulgar has toxins and should not be consumed. Black Trumpet is a choice edible. The others listed above are edible but not very good.

Devil's Urn

Hairy Rubber Cup

Black Bulgar

Common Brown Cup
Peziza phyllogena (also listed as *Peziza badioconfusa*)

HABITAT: These mushrooms are saprobes, getting their nutrients from decaying organic material that may be underground. They are typically found growing from the soil near white pines but are found near other conifers and also in deciduous forests; occasionally found on rotting wood such as downed logs. They grow singly or in clusters.

DESCRIPTION: Although large, these mushrooms often hide under leaves on the forest floor in spring. They are **cup-shaped** or bowl-shaped, narrowing down to the point of attachment; edges sometimes appear flared and trumpet-like but more commonly turn inward. Common Brown Cups have **no stems**, growing directly from the substrate. Individual cups are 1 to 4 inches across and typically as deep as they are wide. Insides are **matte brown**, sometimes with reddish or purplish areas; undersides are **yellowish-tan** and have a **finely granular** texture. Flesh is thin and **brittle**; the cups **crumble easily**. They appear somewhat translucent in the sunlight.

SPORE PRINT: White.

SEASON: Late spring to early summer.

OTHER NAMES: Pig's Ear, *P. badio-confusa*.

COMPARE: Veined Cup (*Disciotis venosa*; also listed as *P. venosa*) grows from the soil and is up to **7 inches** across; it is found only in spring. Its upper surface is yellowish-brown to reddish-brown; the underside is **whitish to tan**. The center is pinched together and has **vein-like wrinkles**. • **Spreading Cup** (*P. repanda*; sometimes referred to as Recurved Cup or Palomino Cup) always grows **on wood**. Young specimens are **pale tan** and cup-like, with a **stem** that becomes less noticeable with age; the outer surface has a whitish bloom. Mature specimens are **flatter** and colored like Common Brown Cup. • *Gyromitra perlata* (also known as *Discina perlata* or *Discina ancilis*) is **reddish-brown**, with a **lumpy, irregular** surface. It is cup-like at first, becoming fairly flat with age. The underside is **pale** and grayish or yellowish-brown. It grows from the soil near conifers.

NOTES: Common Brown Cup is edible but not very tasty; the others here are inedible. It's best to consider Common Brown Cup inedible due to difficulty in identification.

Common Brown Cup

Veined Cup

Spreading Cup (young)

ON DECAYING WOOD

SPRING THROUGH FALL

Wood Ear

Auricularia americana, Auricularia angiospermarum

HABITAT: These saprobes are found on dead and decaying wood, including standing dead trees, stumps, downed logs and branches. *A. americana* fruits on **coniferous** wood, while *A. angiospermarum* is found on **hardwoods**.

DESCRIPTION: Wood Ears are irregularly shaped and look like flattened, wrinkled cups with shallow, irregular folds; they often appear ear-like, accounting for their common name. Individuals are 1 to 6 inches wide. They are usually slightly **puckered** at the point where they are attached to the substrate; the point of connection may be **stub-like**. Flesh is thin and **rubbery**. The spore-producing surface is smooth and brown to reddish-brown. The sterile (non-spore-producing) surface is tan to grayish-brown with a whitish bloom; it is silky or downy and often has **vein-like** wrinkles. Either surface may be facing outward, although the spore-producing surface commonly faces the substrate.

SPORE PRINT: White to cream-colored.

SEASON: Spring through fall.

OTHER NAMES: Tree Ear, Jelly Ear. The two species above were originally considered a single species, listed as *A. auricula* and, in older texts, *A. auricula-judae*.

COMPARE: **Copper Penny** (*Pachyella clypeata*) are rarely wider than 3 inches across and usually closer to an inch. They are **disk-like** and stemless, and much less wrinkled than Wood Ear. The **majority of the disk is attached** to the rotting wood on which these mushrooms grow; the edges are free. The upper surface is reddish-brown to copper-colored and generally shiny; the lower surface is tan. Very young specimens are pillow-like. • **Leafy Brain** (*Phaeotremella frondosa*; also listed as *Tremella foliacea*) has **ruffled, flattened** lobes that are loosely packed and pale to deep **reddish-brown**. It may be up to 8 inches across and 3 inches high; there is no stem. Found on dead hardwoods, it is a parasite that attacks False Turkey Tail (pg. 204) and other *Stereum* species. It is edible, but tasteless. • **Common Brown Cup** (pg. 246) grows as clusters of irregularly shaped brownish cups that may be found on rotting logs but typically grow from the soil; they have a **brittle** texture and **crumble easily**.

NOTES: Like the similarly named (and related) Tree Ears sold in Asian groceries, Wood Ears are edible but act as anticoagulants; caution is advised for persons taking blood-thinning medications.

Wood Ear

Copper Penny

Leafy Brain
parasitizing *Stereum*

Rabbit Ears

Otidea onotica (also referred to as Hare's Ear)

While it doesn't look particularly like rabbit ears, this cup fungus is fairly easy to recognize. It may be cup-shaped, ear-shaped or oval, but it typically has a **cleft down one side** that causes the split edges to **curl inward or roll up**; the top edges are usually rolled inward. The exterior is **yellowish-brown to tan** and may be downy. Inside, the spore-bearing surface is often paler, frequently with **pinkish tinges, splotches or spots**. Individual specimens are typically less than 2 inches across and 3 inches tall. It is typically stemless but may have a small, whitish stem. This saprobe is found in hardwood and mixed forests, often in mossy areas. Its spore print is white; it fruits from summer through fall.

COMPARE: Bladder Cup (*Peziza vesiculosa*) is similar in overall appearance and size, but the outside has a grainy surface; the inside is generally darker than the outside. Although it may be split and folded in on itself, it generally **lacks the cleft** on the side. It grows on **manure, composted straw and compost heaps** and is commonly found in horse pastures. • **Spreading Cup** (pg. 246) grows on **rotting wood**. Young specimens are cup-like, with a **stem** that becomes less noticeable with age. • **Orange Peel Fungus** (pg. 252) is, obviously, **orangish** in color.

NOTES: Orange Peel Fungus is edible; the others listed here are generally considered inedible. Some sources say that Rabbit Ears and Bladder Cup are used medicinally, or are being studied for medicinal properties.

Brown-Haired White Cup

Eyelash Cup

Brown-Haired White Cup

Humaria hemisphaerica (also referred to as Hairy Fairy Cup)

This little cup fungus is fairly common in our area, but easy to miss due to its size. Mature specimens are typically 1 inch across or less and shaped like a deep bowl or cup. The spore-bearing interior surface is **white and smooth**. The exterior is densely covered with **stiff brownish to yellowish-brown hairs** that also ring the top edge of the bowl, projecting over the edge. There is no stem. Brown-Haired White Cup grows scattered or in groups from the soil near hardwood trees, as well as on well-decayed wood and areas with rich humus. It fruits from summer through fall.

COMPARE: Eyelash Cup (*Scutellinia scutellata*) is smaller, typically ½ inch across or less. The interior is **bright orange to red**; the exterior is paler orange to brownish and covered with stiff brownish to blackish hairs, which also form an "eyelash" fringe around the top of the cup. It grows from spring through fall on damp, rotten wood as well as on damp soil. • Bird's Nest Fungus (pg. 275) are typically ½ inch across or less. They are **deeper** and somewhat **cone-shaped**, with shaggy or hairy exteriors. Mature specimens have **tiny flattened spheres** inside, which give the impression of eggs in a nest. They fruit from spring through fall on wood, including downed branches, woodland debris and even old construction lumber.

NOTES: The species listed above are too small to eat; they are enjoyed for their beauty and make splendid candidates for macro photography.

Orange Peel Fungus
Aleuria aurantia

It's a bit of a surprise to see these pretty cup fungi growing in rough, rocky spots, but that's what they like. These saprobes fruit in areas of bare, **hard-packed soil**, and are often found along roads and trails; they also may grow in disturbed areas, including gardens and newly planted lawns. They are shallow, **stemless** cups that may be nearly 4 inches wide but are typically smaller. Edges are often irregular or wavy. The inner surface where spores are produced is **bright orange** and smooth. The outside is whitish and is downy on young specimens. Flesh is thin and brittle; spores are white. Orange Peel Fungus fruits from summer through fall.

COMPARE: False Orange Peel (*A. rhenana*; also listed as *Sowerbyella rhenana*) is similar but less than 1 inch across; it has a **distinct stem** up to 1 inch long. It fruits in **coniferous woodlands**. • Several *Sarcoscypha* species appear similar, but fruit in **spring**. Scarlet Cups (*Sarcoscypha austriaca*) grow on **decaying hardwood branches**, and seldom exceed 2 inches across. The inner spore-producing surface is **bright red** and glossy; outside is downy and pinkish, buff or whitish. They may be stemless, or may have a short, thick stem at the base. The related *Sarcoscypha dudleyi* is indistinguishable from Scarlet Cup without a microscope. (*Sarcoscypha coccinea* is often listed in field guides, but it is a western species that does not grow in our area.) • Eyelash Cup (pg. 251) is bright orange to red and only ¼ to ¾ inch wide; its edges are fringed with **dark hairs**. It grows on **rotten wood**.

NOTES: Orange Peel Fungus is edible; the others listed are inedible.

Stalked Scarlet Cup

Shaggy Scarlet Cup

Stalked Scarlet Cup

Sarcoscypha occidentalis

Although these saprobes are very small, they are so brightly colored that they call attention to themselves. The top is cup-shaped, sometimes flattened and bowl-like; it is typically ¼ to ¾ inch across and smooth on both sides. Edges are often slightly wavy, and the outline of the cup may be rounded, oval or irregularly curved. The spore-bearing surface inside is **vermilion-red**; the outside of the cup is similar but paler, flowing seamlessly into the **whitish stem** that is typically ½ to 1¼ inches tall. White mycelium (threadlike fungal filaments) are often visible at the base of the stem. It grows singly or clustered on fallen hardwood sticks and logs that are above ground or buried, sometimes appearing to fruit from damp leaf litter. Stalked Scarlet Cup first appears in late spring, and can be found into fall.

COMPARE: The exterior of both the cups and stems of **Shaggy Scarlet Cup** (*Microstoma floccosum*; sometimes referred to as Pink-Fringed Faery Cup) are covered with **dense whitish hairs** (*floccus* means "tuft or wisp of wool" in Latin); the overall impression is of a tiny, hairy goblet with a long, thin, curved stem. Cups are typically about ⅜ inch across and pinkish to red inside, with fringed edges; the white stems are up to 1¾ inches tall. They prefer the same habitat as Stalked Scarlet Cup, and are found in summer. • Several other *Sarcoscypha* species are found in our area, but lack distinct stems; please see pg. 252.

NOTES: Edibility is unknown for these tiny fungi, which are best appreciated for their interesting appearance.

ON DECAYING WOOD SPRING THROUGH FALL

Candlesnuff Fungus, Dead Man's Fingers

Xylaria hypoxylon, Xylaria polymorpha

HABITAT: These related species are saprobes, getting their nutrients from decaying deciduous wood that may be buried. Both grow in loose groups.

DESCRIPTION: Candlesnuff Fungus (*X. hypoxylon*) and Dead Man's Fingers (*X. polymorpha*) have two different forms: an immature stage during which they are pale and covered with powdery asexual spores and a mature stage when the surface is dark and covered with small bumps with pores (visible with a hand lens). The pores contain mature spores. • **Candlesnuff Fungus** is smaller and thinner, usually 1 to 3 inches tall and less than ⅜ inch thick. Immature specimens are often **branched**, with two to several thinner forks near the top; they are coated with **whitish** or grayish powder. They are often rounded but may be **somewhat flat**, especially towards the top; they often appear antler-like. Mature specimens are carbon-like, black and pimply and are often unbranched; they appear **spindly or withered**. • **Dead Man's Fingers** are typically **unbranched** even when immature; they may be nearly **4 inches tall** and **1 inch thick**. Immature specimens are rounded, knobby or puffy-looking. They are coated with gray or **bluish** dust except at the very tip, which is white to cream-colored. Mature specimens are carbon-like, black and pimply and are much more **fleshy** than mature Candlesnuff.

SPORE PRINT: Black.

SEASON: The immature stage of both species is present in spring. Mature Candlesnuff is found throughout summer; mature Dead Man's Fingers are present from summer through fall.

OTHER NAMES: *X. hypoxylon* are sometimes called Carbon Antlers.

COMPARE: Several mushrooms are similar to Dead Man's Fingers in color and height. **Stalked Xylaria** (*X. longipes*) is more slender and usually has a **thin stalk** at the base. • **Common Earth Tongue** (*Geoglossum difforme*) is more flattened and **tongue-like**; its surface is **glossy** and may be slimy. • **Velvety Earth Tongue** (*Trichoglossum hirsutum*) has a **flattened oval head** and a **rounded stalk**. Both the head and stalk are covered with stiff hairs.

NOTES: The species listed here are inedible.

Immature Candlesnuff

Mature Candlesnuff

Immature Dead Man's Fingers

Mature Dead Man's Fingers

ON DECAYING WOOD

EARLY SUMMER THROUGH FALL

Crown-Tipped Coral

Artomyces pyxidatus

HABITAT: This lovely coral mushroom is a saprobe, growing **directly on decaying wood** of deciduous trees, particularly willow, aspen and maple.

DESCRIPTION: Although often found growing in large clusters, this coral may grow as a single specimen, making it easier to see its form. Individuals contain numerous branches that **curve away from the base**, similar to a **candelabra**. Specimens are 1½ to 4 inches wide and slightly higher; they are **white to pale yellowish-pink** when young, darkening to tan. Branches may divide into two or more stems at the top. Each stem is tipped with a **shallow, tiny cup** that has three to six points, appearing **crown-like**.

SPORE PRINT: White.

SEASON: Early summer through fall.

OTHER NAMES: *Clavicorona pyxidata*, *Clavaria pyxidata*.

COMPARE: Some *Ramaria* species have branches that split into two or more stems. Stem tips are **pointed or brush-like** rather than crown-like, and branches often grow from a thickened base. The spore print is **yellowish**. **Straight-Branched Coral** (*R. stricta*; formerly listed as *Clavaria stricta*) grows from decaying **conifer** wood that may be buried. Branches are **straight, upright and parallel** and often flattened. It is **buff-colored to yellowish-pink**, bruising purplish-brown; young stem tips are yellow. **Yellow-Tipped Coral** (*R. formosa*) grows **from the ground**. Branches are **pinkish**; stem tips are yellow. With age, the entire specimen turns orangish to tan. • **False Coral** (*Sebacina schweinitzii* or *Tremellodendron pallidum*) grows **from the ground**. It is composed of **very tough**, dry, whitish branching stems that are flattened and **partially fused** together. Found from **spring** through fall. **White Coral Jelly Fungus** (*Tremella reticulata*) resembles False Coral, but it has a **gelatinous** texture; lobes of older specimens are hollow. It grows on rotted wood and from the ground. • **Crested Coral** (*Clavulina cristata* or *Clavulina coralloides*) is whitish and grows **from the ground**. Branches are slightly flattened and have **tooth-like points**. A gray form is also found; some refer to it as *Clavulina cinerea*, while others regard it as a diseased specimen of *Clavulina cristata*.

NOTES: Crown-Tipped and Crested Coral are edible but easy to confuse with Yellow-Tipped Coral, which is **toxic**; the others listed are inedible.

Crown-Tipped Coral

Straight-Branched Coral

Yellow-Tipped Coral

False Coral

Crested Coral

FROM THE SOIL | SUMMER THROUGH FALL

Worm Corals (several)

Clavaria and *Clavulinopsis* spp.

HABITAT: These species are saprobes, getting their nutrients from decaying organic matter. They grow **directly from the ground** in woodlands in clumps or bunches; often found in grassy or mossy woodland spots.

DESCRIPTION: *Clavaria* species tend to be club-like; compared to the species discussed on pg. 256, they branch less frequently if at all. They have a **brittle** texture and **break easily.** • White Worm Coral (*Clavaria vermicularis* or *Clavaria fragilis*) looks like clumps of mung bean sprouts standing upright in the woods; it is generally unbranching, although some stalks may have small branches at the tips. Fresh stalks are **chalk-white**, becoming yellowish with age. They are cylindrical or slightly flattened, typically 2 to 6 inches tall and ⅛ to ¼ inch wide. Tips are **softly pointed** and may turn brownish. • Sometimes called **Smoky Spindles**, *Clavaria fumosa* are shaped like White Worm Coral but are **grayish, yellowish-tan or pinkish**; they are 1 to 5 inches tall. • **Spindle-Shaped Yellow Coral** (*Clavulinopsis fusiformis*) is similar in size and shape to White Worm but is **bright yellow**; it is more common in the northern part of our area than in the south. • **Golden Fairy Club** (*Clavulinopsis laeticolor*; also referred to as Handsome Club) is **yellowish-orange to orangish** and typically less than 2 inches tall. The upper portion is up to ³⁄₁₆ wide and often somewhat flattened, with a **blunt, squared-off tip** that darkens with age; there may be a groove or fold running from the top towards the base. It is club-shaped and typically unbranched, but may fork once. The club narrows towards the base, which is whitish at the very bottom and often surrounded with white mycelium (thread-like fungal filaments); the club often curves a bit, particularly towards the base. It grows in loose clusters rather than tight bunches.

SPORE PRINT: White.

SEASON: Summer through fall.

OTHER NAMES: White Worm Coral is also called Fairy Fingers.

COMPARE: Violet Coral (*Clavaria zollingeri*) is **purple** and less than 4 inches high; unlike the other *Clavaria* species discussed above, its stalks **fork repeatedly**.

NOTES: White Worm Coral and Spindle-Shaped Yellow Coral are edible but unremarkable; Spindle-Shaped Yellow Coral may be bitter. Golden Fairy Club is too small to be of interest. The others are generally regarded as inedible.

White Worm Coral

Spindle-Shaped Yellow Coral

Golden Fairy Club

Violet Coral

Club-Shaped Coral

Clavariadelphus pistillaris (also known as Pestle-Shaped Coral)

Found growing from the soil in association with **deciduous** trees, particularly beech; they grow in loose clusters, looking like a collection of **tiny baseball bats**. Individuals are commonly 3 to **6 inches** high, although they may grow much **taller**. They are **club-shaped**, with a swollen, rounded top that narrows to a thick, rounded base; younger specimens are less club-like. Colors vary from yellowish to tan to orangish-brown, darkening with age; they turn brownish when bruised. The surface of young specimens is dry and smooth, becoming wrinkled or somewhat pockmarked. They grow from summer through fall and have a white to yellowish spore print.

COMPARE: *C. americanus* is virtually identical, but it grows under oaks and **conifers**. · Flat-Topped Coral (*C. truncatus*) has a **flattened** top; the edge is generally softly rounded but may also be somewhat abrupt, giving the impression of a small, solid trumpet. They are up to 6 inches tall; the top may be 3 inches across. Tops are **yellowish**; the stalks are **orangish** and often wrinkled. They are found near conifers. · Strap-Shaped Coral (*C. ligula*) are less than 4 inches tall, with a **slender** profile; they are usually less swollen at the top and may be somewhat flattened. They are salmon-colored to yellowish-brown and are found in mixed woods, often growing in conifer needles.

NOTES: Club-Shaped Coral and *C. americanus* are edible but often bitter. Flat-Topped Coral is a good edible; Strap-Shaped Coral is not eaten.

Velvet-Stalked Fairy Fan

Spathulariopsis velutipes (also known as *Spathularia velutipes*)

These pretty little mushrooms look like spatulas or fans that might be used by fairies. They are saprobes, growing on decaying wood that may be underground; they are typically found in loose clusters or groups, often under pine trees. Mature specimens are up to 2¼ inches tall; they are fairly soft and flexible. The stalk is brownish and has a **velvety** texture; orange mycelium (threadlike fungal filaments) may be seen at the base. Topping the stalk is a **flattened head** that is fan-shaped to spoon-shaped. It is pale yellow to yellowish-brown and usually wavy; it is up to 1¾ inches wide. The bottom of the head runs alongside the stalk; the top of the head fans around the top of the stalk, forming a **flattened, partial ring** that encircles the top of the stalk. The heads are smoothly textured but may have wrinkles running from the stalk to the outer edges. Occasionally, stalks divide into two branches, each with its own head. Its spore print is white, and it is found from late summer to fall.

COMPARE: Yellow Fairy Fan (*Spathularia flavida*) is very similar, but its stalk is **smooth** rather than velvety and it is **yellowish overall**. It is found in the northern parts of our area. • Fan-Shaped Jelly Fungus (*Dacryopinax spathularia*) has a similar shape, but is less than 1 inch tall; it is **orange overall** with a **jelly-like texture**. It grows from cracks in bare dead wood and may grow from construction lumber.

NOTES: Fairy Fans have not been reported as edible; they are best enjoyed for their unique, charming appearance.

Tooth Mushrooms (several)

Hydnellum spp.

HABITAT: This group of mushrooms grows from the ground under deciduous trees and conifers. They are mycorrhizal, growing in a symbiotic relationship with living trees. Due to their habit of enveloping surrounding debris, they may be attached to sticks or plants.

DESCRIPTION: It is hard to describe the shape of these mushrooms because they change drastically as they grow. Individual caps spread and may **fuse together**, engulfing anything in their path. The **velvety** cap surface may change color or texture as it grows. Undersides are covered with short spore-bearing **teeth**, which extend down the top of the stubby stem; the stem is often so short that specimens appear stemless. Many Hydnellum are pale and similar when young, but each species has at least one unique trait to distinguish it, especially at maturity. • Orange Hydnellum (*H. aurantiacum*) is the most common in our area, growing in large groups under conifers. Its **orange to brownish** caps have a **paler outer edge**; mature specimens are up to 6 inches across and extremely **bumpy**. Teeth are white, turning brown with age except on the **tips**, which remain **white**. • Caps of **Blue Tooth** (*H. caeruleum*) are up to 4 inches across. When young they are **whitish with bluish** tinges, particularly around the edge; they turn tan or brown with age. They ooze **drops of blue liquid** that sit on top, leaving a potholed surface when they evaporate. Teeth are bluish-gray to white, turning brown with age; stems are orange. The cut flesh has blue zones and **smells like cucumber**. Blue Tooth are found in mixed woods. • **Zoned Tooth** (*H. concrescens*) is up to 4 inches across and **brownish to pinkish-brown** on top, typically with **concentric bands** of color. Teeth are whitish to pale pinkish at first, becoming brownish with age. Found near oaks. • Spongy Foot (*H. spongiosipes*) has a flat, brown cap that is up to 4 inches across. They have a **spongy brown stem** and brown teeth that **bruise darker brown**. It is also called Velvet Tooth and grows with oaks; it is uncommon in our area.

SPORE PRINT: Brown.

SEASON: Summer through fall.

OTHER NAMES: Stiptate Hydnum (meaning, having a stem and teeth).

COMPARE: See Hedgehogs on pgs. 52–53.

NOTES: *Hydnellum* species are inedible but are used by dyers.

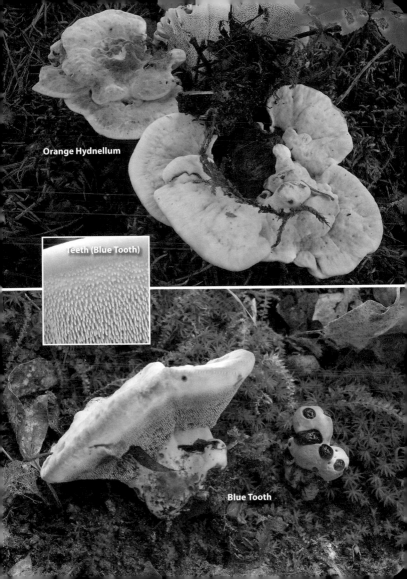

Orange Hydnellum

Teeth (Blue Tooth)

Blue Tooth

ON DECAYING WOOD   SPRING THROUGH FALL

Jelly Fungus
Various species

HABITAT: These jelly-like fungi are found on dead and decaying wood, including fallen logs, sticks and branches; all but one are found on wood from deciduous trees. Most here are saprobes that feed on the wood; the *Tremella* species are parasitic on other fungi that are present on the wood.

DESCRIPTION: These fungi look like clusters of glossy to shiny lobes; they are gelatinous when fresh and moist. Most here are 1 to 3 inches across. • **Orange Jelly** (*Dacrymyces chrysospermus* or *Dacrymyces palmatus*) fruits on **conifer** wood. It is **orangish** to orangish-yellow and typically brainlike, although it may appear folded. Clusters are **white** at the point of attachment to the wood. • Two *Tremella* species that resemble Orange Jelly are referred to as **Witches' Butter.** Both are **yellow to yellowish-orange** clusters that are found on **deciduous** wood, where they attack other fungi which may not be visible. *T. mesenterica* parasitizes the *Peniophora* genus (pg. 242) and is less than 2 inches across; *T. aurantia* parasitizes *Stereum* species, particularly Hairy Curtain Crust (pg. 204) and is up to 4 inches across. • **White Jelly Fungus** (*Ductifera pululahuana* or *Exidia alba*) is **white,** darkening with age; it has **tightly packed** lobes that are often flattened. **Snow Fungus** (*T. fuciformis*) is similar but **translucent** and shinier, with a less bunched appearance. It fruits after heavy rainfall. • **Amber Jelly Roll** (*E. crenata* or *E. recisa*) resembles a mass of **shiny, puckered brownish cups**. Individual lobes are up to 1½ inches across and attached to the wood by a stem-like point where the wrinkles come together.

SPORE PRINT: Not used for identification; microscopic study is more helpful.

SEASON: Spring through fall.

OTHER NAMES: Orange Jelly is also occasionally referred to as Witches' Butter.

COMPARE: Black Witches' Butter (*E. glandulosa*; also called Black Jelly Roll) looks like **small, wrinkled black blobs**, each less than ½ inch across, fused together in a long, **linear cluster**. It grows on deciduous wood. • Leafy Brain (pg. 248) has **ruffled, flattened lobes** that are pale to deep **reddish-brown**.

NOTES: Snow Fungus is commercially raised and sold in Asian markets for use in soup, as well as medicinally; Orange Jelly and Witches' Butter (yellow) are also used in soup. The others listed above are generally considered inedible.

Orange Jelly

White Jelly Fungus

Snow Fungus

Amber Jelly Roll

FROM THE SOIL NEAR TREES

LATE SUMMER THROUGH FALL

Lobster Mushroom

Hypomyces lactifluorum

HABITAT: Grows from the ground singly or in loose groups in mixed woods. It is a parasite of *Russula* and *Lactarius* species, so it is found near fruiting bodies of those mushrooms.

DESCRIPTION: This unmistakable mushroom is colored like a cooked lobster shell; it also may smell somewhat fishy. The hard red shell is created when the *Hypomyces* parasite infects the fruitbody of the host mushroom, creating a new species; some mycologists believe that only white *Russula* and *Lactarius* species are parasitized by *H. lactifluorum*. The distinct cap and stem of the host species become a **misshapen** body with a hard, minutely **pimpled orangish-red surface**. Subtle gill-like folds are evident on some specimens; others appear like featureless, misshapen blobs. The spores are white and may cover the entire surface of the mushroom as well as the surrounding dirt or plants. Lobsters are notoriously dirty, but the white flesh is so **firm** that they can be scrubbed clean without damage. Older specimens turn darker red to bright magenta and become soft inside.

SPORE PRINT: White.

SEASON: Late summer through fall.

OTHER NAMES: None.

COMPARE: Other red- to orange-colored mushrooms include the red *Russula* species (pg. 134) and orange *Lactarius* species (pg. 128). These have well-defined gills and the classic cap-and-stem shape. • *H. chrysospermus* (pg. 270; also called Bolete Mold) attacks edible and choice Boletes, making them toxic and inedible.

NOTES: Experts have determined that the main hosts of the Lobster fungus are *R. brevipes* (pg. 80) and *L. piperatus* (pg. 80), but it is impossible to determine the host of any specific Lobster with certainty. Although concerns have been raised about eating Lobsters when the identity of the host is unknown, they have been safely consumed for a long time and are sold commercially in some areas. The host species probably affects the flavor of the Lobster. Some Lobsters taste like seafood, while others are bland; some may be peppery. Lobster mushrooms should be fresh and firm; they should not be eaten if they are old and soft, or if they lack the bright orange, pimply surface.

Closeup

Misshapen specimens

ON DECAYING WOOD AND OTHER HOSTS

SPRING THROUGH FALL

Slime Molds (several)

Various species

HABITAT: This common but peculiar fungus-like organism is often found on decaying wood such as fallen trees but also grows on other hosts; see the text below. It appears after rain.

DESCRIPTION: Slime molds start out as single cells that mate to become a plasmodium, a **slimy** mass of millions of cell nuclei surrounded by one membrane. Some slime molds can expand and move in search of nutrients, climbing up and enveloping plants, fences, trees or anything they encounter; they may also exist under bark or dead leaves. The second stage of growth occurs when fruiting bodies are formed; these may be yellow, white or brightly colored. The fruiting bodies exist to disperse spores. There are four types of fruiting bodies. • *Sporangia*, the most common, are individual bodies that typically look like a tiny ball or cylinder on a very thin stalk; a hand lens is necessary to see the shape of individual sporangium (the singular term for sporangia). Chocolate Tube Slime (*Stemonitis axifera*) is a good example; in this case, the entire sporangium appears stalk-like, with a black stalk topped by a chocolate-brown spore-producing structure. • *Aethalia* are stalkless and cushion-like or lacy; Scrambled Egg Slime (*Fuligo septica*; also known as Dog Vomit Slime Mold) is easy to spot due to its yellowish color and the size of the mass, which may be up to 8 inches across. • *Pseudoaethalia* are also stalkless and cushion-like but they are formed from stalked sporangia that fuse together; they are difficult to separate visually from aethalia. Red Raspberry Slime (*Tubifera ferruginosa*) is a stunning bright pink but quickly turns brownish. • *Plasmodiocarps* form into thickened, irregular veins with a hard external crust. Pretzel Slime Mold (*Hemitrichia serpula*) is a very distinct example.

SPORE PRINT: Not used for identification.

SEASON: Spring through fall.

OTHER NAMES: Many slime molds have no common name.

COMPARE: Wolf's Milk Slime (pg. 242) are aethalia. • Crust Fungi (pg. 272) may resemble aethalia, but they are **dry** rather than slimy.

NOTES: Slime molds can be found all over the globe in a wide variety of habitats. They are not eaten.

Chocolate Tube Slime (sporangia)

Scrambled Egg Slime (aethalia; shown in plasmodial stage)

Red Raspberry Slime (pseudoaethalia)

Pretzel Slime Mold (plasmodiocarp)

Parasitic Fungi (several)
Various species

HABITAT: Numerous types of fungi grow on other mushrooms, parasitizing them and, in some cases, transforming them into another type of fungus. Each parasitic mushroom attacks a particular species (or genus), so they will be found where (and when) those mushrooms grow.

DESCRIPTION: Collybia Jelly (*Syzygospora mycetophila*; also listed as *Christiansenia mycetophila*) attacks **Oak Collybia** (pg. 94). It causes **gelatinous yellowish tumor-like growths** to develop on the host mushroom, frequently on the cap but also on the gills and stem. The tumors often fuse, appearing brain-like; they may also grow in large clusters around the base of the Oak Collybia. • The *Asterophora* genus contains two species, *A. lycoperdoides* and *A. parasitica*; these grow on the caps of old Russula and Lactarius specimens. *Asterophora* develop as small white cap-and-stem mushrooms; *A. parasitica* has **gills** under a **silky** cap, while *A. lycoperdoides* has **deformed gills or no gills** under its **rough-textured** cap. As the *Asterophora* mature, they produce powdery, buff-colored spores; the spores of *A. parasitica* develop **from the gills** under the cap, but spores of *A. lycoperdoides* appear **on top** of the cap. • **Parasitic Bolete** (*Pseudoboletus parasiticus*; also listed as *Boletus parasiticus*) **grows from Common Earthballs** (pg. 240). The bolete has a dry, tan to yellowish cap up to 3 inches wide. The stem is short and cream-colored and covered with fine brown fibers; it may curve as it grows around the Earthball. The pore surface under the cap is dirty yellowish. • **Bolete Mold** (*Hypomyces chrysospermus*) attacks boletes (including Parasitic Bolete, above). The mold first appears on the pore surface as a white powder that soon covers the entire mushroom with a **cottony white blanket** that turns yellow before turning brown; even choice Boletes become disgusting, misshapen and toxic.

COMPARE: Lobster Mushrooms (pg. 266) are created when *Russula* or *Lactarius* species are attacked by another species of *Hypomyces*.

NOTES: Parasitic Bolete is edible but requires caution and thorough washing since the huge amount of **toxic** spores released from the Earthball may spread onto the bolete. The other fungi and host mushrooms discussed here should not be eaten; Boletes attacked by Bolete Mold may be **toxic**.

Collybia Jelly

A. parasitica

A. lycoperdoides

Parasitic Bolete

Bolete Mold

Crust Fungi (several)
Various species

HABITAT: Crust Fungi are saprobes, getting nutrients from the dead and decaying wood of deciduous trees and, sometimes, conifers.

DESCRIPTION: These fungi have a texture and shape that is not what comes to mind when you think of mushrooms. Many are related to polypores but don't always grow into a shelf form. They have no stems and fuse to the material they are growing on. • **Crowded Parchment** (*Stereum complicatum*; also listed as *S. rameale*) covers logs, mainly oak, with sheets of flat to ruffled fungus that sometimes form **small fan-shaped brackets**. The top side is silky and colored with **orange to reddish-brown banding**; the spore-bearing surface below is **solid orange to cream** with a smooth texture. • **Ceramic Parchment** (*Xylobolus frustulatus*; also listed as *S. frustulosum*) looks like **white to buff-colored ceramic tiles** that may completely cover branches and logs, usually oak. Individual fruiting bodies are generally less than ½ inch across; they **turn black** with age. • **Milk-White Toothed Polypore** (*Irpex lacteus*) is a white to tan mass with hard spore-bearing **teeth** up to ¼ inch long. It sometimes develops a series of overlapping brackets, or can be a flat, toothy crust. It is found on deciduous trees, sometimes living trees.

SPORE PRINT: White (Crowded Parchment, Milk-White Toothed Polypore) or pinkish (Ceramic Parchment). Spore prints are difficult to obtain.

SEASON: Adds new growth annually but found year round.

OTHER NAMES: Commonly called Crusts or Parchment Fungus.

COMPARE: False Turkey Tail (pg. 204) is so closely related to Crowded Parchment that it has been found to occasionally cross (mate). Some experts regard them as varieties of the same species. • **Hairy Curtain Crust** (pg. 204) could be confused with Crowded Parchment, but it is composed of densely **velvety caps** that form a crust-like layer with wavy edges. • **Ochre Spreading Tooth** (*Steccherinum ochraceum*) is a spreading, toothy mass similar to *Irpex lacteus*, but its teeth are **orangish**. The edges of the crust are often **folded over**, forming velvety white cap-like edges. • Young growth of **Purple Tooth** (pg. 232) is sometimes flat and crust-like.

NOTES: Most crusts are not edible due to their texture. The species listed here cause white rot of wood.

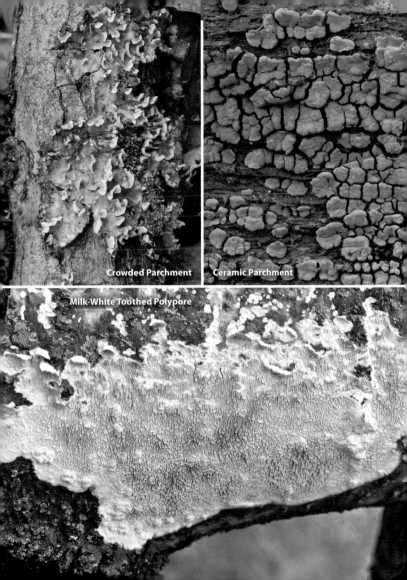

Crowded Parchment

Ceramic Parchment

Milk-White Toothed Polypore

Cedar-Apple Rust

Gymnosporangium juniperi-virginianae

This unusual-looking fungus is found on living Eastern red-cedar trees, which are actually a member of the juniper family (*Juniperus virginiana*). The life cycle starts when the fungus that causes this growth infects apple, crabapple or hawthorn trees, manifesting itself as yellow or orange blisters on the leaves. In midsummer, spores from the fungus are blown by the wind and land on red-cedar trees. The infected leaves on the apple or other host trees may then drop off, weakening the tree. The next spring, the spores on the red-cedar leaves (needles) develop into **swollen, brownish to dull reddish galls**. Spring rains cause the galls to produce **soft orange spore-bearing tendrils** that are up to 1½ inches long. Later in spring, the tendrils release fresh spores that are blown to apple or other susceptible trees, continuing the cycle for another year. The galls dry out but remain on the red-cedar trees for several years, causing some twig dieback.

COMPARE: Similar, related fungi in the *Gymnosporangium* genus also attack pears, mountain ash and quince; the galls and tendrils are smaller and less obvious.

NOTES: Cedar-Apple Rust infects not only the leaves but also the fruits of the host trees, appearing as large orange to yellow spots on the skin; this adversely affects the quality of the fruit and also may cause premature fruit drop. Both authors have seen these fungi on red-cedar trees while gathering morels in the spring.

Striate Bird's Nest

Bird's Nest Fungus (several)
Crucibulum and *Cyathus* spp.

Although they are tiny, these unusual fungi are fascinating and lovely. They are easiest to identify in the mature stage, when they look like **tiny, cone-shaped nests** ½ inch or less across, with even tinier **flattened spheres inside**. On young specimens, a dome-like lid covers the top, appearing cushion-like. The lid eventually falls away, revealing the interior with two to numerous "eggs" that are less than ⅟₁₆ inch wide and contain the spore-producing structures. Bird's Nest Fungus grows singly, scattered or in dense clusters on downed branches, woodland debris and even on old planks. They are found from spring through fall. Several varieties appear in our area. • **White-Egg Bird's Nest** (*Crucibulum laeve*) are **yellowish to tan** and often **velvety** on the outside; the inside is smooth and tan to grayish. Eggs are **white**. • **Dung-Loving Bird's Nest** (*Cyathus stercoreus*) is **brownish** and **shaggy** outside, with smooth **grayish interiors and eggs**; it is often found on manure but also grows on woody debris. • **Striate Bird's Nest** (*Cyathus striatus*) is more vase-shaped. The outside is dark grayish-brown to brownish and covered with **shaggy hairs**; the interior is distinctly **ribbed** and shiny and ranges from tan to gray. Eggs are grayish to whitish.

COMPARE: Little Nest Polypore (pg. 222) has a cup-like stage but lacks "eggs." • Additional Bird's Nest species include the *Nidula*, *Nidularia* and *Mycocalia* genera

NOTES: Bird's Nest are best appreciated when viewed with a hand lens. They are inedible.

Fresh specimens   Attacked by mold

Ochre Jelly Club

Leotia lubrica

These saprobes grow from the soil or from well-rotted wood, usually in profuse **clusters**, from early summer through fall. Also called Jelly Babies, these little fungi appear to have a long stem with a pillowy little cap. In actuality, they are a stemmed club with an **asymmetrical and often furrowed top** that may be rolled under to look like a cap. The colorless spores are produced on the surface of the cap-like top. Stems are up to 3 inches tall and may be minutely scaly on the outside; they are hollow or filled with jelly inside. The top is also **gelatinous** and is less than 2 inches across. The classic form has a cap that ranges from dull yellow, orange, tan to olive with a light yellow stem. With age, it darkens and becomes green. In the past, this green-headed form was considered a separate species, *L. viscosa*; however, recent DNA studies have suggested that this is simply a form of *L. lubrica* which has been attacked by a mold that turns the cap green. Another form is **green overall**; this is often listed as *L. atrovirens* but again, some experts believe that this is just another variation of *L. lubrica*. Some references list the all-green form as *Coryne atrovirens*.

COMPARE: Other small, shiny mushrooms such as Waxy Caps (pgs. 122, 150), Fuzzy Foot (pg. 124) and Velvet Foot (pg. 130) have **gills** under the caps.

NOTES: The edibility of Jelly Babies is unknown. They are related to Morels (pgs. 24-27) and other ascomycetes (see pg. 19).

Highly magnified

Lemon Drops

Bisporella citrina (also known as Lemon Disco and Yellow Fairy Cups)

Lemon Drops are saprobes, getting nutrients from decaying or dead organic matter. They are found from summer through fall growing prolifically on the decaying wood of deciduous trees and conifers. These tiny fungi are usually not overlooked, even though individual cups are **⅛ inch** wide or less! Their **bright yellow** color and sheer numbers will make you take notice. With a hand lens, you can see the distinct **cup shape**, which may have a minute stem attaching it to the wood; some individuals may be flatter and more disc-like. Like other cup fungi (pgs. 252-253) the spores are produced on the inner surface of the saucer. The discs become darker yellow to almost orange when old or dried out. The spores are colorless.

COMPARE: *Chlorencoelia versiformis* is larger, growing up to **1 inch** across; with age, the yellow cups develop a **green color inside**. • Some **Slime Molds** (pg. 268) are yellow and can completely cover a dead log, but the mass is not comprised of individual cups, even when viewed through a hand lens. • **Witches' Butter** (pg. 264) may be bright yellow and grows on decayed wood, but it is more **wavy and folded**, lacking the distinct cups. It is **gelatinous** in wet weather. • **Fuzzy Foot** (pg. 124) is bright yellow and also known to swarm on a log, but individual caps are **¼ to 1 inch** across; they have a distinct cap and stem, with **gills** under the caps.

NOTES: The edibility of Lemon Drops is unknown; they are too small to eat.

Pig's Ear Gomphus   Scaly Chanterelle

Pig's Ear Gomphus
Gomphus clavatus

Found on the ground near conifers, these mushrooms are somewhat funnel-like, with a flared-out top and narrower base. The base may be fairly broad and neck-like, or it may be much narrower, appearing like a stem. Pig's Ear may grow alone, scattered or in groups; several individuals may fuse together at the base. They are up to 4 inches tall; mature specimens may be up to 6 inches across at the top. Its exterior is yellowish-tan to purplish-brown; the base is generally paler. The upper portion is covered with **shallow wrinkles** that descend partway down the base; the margin is wavy or even ruffled. The top has a **cup-like depression** that becomes more funnel-like with age. The surface of the cup is **pale brown to lilac-colored**. It is smooth or sometimes has a few small scales. The flesh is solid and thick; it is whitish to buff-colored. The base may bruise faintly rust-colored. The spore print is brownish-yellow. Pig's Ear is found from midsummer through fall.

COMPARE: Scaly Chanterelle (*Turbinellus floccosus* or *G. floccosus*) is more **vase-shaped**, with a deeper central cavity. It is up to 5½ inches tall and the top may be nearly as wide. The interior is **yellowish-orange, orange** or **reddish-orange** and finely scaly. The outside is cream-colored on young specimens, darkening with age; the surface has **prominent wrinkles** running from the top to the base.

NOTES: Pig's Ear Gomphus is edible and often considered choice, although it may be compromised with insect larvae. Some people eat Scaly Chanterelle, but others find them unpalatable; some people become sick after eating them.

Jelly Tooth
Pseudohydnum gelatinosum

These unusual saprobes are found singly, scattered or in small groups on rotting conifer wood, including stumps and logs; they also fruit from woody debris and duff under conifers. The entire fruiting body is **translucent**, with a **rubbery, gelatinous texture**. Caps are fan-shaped to broadly tongue-like; they are typically 1 to 2 inches across, and often have wavy or irregular edges. The tops are white, grayish or brownish, with a dull, rough texture. A thick stem flows smoothly from one edge of the cap. The stem is colored like the cap or paler; it is similarly roughened, and is typically about as tall as the cap is wide. **Short, soft, pointed spines** cover the underside of the cap; they are translucent and white to pale gray. Spores are white. Jelly Tooth can be found from late summer through fall. They are sometimes called Cat's Tongue, due to their roughened texture.

COMPARE: Jelly Fungi (pg. 264) are also soft, gelatinous and translucent, but they are **clusters of lobes** and have **no spines**. • Marshmallow Polypore (pg. 230) is whitish; the pore surface of older specimens becomes distended, forming long tooth-like projections. It fruits on **hardwoods**. • Tooth Mushrooms (pg. 262) are not translucent; they have a **firm** texture and are **much larger**.

NOTES: Jelly Tooth are edible but have almost no flavor; however, their rubbery, gelatinous texture is interesting. Some people eat them raw with cream and honey (or sugar); others marinate them for use in salads. They can also be cooked with sugar and lemon juice to create gummy candies.

Dog's Nose Fungus
Camarops petersii

This saprobe can be found from summer through fall, growing singly or in small clusters on well-rotted oak logs. It begins as a **flattened, often irregularly shaped disc** with an exterior skin, called a veil or peridium. The skin is a mottled tan to gray to dark brown color, splitting open as it grows to reveal a **slimy, pimply black surface** that looks like a dog's nose! This pimply surface produces spores, and soon turns into an **ink-like fluid** (similar to that produced by *Coprinus* species, pgs. 28–29) that can leave a mess on your hands, if handled. Several specimens can fuse together, creating misshapen masses up to 3 inches or more across, which remain less than 1 inch in height. Typically not entirely fused to the log, it may be attached by a poorly formed stub of a stem. Skin remnants become curled back and are often stained by the black spore slime, which eventually dries out, retaining the black color and dog nose texture.

COMPARE: Carbon Balls (pg. 243) are more **spherical**, with **dry and sooty spores** accumulating on the surface. • Black Bulgar (pg. 244) has a similar shape and colors but the center is **smooth, shiny and rubbery**. • Devil's Urn (pg. 244) grows in early **spring**; it is fragile and **cup-shaped**, with a **hollow interior**.

NOTES: This fungus is not edible but is fun to find and photograph. Its absence in field guides may be more related to its peculiarity than its rarity. Some sources say records from the 1800s describe it growing on American Chestnut, which is now essentially extinct due to Chestnut blight fungus, *Cryphonectria parasitica*.

Chaga

Inonotus obliquus

Also called the Clinker Polypore or Birch Conk, this unusual, homely fungus would generate no notice at all if it were not used to make a highly regarded medicinal tea. It typically grows as a **bulging canker** on living trees, primarily birch; it may also grow as a snout-like or irregular projection rather than a bulge. Chaga may be a foot or more across. The surface is **black and heavily cracked**, often with brownish areas showing between the cracks; it looks **charred or burned**. The interior is yellowish-brown, with a **corky** texture. At this stage the fungus is sterile and does not produce spores. The fertile stage comes only after the host tree has died and a layer of tubes develops under the bark. These spore-producing tubes are quickly attacked and destroyed by beetles. Chaga grows in the fall but is present year-round. It is a parasite that will eventually kill the host tree in less than a decade.

COMPARE: Decayed *Phellinus* species (pg. 223) look like misshapen Chaga, but the interior is black and rotted, with a crumbly texture.

NOTES: Chaga is widely used in Slavic countries, Eastern Europe and some parts of Asia to make a tea that is believed to both prevent and cure cancer. It is rich in antioxidants and is also used to fight viruses, to cure disorders of the digestive system and as a general health tonic. A hatchet is generally needed to remove it from the host tree; the entire fungus is then pounded or ground and the resulting material is steeped to make tea.

Helpful Resources and Bibliography

Information on mushrooms is readily available in books, magazines and on the Internet; note, however, that some websites are less reliable than others. Here is a list of some websites and books that provide reliable information that may be of interest to readers.

WEBSITES

Mycological societies, including the national society (NAMA) and affiliates

North American Mycological Association (namyco.org)

Illinois Mycological Association (illinoismyco.org)

Indiana: The Hoosier Mushroom Society (hoosiermushrooms.org)

Iowa: Prairie States Mushroom Club (iowamushroom.org)

Michigan Mushroom Hunter's Club (michiganmushroomhunters.org)

Minnesota Mycological Society (minnesotamycologicalsociety.org)

Wisconsin Mycological Society (wisconsinmycologicalsociety.org)

Note: There are no NAMA affiliates in North Dakota or South Dakota.

University or independent websites

American Mushrooms, David Fischer (americanmushrooms.com/basics.htm)

Fungi magazine (fungimag.com)

Illinois Mushrooms, Joe McFarland (illinoismushrooms.com)

Indiana Mushrooms (indianamushrooms.com)

Iowa State University Herbarium, Fungi of Iowa (herbarium.iastate.edu/fungi-iowa)

Messiah College, Gary Emberger, fungi on wood (messiah.edu/Oakes/fungi_on_wood/index.htm)

Mushroom Expert, Dr. Michael Kuo (mushroomexpert.com)

MykoWeb: Mushrooms and Other Fungi on the Web (mykoweb.com)

University of Wisconsin/LaCrosse, Tom Volk's page (botit.botany.wisc.edu/toms_fungi)

Urban Mushrooms (urbanmushrooms.com)

BOOKS

Arora, David. *Mushrooms Demystified*. Berkeley: Ten Speed Press, 1986.

— *All That the Rain Promises and More: A Hip Pocket Guide to Western Mushrooms*. Berkeley: Ten Speed Press, 1991.

Baroni, Timothy J. *Mushrooms of the Northeastern United States and Eastern Canada*. New York: Timber Press Field Guides, Workman Publishing, 2017.

Barron, George. *Mushrooms of Northeast North America, Midwest to New England*. Auburn, WA: Lone Pine Publishing, 1999.

Bessette, Alan E. and Arleen R. and David W. Fischer. *Mushrooms of Northeastern North America*. Syracuse, NY: Syracuse University Press, 1997.

Bessette, Alan E. and Arleen R. and Michael Beug. *Ascomycete Fungi of North America: A Mushroom Reference Guide*. Austin, TX: University of Texas Press, 2014.

Kuo, Dr. Michael. *Morels*. Ann Arbor: The University of Michigan Press, 2005.

—*100 Edible Mushrooms*. Ann Arbor: The University of Michigan Press, 2007.

—*Mushrooms of the Midwest* (with Andrew S. Methven). Urbana, Chicago and Springfield: University of Illinois Press, 2014:

Lincoff, Gary H. *National Audubon Society® Field Guide to North American Mushrooms*. New York: Alfred A. Knopf, 2011 (24th printing).

—*The Complete Mushroom Hunter*. Beverly, MA: Quarry Books (Quayside Publishing Group), 2010.

McFarland, Joe and Dr. Gregory M. Mueller. *Edible Wild Mushrooms of Illinois & Surrounding States: A Field-to-Kitchen Guide*. Urbana and Chicago: University of Illinois Press, 2009.

McKnight, Kent H. and Vera B. *A Field Guide to Mushrooms, North America* (A Peterson Field Guide). New York: Houghton Mifflin Company, 1987.

Pacioni, Giovanni; Gary Lincoff, U.S. editor. *Simon & Schuster's Guide to Mushrooms*. New York: A Fireside Book, published by Simon & Schuster Inc., 1981.

Spahr, David L. *Edible and Medicinal Mushrooms of New England and Eastern Canada*. Berkeley: North Atlantic Books, 2009.

Glossary

Aborted: A mushroom whose growth is stunted, deformed or mutated. This often occurs after contact with another organism, possibly even another mushroom.

Agarics: A large family of mushrooms (both edible and poisonous) with a stem and a distinct cap with gills. Sometimes used as a general term for multiple species.

Amatoxins: Lethal toxins present in some species of mushrooms, including some *Amanita, Galerina, Lepiota* and *Conocybe* species. Ingestion causes extreme sickness and may cause death.

Annual: A mushroom whose fruitbody appears once a year in a particular season. (*Compare:* Perennial)

Ascomycete: Scientific name for a group of mushrooms whose spores develop in a sac-like container called an ascus. When the spores are ripe, the end of the sac opens to eject them. (*Compare:* Basidiomycete)

Ascus: The sac-like container that produces spores on the group of mushrooms called ascomycetes. (*Plural:* asci)

Attached gills: Gills that are attached to both the underside of the cap and to the stem. (*Compare:* Free gills)

Basidiomycete: Scientific name for a group of mushrooms whose spores develop on microscopic club-shaped appendages called basidia. This includes most mushrooms with gills and pores, as well as puffballs. (*Compare:* Ascomycete)

Basidium: Microscopic club-shaped appendage with tiny prongs that carry spores. (Plural: Basidia) *See also* Basidiomycete.

Biological species: Organisms that can interbreed to produce fertile offspring.

Bolete: General name used for mushrooms that have a cap and stem with a pore surface under the cap rather than gills or teeth. Many are in the *Boletus* genera; others are not but are still commonly referred to as "boletes."

Bracket: Term used to describe mushrooms that grow laterally (sideways) from a tree or another object, usually without an obvious stem. (*Synonym:* Shelf)

Branching: The growth habit of a mushroom or part of a mushroom that has multiple stems or limbs, resembling the branches of a tree. (*Compare:* Unbranching)

Brown rot: A condition where a fungal organism breaks down and consumes the cellulose of a tree, leaving behind the lignin as a brown, corky material. (*Compare:* White rot)

Bruise/bruising: A color transformation, usually in the cut or damaged flesh, gills or pore surface of a mushroom.

Bulbous: Abruptly swollen or rounded; generally refers to the base of a mushroom stem. (*Compare:* Club-shaped)

Button: An immature or newly emerging mushroom on which the gills or pores underneath the cap are not visible yet. Usually spherical or egg-shaped.

Canker: A sore or tumor-like growth, derived from the Latin word *cancer.*

Cap: The top or head of the mushroom, usually used in reference to mushrooms with a stem. In forms with lateral (sideways) or less prominent stem growth, the cap may be more shelf-like. Called the pileus in some sources.

Chambered: A cavity that is broken into multiple enclosed spaces. In mushrooms, it may occur in the stem or inside the entire fungus.

Close gills: Numerous gills that are closely spaced but still have slight separation from one another.

Club-shaped: Gradually swollen; refers to the base of a mushroom stem. (*Compare:* Bulbous)

Concentric: Usually refers to ridges, lines or other bands of texture or color that are circular and parallel, surrounding a central point. (*Compare:* Radiate)

Coniferous: A tree or shrub with needle-like or scale-like leaves (usually evergreen) whose seeds are contained in cones. (*Compare:* Deciduous, Hardwood)

Cortina: A partial veil over the gills that resembles cotton fibers or a spiderweb.

Cross-veins: Connecting ridges between the gills or gill-like folds of some mushrooms; appears as a net-like pattern.

Crowded gills: Numerous gills that are so tightly packed that the spaces between them are not visible.

Crust: Mushrooms growing as a thin layer covering a surface, usually on dead or decaying tree branches or logs.

Cup: Multiple meanings. Usually refers to the shape of a mushroom whose cap or entire body is concave, like a bowl. Also used to describe the sac-like structure found at the base of the stem on some species (especially Amanita). Cup Fungi is additionally used as a general term for members of the Ascomycete group, which have sac-like structures that produce spores. *See also* Ascus, Volva.

Deciduous: Trees and shrubs that lose their leaves each year, rather than being evergreen; also referred to as hardwoods. (*Compare:* Coniferous)

Decomposer: Something that hastens or facilitates decay or decomposition.

Decurrent gills: Gills that are attached to the stem and run down it. (*Compare:* Free gills) *See also* Attached gills.

Deliquesce: To dissolve, turning to liquid.

Eccentric: Off-center; for mushrooms it is usually used in reference to the placement or the growth of the stem in relation to the cap.

Egg: The immature stage of growth where a mushroom is entirely covered by a thin membrane called a universal veil.

Fairy ring: A group of mushrooms growing in a circle or an arc.

Fertile: Capable of reproduction; for mushrooms, "fertile surface" refers to the surface that holds and releases spores. (*Compare:* Sterile)

Filament: A thin, string-like piece of material.

Flesh: For mushrooms, a term describing the interior that is revealed when the mushroom is cut.

Folds: Gill-like ridges found under the cap of some mushrooms (notably Chanterelles); like gills, the folds contain the microscopic spore-bearing structures.

Forked gills: Gills that branch into two (or more) sections, often near the cap edge.

Free gills: Gills that are attached to the underside of the cap but are not attached to the stem. (*Compare:* Attached gills)

Fruit/fruiting body: The part of a fungal organism that is visible above the ground or other growing medium; another word for what we generally call a mushroom.

Fungus: The scientific Kingdom that is neither plant nor animal; includes yeasts and molds as well as the fleshy fruit bodies we commonly call mushrooms. (*Plural:* fungi) *See also* Kingdom.

Gastrointestinal: The lower digestive tract of the body. "Gastrointestinal problems" refers to a stomachache, cramps and/or diarrhea.

Genus: Scientific classification in biology; the second-to-last level of Latin naming for a living organism. Could be considered the Latin "last name" for a living organism but is listed before the species name. (*Plural:* genera. *Compare:* Phylum, Species) *See also* Kingdom.

Gills: Blade-like or plate-like structures attached to the cap underside of some mushrooms; the gills contain the microscopic spore-bearing structures. Some sources refer to gills as lamellae (*singular:* lamella).

Glandular dots: Textural markings that are minutely raised and usually of a different color than the background; found on the stem of some mushrooms. Glandular dots are smaller than scabers. *See also:* Scabers.

Habitat: A term used to describe the area where a mushroom grows, including geography, type of soil or other substrate, and other species of plants (usually trees) nearby. In our area, elevation does not play a prominent role.

Hand lens: A small, hand-held magnifying glass, used to see minute but not microscopic features. (*Synonym:* Loupe)

Hardwood: A broad-leaved tree whose seeds are contained in fruits or nuts; also referred to as deciduous trees. (*Compare:* Coniferous)

Host: A term used to describe an organism on which a mushroom (or other organism) is growing; the host may be a tree, plant or another mushroom. *See also:* Parasite.

Humus: Decayed leaves and organic matter.

Hygrophanous: An adjective that describes a type of mushroom whose tissue changes appearance (color or texture) based on the amount of moisture present.

Kingdom: Scientific classification in biology; the first level of Latin naming for a living organism. Fungi are called the third kingdom, after plants and animals. The 7 levels of this classification are: Kingdom, Phylum, Class, Order, Family, Genus, Species.

Latex: Thickened fluid that comes from slicing the flesh or gills of *Lactarius* and some other species of mushrooms.

Loupe: A small, hand-held magnifying glass, used to see minute but not microscopic features. (*Synonym:* hand lens)

Margin: The edge, usually referring to the outer portion of a mushroom's cap.

Marginate: To have a well-defined border; with mushrooms, usually in reference to the bottom edge of the gills being a different color than the sides of the gills.

Membrane: Skin-like tissue; with mushrooms, usually used in reference to a partial or universal veil.

Milky: A term use to refer to some species of mushrooms that ooze a fluid when cut or scored across the gills or flesh. *See also* Latex.

Mixed woods: An area that has both deciduous and coniferous trees.

Monotype: A genus with only one representative species.

Morphology: The study or categorization of an organism based on its physical structure or appearance. (*Compare:* Taxonomy)

Mushroom: The general term for the fleshy fruitbody of a fungal organism.

Mycelium: The collective name for the root-like filaments of a fungal organism.

Mycology: The study of mushrooms.

Mycorrhizal: An adjective that describes a mushroom that grows from the ground but has a symbiotic relationship with the roots of trees. (*Compare:* Saprobe)

Notched Gills: Having a notch or cutout where the gills attach to the stem. (*Compare:* Attached gills, Decurrent gills) *See also* Free gills.

Parasite: An organism that grows on another living organism in a relationship that benefits one organism to the detriment of the other; feeding off something while it is still alive with no benefit to the host. *See also:* Host.

Partial veil: A membrane on the underside of the cap of some immature mushrooms; it stretches from the stem to the cap edge, covering the gills or pores. When the cap expands as the mushroom matures it breaks the partial veil, sometimes leaving fragments on the cap edge and a ring on the stem. (*Compare:* Universal veil) *See also* Ring, Ring zone.

Patches: Small to medium-sized, irregularly shaped pieces of tissue attached to the surface of a mushroom cap; they are remnants of a universal veil. *See also* Warts.

Perennial: A mushroom whose fruitbody persists over several years; new growth layers are added to the existing fruitbody each year. (*Compare:* Annual)

Phylum: Scientific classification in biology; the second level of Latin naming for a living organism. (*Plural:* phyla. *Compare:* Genus, Species) *See also* Kingdom.

Polypore: Literally means "having many pores;" refers to a group of mushroom species that release their spores from a surface covered with minute holes.

Pores: Minute holes or openings. In mushrooms, usually part of the fertile, or spore- producing, surface. *See also* Polypore

Pubescent: Having minute hairs.

Radiate: With mushrooms, refers to lines, ridges or grooves that emanate from a central point, like the spokes of a wheel. The lines, ridges or grooves are often faint and only the outer portions may be visible. (*Compare:* Concentric)

Redlist: List of threatened animal, fungi and plant species. Established in 1964 and maintained by the International Union for Conservation of Nature (IUCN). More information at https://www.iucnredlist.org/

Resupinate: A stemless fruitbody that appears to grow upside-down, with its back fused onto the substrate and its fertile surface facing upward. Usually found growing on fallen logs or other horizontal surfaces. *See also* Crust.

Reticulation: A netlike pattern of raised ridges.

Rhizomorph: Cord-like strands composed of multiple fungal filaments.

Ring: A band of tissue encircling the stem of mushrooms that have a partial veil. It may be large and skirtlike, or small and fragile; it may be firmly attached to the stem or free. Also called an annulus. (*Compare:* Ring zone) *See also:* Partial veil.

Ring zone: The place on a mushroom stem where a partial veil was once attached. The ring (see above) may move or deteriorate with age, leaving a zone where the stem texture or color may be different. It may also collect the spores that have been released from above. *See also:* Partial veil.

Rosette: Growing in a circular and layered pattern, like a flower; rose-like.

Saprobe: Mushrooms that get their nutrients from dead or decaying organic matter are called saprobic. (*Compare:* Mycorrhizal)

Scabers: Minute raised scales on the stems of some mushrooms; often a different color than the stem. Scabers are larger than glandular dots. They are a key ID feature for some mushrooms, especially the *Leccinum* species, which are called scaber stalks. *See also* Glandular dots.

Scales: Raised growths that are generally minute to small. There are various textures possible, from fibrous and tufted, to pointy and sharp. The nature of the scales is usually a key ID feature. May be called scabrous in some sources.

Serrate: Jagged in appearance, like the edge of a saw blade. Usually in reference to the edges of gills.

Shelf: Term used to describe mushrooms that grow laterally (sideways) from a tree or another object, usually without an obvious stem. (*Synonym:* Bracket)

Species: Scientific classification in biology; the final or last level of Latin naming for a living organism. Could be considered the Latin "first name" for a living organism but is listed after the species name. (*Compare:* Genus, Phylum) *See also* Kingdom.

Spore deposit: Visible ripe spores that have been released by a mushroom; may be seen on nearby plants, objects or other mushrooms. *See also* Spore print.

Spore print: A spore deposit deliberately caught on a piece of paper; spore prints are made by mushroom enthusiasts for purposes of identification.

Spores: Microscopic reproductive structures, like the "seeds" of mushrooms. Spores are part of sexual reproduction in fungi, as opposed to the same organism growing and spreading to produce additional fruit bodies.

Stem: The part of the mushroom on some species that grows to support a cap. Referred to as the stipe in some sources.

Sterile: Incapable of reproduction; for mushrooms, "sterile surface" refers to the non-spore-producing surface. (*Compare:* Fertile)

Striate: Lines or ridges on a mushroom, usually visible on the cap surface or on the stem.

Substrate: The material or medium on which a mushroom is growing: wood, soil, leaves, straw, compost, wood chips, etc.

Symbiotic: A mutually beneficial relationship, where one organism provides benefits to another in exchange for something it needs. (*Compare:* Parasite) *See also* Mycorrhizal.

Tawny: A color that ranges from tan to light brown, sometimes having a yellowish or reddish hue.

Taxonomy: The science of classifying and naming living organisms based on biological characteristics and relationships. Groups such as genus and species are called taxa (*singular:* taxon). *Compare:* Morphology

Terrestrial: Growing from the ground. *See also:* Substrate, Habitat.

Tomentose: Having a dense covering of fine, short hair.

Tubes: Hollow cylindrical structures on some mushrooms, especially boletes, that contain the spore-producing structures. The pores are packed tightly together under the cap; openings in the bottoms of the tubes create a spongy texture known as a pore surface.

Umbo: A bump, knob or nipple-like protrusion at the top of a mushroom cap; a cap with this feature is called umbonate.

Unbranching: The growth habit of a mushroom or part of a mushroom that has a single stem or member. (*Compare:* Branching)

Uniform: Even all over. Usually in reference to a color, texture, size or other growth pattern.

Universal veil: A thin membrane that completely surrounds an immature or developing mushroom. As the mushroom grows, it breaks the partial veil, sometimes leaving fragments on the cap surface and around the base of the stem. (*Compare:* Partial veil) *See also* Button, Egg, Patches, Volva, Warts.

Veil remnants: The remains of a partial or universal veil on a mature mushroom. Partial veil remnants are typically shaggy, tissue-like pieces hanging from the cap edges. Universal veil remnants may appear as warts or patches on the top of a cap.

Viscid: Having a sticky, but not slimy, surface. The caps of some mushroom species react to moisture in the air and are tacky when wet.

Volva: The fragile, sac-like structure that remains at the base of the stem on species that have a universal veil. As the mushroom grows, it breaks through the membrane, leaving this sac at the base of the stem. It is a common feature of *Amanita* and *Volvariella* species and is sometimes called a cup.

Warts: Small, irregularly shaped pieces of tissue attached to the surface of a mushroom cap; they are remnants of a universal veil. *See also:* Patches.

White rot: A condition where a fungal organism uses the lignin of a tree, leaving the lighter cellulose behind, as a soft, rotted substance. (*Compare:* Brown rot)

Zonate: Having distinct stripes, bands or zones of color or texture.

Index

Note: **Bold text** indicates complete species description

Additional photo credits

The Mushroom Observer website, mushroomobserver.org, is owned and operated by the Massachusetts-based non-profit, Mushroom Observer, Inc. The website's purpose is to record information about mushrooms—their location, appearance and other information—by allowing members to post photos of their fungal finds and to discuss them with other enthusiasts. It can be used as an aid in identifying unfamilar mushrooms, a research tool to study photos of mushrooms in various stages and locations, and a record of dates and locations of various species. This site currently has over 10,000 members, ranging from amateurs to professional mycologists. According to the site's owners, it is "a living field guide for mushrooms or a collaborative mushroom field journal."

Entries below that include a number in parentheses were originally posted on Mushroom Observer; photographers' names (or handles) are listed below, along with the Mushroom Observer image number in parentheses. The publisher, and authors, wish to acknowledge the importance of the website, and the generosity of its contributing members.

TOP EDIBLES & TOP TOXICS: 13, Velvety: AmatoxinApocalypse (32731). **19, top**: Linas Kudzma (350222); **bottom**, Tom Bruns (64908). **23**, Shelf/other: Wikipedia User Norbert Nagel. **25**, *M. diminutiva*: Ryan Pridgeon (732801). **26**, *M. angustifolia*: Dave Wasilewski (867102); Half-free Morel, split: Patrick Harvey (141479). **27**, *V. bohemica & V. bohemica, split*: Eva Skific (419059 & 868905); *V. conica*: Brad Bomanz/Missouri Mycological Society Herbarium (263541). **30**, *S. spathulata*: Glenn Murray and Susan Keith (253078). **35**, *Pleurotus pulmonarius*: HuaFang (931681). **36**, *Pleurotus dryinus*: Dave Wasilewski (737369). **37**, Stalkless Paxillus: Alan Rockefeller (163045). **39**, Red Chanterelle: Scott Hamilton (262051); Smooth Chanterelle: Dan Molter CC 3.0 (16351); Yellow-Foot Chanterelle: Devin B. (799065). **42**, Interior of Puffball: Bob Zuberbuhler (111776). **43**, Purple-Spored Puffball: Ron Kerner. **44**, King Bolete: Lindner Imagery. **45**, Reticulation on stem: Alan Rockefeller (359398). **46**, *B. variipes*: Eva Skific (917256); Lilac Bolete: dario.z (539981). **47**, Bluing Bolete: Renée Lebeuf; *X. purpureum*: Eva Skific (917885). **48**, *H. erinaceus*, Gerard Schuster/lebrac.de. **51**, Fragrant Black Trumpet: David Fischer, Americanmushrooms.com. **53**, *H. umbilicatum*, Ryane Snow (72990). **56**, Big Red: Patrick Harvey (323007). **57**, Gabled False Morel: Ron Spinosa; Bull-Nose False Morel: AJ (323152). **59**: Yellowish gills: Martin Livezey (201523); Velvet Foot: AmatoxinApocalypse (32731). **64**, False Death Cap: Ron Pastorino (380609). **65**, Cleft-Foot Amanita: Eva Skific (1068627). **66**, *A. multisquamosa*, Jimmie Veitch (262411). **67**, *A. russuloides*: Richard Kneal (428869). **68, left**: The 3 Foragers (260428). **69**, Brick-Cap Bolete: Dan Molter CC 3.0 (99992). **70**, Frost's Bolete: Dan Molter CC 3.0 (99984). **71**, Brown Roll-Rim: Devin B. (786273); Velvet-Footed Pax: I.G. Safonov (56653).

CAP & STEM WITH GILLS: 75, *Mycena subcaerulea*: Dan Molter CC 3.0 (86928). **77**, Sweetbread Mushroom: Jimmie Veitch (649649). **79**, American Parasol: Judi Thomas (636303); Sharp-Scaled Parasol: Ann F. Berger (167872). **81**, Peppery Milky: Ann F. Berger (652075). **83**, Meadow Mushroom: Scott Hamilton (160869); Wood Mushroom: Ron Pastorino (223223); Spring Agaricus: Terri Clements/Donna Fulton (320426); Eastern Flat-Topped Agaricus: Martin Livezey (175032). **85**, Decorated Mop: Paul Derbyshire (110702); Man on Horseback: Alan Rockefeller (357517); *Tricholoma odorum*: Dave Wasilewski (271357). **87**, Destructive Pholiota: T. Nelson (269643). **89**, Maple Agrocybe: HuaFang (908610); Common Fieldcap: AmatoxinApocalypse. **93**, Pleated Pluteus: Bill Sheehan (523452). **95**, Oak Collybia: AJ (354193); Buttery Collybia: Dave Wasilewski (293989). **97**, Common Mycena: Devin B. (799064); Clustered Bonnet (both): HuaFang (928237, 928241); *M. leptocephala*: Eva Skific (570101). **101**, Mica Caps: Dan Molter CC 3.0 (41717). **105**, *A. ceciliae*: Ann F. Berger

302

(356903). **115, Black-Staining Russula**: Caleb Brown (359068); **Red staining**: Erlon Bailey (53538). **117**, *C. trivialis*: Evica Skific (562433); *C. corrugatus*: Devin B. (758962); *C. distans*: Dave Wasilewski (955306). **119**, *A. flavorubens*: dario.z (878017); **Eastern American White Blusher**: Dave Wasilewski (153742). **121, Chocolate Milky**: Walter J. Doyle (157047); *L. fumosus*: Damon Brunette (95495). **123**, *H. flavescens*: Devin B. (915963); *E. murrayi*: Ann F. Berger (356820). **127**, *C. hesleri*: Devin B. (935030). **129**, *Lactarius thyinos*: Dave Wasilewski (97802); *Lactarius psammicola*, **Lactarius deliciosus var. deterrimus**: Eva Skific (824235, 784682); *Lactarius hygrophoroides*: Dan Molter CC 3.0 (48685). **131, main**: AmatoxinApocalypse (32731). **133**, *H. punicea*: Eva Skific (790896). **135**, *R. mariae*: I.G. Safonov (554766); **Rosy Russula**: Eva Skific (1065774). **137, Brick Tops**: Dan Molter CC 3.0 (65279); **Sulfur Tuft**: Britney Wharton-Ramsey (179585); *H. capnoides*: Scott Hamilton (172730). **139, Bleeding Mycena**, top left: Heather Waterman (1013318); **"Bleeding"**: Jacob Kalichman (952288); **Attacked by** *Spinellus fusiger*: Judi Thomas (665377); **Lilac Mycena**: Dan Molter CC 3.0 (621248). **141, Purple-Gilled Laccaria**: Ron Pastorino (380602). **143, Maturing Blewits**: Dan Molter CC 3.0 (60809); **Lilac Bonnet**: Britney Wharton-Ramsey (213962). **147, Indigo Milky**: Benjamin J. Dion (290785). **149, Smooth Volvariella**: TaxoNerd (296039). **150**: Wikipedia User Strobilomyces. **151**: Ron Pastorino (119313). **153, Train Wrecker**: Richard Kneal (248446). **157**: Dave Wasilewski (468791). **161**: Troy Kling (484551). **162**: Jimmie Veitch (271079). **165**: Paul Derbyshire (105143). **166, left**: AJ (337567). **167**: Ann F. Berger (183478). **168**: Crystal Davidson (1041576). **169, left**: Brian Adamo (122662); **right**, Jon Shaffer (896647).

CAP & STEM WITH PORES: 175, Rooting Polypore: Dave Wasilewski (362017). **177, White Birch Bolete**: Erlon Bailey (108223). **179, Butter Foot Bolete**: Patrick Harvey (90457); *Aureoboletus auriporus*: Adam Bryant (920547). **186, Wrinkled Bolete**: Dan Molter CC 3.0 (53741). **187, both**: HuaFang (926352, 912938) **188**: Scott Hamilton (161597). **191**: Jimmie Veitch (657426).

ATYPICAL CAPS: 199, Dog Stinkhorn: Erica Urbanovitch (45277). **201, Smooth-Stalked Helvella**: Sava Krstic (144692); **Fluted Black Helvella**: Alan Rockefeller (301338); **Saddle-Shaped False Morel**: John Kirkpatrick (302281).

SHELF WITH PORES: 205, Hairy Turkey Tail, False Turkey Tail: Aaron Carlson (1031854, 871730); **Hairy Curtain Crust**: HuaFang (851483). **211, Cluster of Oak Bracket**: Alden Dirks (926329). **213**: Keith A. Bradley (454749). **214**: Roseanne Healy. **221**: Scott Hamilton (116429). **222, both**: Sylvia Hosler (451502, 558262).

SHELF WITH GILLS: 225, Hairy Panus: Martin Livezey (322525); **Smooth Panus**: Byrain (202240). **229**: Scott Hamilton (200810).

SHELF/OTHER: 230: Patrick Harvey (267700). **231, right**: David Fischer, Americanmushrooms.com. **233, main**: Wikipedia User Norbert Nagel. **234**: Jason Hollinger (282853).

SPHERICAL MUSHROOMS: 239, Rounded Earthstar: Richard Kneal (240755); **Collared Earthstar**: Lucy Albertella (215164).

CUP-SHAPED MUSHROOMS: 245, Hairy Rubber Cup: Ryan Pridgeon (747976). **249, Copper Penny**: HuaFang (855703). **250**: Ann F. Berger (544802). **251, Brown-Haired White Cup**: HuaFang (928293).

CORAL AND CLUB FUNGI: 257, Straight-Branched Coral: Damon Brunette (102150); **Yellow-Tipped Coral**: Brian Adamo (147815); **Crested Coral**: Scott Hamilton (267500). **259, Spindle-Shaped Yellow Coral**: Karen Hardy (250127); **Golden Fairy Club**: Greg Giannone (914100). **260**: Jean-Luc Fasciotto. **261**: vjp (159725).

MISCELLANEOUS MUSHROOMS: 265, Orange Jelly: Dr. Lorne Stobbs (353452); **Snow Fungus**: James Craine (563419). **269, Pretzel Slime Mold**: Jon Carl Jacobs (57955). **271, Collybia Jelly**: Alan Rockefeller; **Parasitic Bolete**: Scott Hamilton (158792). **281, Chaga**: Andrew Parker.

About the Authors

Teresa Marrone has been gathering, preparing and writing about wild edibles for three decades. She is the author of more than a dozen outdoors themed books, including the *Wild Berries & Fruits Field Guide* series (currently available for four regions of the U.S.) and numerous cookbooks and is also the co-author of two other regional mushroom ID guides (*Mushrooms of the Northeast* and *Mushrooms of the Northwest*). She lives in Minneapolis with husband Bruce and enjoys shooting photos of mushrooms, berries and all things wild in the area surrounding their property, abutting Minnesota's Boundary Waters Canoe Area Wilderness.

A serious mushroom enthusiast, **Kathy Yerich** has been hanging out with the Minnesota Mycological Society (MMS) for nearly 15 years. Current MMS and NAMA (North American Mycological Assn.) board member, her mission in those organizations is to make learning about mushrooms fun and accessible to everyone. She lives in Forest Lake, MN with her potter and mushroom scout husband Fred and is still astounded by the opportunity to collaborate on this book with Teresa.

Consultant and reviewer **Ron Spinosa** is a past president of the Minnesota Mycological Society, having served four years in that position. He has a Master of Science degree in Zoology with paleontology and evolutionary biology as areas of special interest and has been studying and enjoying mushrooms for over 25 years. Mushroom cultivation is one of his special interests. Ron is currently the Chair of the Cultivation Committee of the North American Mycological Association. He has given many presentations and workshops on mushrooms at nature centers, museums, schools and garden clubs. He was recently awarded *The Harry and Elsie Knighton Service Award* by the North American Mycological Association.